Lenka Ivantysynova

RFID in Manufacturing

Lenka Ivantysynova

RFID in Manufacturing

Mapping the Shop Floor to IT-Enabled Business Processes

Südwestdeutscher Verlag für Hochschulschriften

Impressum/Imprint (nur für Deutschland/ only for Germany)
Bibliografische Information der Deutschen Nationalbibliothek: Die Deutsche Nationalbibliothek
verzeichnet diese Publikation in der Deutschen Nationalbibliografie; detaillierte bibliografische
Daten sind im Internet über http://dnb.d-nb.de abrufbar.
 Alle in diesem Buch genannten Marken und Produktnamen unterliegen warenzeichen-, marken-
oder patentrechtlichem Schutz bzw. sind Warenzeichen oder eingetragene Warenzeichen der
jeweiligen Inhaber. Die Wiedergabe von Marken, Produktnamen, Gebrauchsnamen,
Handelsnamen, Warenbezeichnungen u.s.w. in diesem Werk berechtigt auch ohne besondere
Kennzeichnung nicht zu der Annahme, dass solche Namen im Sinne der Warenzeichen- und
Markenschutzgesetzgebung als frei zu betrachten wären und daher von jedermann benutzt
werden dürften.

Verlag: Südwestdeutscher Verlag für Hochschulschriften Aktiengesellschaft & Co. KG
Dudweiler Landstr. 99, 66123 Saarbrücken, Deutschland
Telefon +49 681 37 20 271-1, Telefax +49 681 37 20 271-0
Email: info@svh-verlag.de
Zugl.: Berlin, Humboldt-Universität zu Berlin, Dissertation, 2008

Herstellung in Deutschland:
Schaltungsdienst Lange o.H.G., Berlin
Books on Demand GmbH, Norderstedt
Reha GmbH, Saarbrücken
Amazon Distribution GmbH, Leipzig
ISBN: 978-3-8381-1271-8

Imprint (only for USA, GB)
Bibliographic information published by the Deutsche Nationalbibliothek: The Deutsche
Nationalbibliothek lists this publication in the Deutsche Nationalbibliografie; detailed
bibliographic data are available in the Internet at http://dnb.d-nb.de.
 Any brand names and product names mentioned in this book are subject to trademark, brand
or patent protection and are trademarks or registered trademarks of their respective holders.
The use of brand names, product names, common names, trade names, product descriptions
etc. even without a particular marking in this works is in no way to be construed to mean that
such names may be regarded as unrestricted in respect of trademark and brand protection
legislation and could thus be used by anyone.

Publisher: Südwestdeutscher Verlag für Hochschulschriften Aktiengesellschaft & Co. KG
Dudweiler Landstr. 99, 66123 Saarbrücken, Germany
Phone +49 681 37 20 271-1, Fax +49 681 37 20 271-0
Email: info@svh-verlag.de

Printed in the U.S.A.
Printed in the U.K. by (see last page)
ISBN: 978-3-8381-1271-8

Copyright © 2010 by the author and Südwestdeutscher Verlag für Hochschulschriften
Aktiengesellschaft & Co. KG and licensors
All rights reserved. Saarbrücken 2010

To Tobias, and my loving parents.

Contents

1	**Introduction**	**1**
1.1	Motivation	1
1.2	RFID Technology: An Overview	4
1.3	IT Infrastructures in Manufacturing	6
1.4	Principal Contributions	9
1.5	Organization	10
2	**Potential Benefits of RFID on the Shop Floor**	**12**
2.1	Automatic Identification Technologies	13
2.2	RFID Applications	16
2.3	Case Studies	19
	2.3.1 Production of Airbags	21
	2.3.2 Production of Sliding Clutches	28
	2.3.3 Production of Engine-Cooling Modules	34
	2.3.4 Production of Cast Parts	39
	2.3.5 Production of Electronic Connectors	43
	2.3.6 Production of Aluminum Foils for Packaging	50
2.4	Lessons Learned	56
	2.4.1 Evaluating Potential Benefits	56
	2.4.2 Comparing RFID with other Auto-ID Technologies	66
	2.4.3 Evaluating Current Motives and Open Potentials	70
2.5	Conclusion	74
3	**Challenges of Embedding RFID into Shop-Floor Processes**	**77**
3.1	Reference Model for Production Processes	78

3.2	Hindrances on the Shop Floor	81
	3.2.1	Hostile Physical Conditions	81
	3.2.2	Presence of Metal	81
	3.2.3	Demand for Wireless Communication	82
	3.2.4	Processes in Close Spatial Proximity	83
3.3	Required RFID Functionalities	83
	3.3.1	Filtering and Enriching RFID Data	84
	3.3.2	Storing RFID Data	85
	3.3.3	Exchanging RFID Data	87
	3.3.4	Detecting Events in RFID Data	88
3.4	Constraints for IT Infrastructures	90
	3.4.1	Distributing Business Logic and Data	91
	3.4.2	Supporting Heterogeneous Data Sources	94
	3.4.3	Dealing with Noise and Uncertainty	95
	3.4.4	Supporting Process Analysis	95
	3.4.5	Supporting Asset Tracking	96
	3.4.6	Providing RFID Data to Components of the Middle Layer	96
3.5	Conclusion	98

4 IT Infrastructures Deployed in Manufacturing — 99

4.1	Flow of Information between Shop Floor and Top Floor	100
	4.1.1	The Purdue Reference Model for Computer-Integrated Manufacturing	101
	4.1.2	ISA-S95	104
	4.1.3	OPC	107
4.2	Case Studies	109
	4.2.1	Production of Milk Products	110
	4.2.2	Production of Cooling Engines	117
	4.2.3	Production of Refractories	123
	4.2.4	Production of Engines	127
	4.2.5	Production of Chemicals	138
	4.2.6	Production of Power Plants	149

	4.2.7	Production of Tires 152
4.3	Lessons Learned 156	
	4.3.1	Data Acquisition and Dataflow in IT Infrastructures . . 156
	4.3.2	Mapping Analyzed IT Infrastructures to ISA-S95 . . . 157
	4.3.3	Central Versus Local Production Control 159
	4.3.4	Activities Supported by RFID 161
	4.3.5	Requirements for the ISA-S95 Level 3 162
4.4	Conclusion 164	

5 Design Guidelines for Embedding RFID into IT Infrastructures — 165

- 5.1 Related Work 166
- 5.2 RFID in Manufacturing: Common Functionalities 167
  - 5.2.1 Identifying Requirements 167
  - 5.2.2 Analyzing Similarities and Variations 169
  - 5.2.3 Estimating Commonalities of Requirements 170
  - 5.2.4 Modeling the Flow of Common Activities 171
- 5.3 Implementation Issues 172
  - 5.3.1 Technologies for Implementing the Common Activities 173
  - 5.3.2 Distributing Data and Logic 177
- 5.4 Conclusion 180

6 Costs and Benefits of RFID Investments — 182

- 6.1 Related Work 184
- 6.2 Quantifiable Costs and Benefits 187
  - 6.2.1 Fixed Costs 187
  - 6.2.2 Variable Cost 188
  - 6.2.3 Benefits 190
- 6.3 Non-Quantifiable Costs and Benefits 194
  - 6.3.1 Operational Benefits 195
  - 6.3.2 Strategic Benefits 197
  - 6.3.3 Risks and Costs 199
  - 6.3.4 Assessment 201

6.4	How to Combine Tangible and Intangible Costs and Benefits	203
6.5	Conclusion	206

7 Beyond Manufacturing: RFID in the Automotive Supply Chain   209

7.1	Related Work	210
7.2	Toward an RFID Adoption Model in the Automotive Industry	211
	7.2.1 Technology-Related Factors	211
	7.2.2 Organizational Readiness Factors	213
	7.2.3 External Environment Factors	214
	7.2.4 Inter-Organizational Pressure Factors	214
7.3	Method and Results	216
	7.3.1 Technology-related Factors	218
	7.3.2 Organizational Readiness Factors	220
	7.3.3 External Environment Factors	220
	7.3.4 Inter-Organizational Pressure Factors	221
7.4	Conclusion	223

8 Conclusion   227

Bibliography   231

Appendix   244

Abbreviations   245

Acknowledgment   248

Chapter 1

Introduction

Radio-frequency identification (RFID) can increase the accessibility of fine-grained process data. RFID technology enables the exchange of data with tagged physical objects in environments in which alternative technologies cannot effectively be deployed. It therefore possesses the potential to bridge the gap between the real world and the virtual world of IT systems. By increasing the accessibility of precise data, RFID promises to alleviate existing business problems (Floekermeier, 2006). The term *real-world awareness* is used to characterize this convergence between the physical and virtual worlds and the availability of timely and accurate information.

In this chapter I outline the need for an analysis of the potential benefits of RFID on the shop floor. Subsequently this chapter gives a short overview of RFID technology and IT infrastructures in manufacturing. Then I outline my principal contributions and conclude the chapter with an overview of this thesis.

1.1 Motivation

During recent years, increased data storage capabilities on RFID chips, reduced tag prices, and improved robustness of tags have made RFID-based applications increasingly appealing to a wide range of industries. In logistics, RFID is already used for numerous applications. Examples include the autonomous and decentralized management of logistic processes (Scholz-Reiter et al., 2004), tracking and tracing (Fruness, 2006), and the management of perishable goods throughout supply chains (Kärkkäinen, 2003).

The characteristics of RFID technology include the capability to detect tags without a line of sight, the possibility to store data on the tag, and the physical robustness of the tags. Even though the possibility of applying RFID applications on the shop floor has recently gained attention (Chappell et al., 2003; MCBeath, 2006), little experience with such applications currently exists. Therefore, it is often unclear if and when RFID technology really is a better basis for a solution than alternative technologies such as bar codes. Hence, there is a clear need for a profound analysis of RFID benefits and an evaluation of RFID use cases in manufacturing. In addition to the benefits one also has to study hindrances that prevent a ubiquitous use of RFID in manufacturing today.

When applying RFID in production, it needs to be integrated into the used IT systems. Here, each manufacturer has to deal with the same challenges: No consolidated findings on how to integrate RFID into the IT infrastructure exist. The consequence is that each IT department has to develop a solution from scratch, without the foundation of a design framework. This generally increases the complexity of RFID introductions and hampers RFID investments in the manufacturing domain (Strüker et al., 2008, p.8). There are several recurring challenges. First the IT staff needs to know which functionalities they have to assure in the IT infrastructure when embedding RFID. Secondly it is also essential to know what technologies are best suited for the implementation. Additionally, they have to decide what the most efficient distribution of data and logic within the IT infrastructure is.

Even though each solution for embedding RFID is unique, manufacturers deal with some common design structures. Therefore, it is possible to derive commonalities and variations for IT systems that support RFID applications in manufacturing. This should cover reusable assets including requirements and functional components. Beyond this, manufacturers need guidance for implementing the required functionality and heuristics for mapping the software components to the hardware infrastructure.

Another hindrance for an RFID adoption is that managers lack dedicated models that assess RFID investments. Lacking the possibilities for forecasting and measuring benefits is seen as one of the top three barriers regarding RFID deployments in enterprises (Strüker et al., 2008, p.26). When investing in RFID, companies face the dilemma of most information communication technology investments: these investments often do not have a "direct value in [their] own right"; they rather open up "a potential for derived value", stemming from a reorganization of business processes supported by the new technology (Remenyi et al., 2000). As a result, it is often impossible to make reliable ROI calculations ex-ante. According to Lucas (1999), the likelihood that IT investments generate a positive ROI is 50% or even below for most investment types (infrastructure investments, investments focusing on indirect returns, strategic applications, transformational IT *etc.*).

However, does this really mean that such investments tend to be problematic, or does the problem rather lie within the purely monetary focus of the selected performance indicator (*i.e.*, ROI)? Many benefits – but also some risks – of RFID are difficult to measure in monetary terms. RFID investments might, for example, affect the company's image, its relationships with customers and suppliers or the employees' motivation. All these effects are hardly quantifiable in advance.

A holistic evaluation approach that takes both monetary and intangible aspects of the investment into account would help manufacturers decide whether an investment in RFID is advantageous. Guidelines that would assess both the quantifiable and the non-quantifiable aspects of RFID in manufacturing would help to reduce the main obstacle that leads to decisions against RFID; that is, the lack of predictable benefits (Schmitt and Michahelles, 2008).

RFID technology can also be implemented as an inter-organizational system along the supply chain to ensure real-time information sharing (Sharma et al., 2007). For instance Strassner and Fleisch (2003) have shown that the use of RFID technology in such a collaborative manner can bring significant benefits for the automotive supply chain. However, even though some original equipment manufacturers (OEMs) are currently engaged in RFID-related pilot projects, which involve both intra- and inter-organizational system scenarios, the technology has not yet made a decisive step from the meeting room to real-life implementations. It is therefore valuable to understand which factors influence RFID adoption.

1.2 RFID Technology: An Overview

Radio-frequency identification (RFID) is an automatic identification method that uses electromagnetic waves to remotely retrieve data stored on transponders. These transponders can be associated with physical objects. Therefore, the retrieved data can be used to identify these objects. This concept was explored with several RFID-related technologies in the first part of the 20th century. One prominent example is the "friend or foe" transponder systems for military aircraft first used during World War II. In general, the development of RFID can be traced back to the landmark paper by Stockman (1948). In his paper Stockman writes:

> Point-to-point communication, with the carrier power generated at the receiving end and the transmitter replaced by a modulated reflector, represents a transmission system [...]. Radio, light, or sound waves (essentially microwaves, infrared, and ultrasonic waves) may be used for the transmission...

Today, the hardware of such a transmission system comprises RFID readers as carriers generating the power, and transponders (also referred to as tags). The tags receive signals from the readers. Readers have the ability to read from as well as write to the transponders' memory.

Each tag consists of an inlay and a casing for the inlay. Popular forms of casings are made out of paper labels and glue which allow the tag to be applied in the manner of a sticker. Other casings (*e.g.*, made of plastics) are designed for protecting the inlay from hostile environmental conditions. The inlay itself typically comprises a computer chip with a memory and communication logic as well as an antenna. Mass-produced versions of RFID inlays are already available below 10 euro cents. Fully converted tags (*e.g.*, in the form of a sticker), usually cost from 20 euro cents upwards.

I categorize RFID tags according to their (i) energy supply, (ii) data storage capabilities and (iii) communication frequency. Finkenzeller (2003) gives a detailed description of each of these attributes. Table 1.1 shows some exemplary tags and their corresponding attributes.

Table 1.1: Exemplary tags with their attributes *energy supply* (battery), *data storage capabilities* (memory and access to memory), and *frequency*.

TAG	BAT.	DATA STORAGE		FREQ.
		MEM.	ACCESS	
VOLCANO TAG 231 (Assion Electronic)	no	64Bit	read only	125 kHz
BIS L (Balluff)	no	192Byte	read/write	125 kHz
TFM 05 2205.210 (Leuze electronic)	no	44Byte	read/write	13.56 MHz
Short Dipole Label (Intermec)	no	96Bit	read only	868 or 915 MHz
AD-220 9 (avery dennison)	no	96Bit	read/write	902-928 MHz
Beacon Tag 137001 (Gao RFID Inc.)	yes	9Byte	read only	868 or 915 MHz

Tags without batteries are referred to as passive tags. These tags harvest energy from the communication signal sent by the RFID reader to run their operations. By contrast, active tags use a battery for energy supply.

RFID tags can have diverse storage capabilities starting at a few bits and going up to several megabytes. Furthermore, one can distinguish between read-only and rewritable tags, according to the properties of their memory.

Regarding the communication frequency, RFID tags are usually categorized into low-frequency (LF), high-frequency (HF) or ultra-high-frequency (UHF) transponders. Low-frequency tags typically operate on frequencies around 125 kHz and have communication ranges which are commonly below 0.5 meters. HF tags operate on the frequency of 13.56 MHz and typically reach communication ranges of 0.5 meters to approximately one meter. Both,

LF and HF tags use inductive coupling for communication. By contrast, UHF tags operate using backscattering and reach ranges of up to approximately 7 meters. UHF tags operate in a frequency range between 860 and 960 MHz. For more details see Finkenzeller (2003).

The communication via air interface is regulated by standardized protocols. A popular standard for RFID tags is the Gen 2 standard from EPCglobal (2005). It is specified for UHF tags and ratified as the ISO standard 18000-6c (ISO/IEC-18000, 2004b). This standard is commonly used for logistics applications which are based on the electronic product code (EPC). EPC numbers of 96-bit size can be read from and written to Gen 2 tags. Additionally, an optional user memory is specified for arbitrary use (EPCglobal, 2005).

The software of an RFID system can be divided into applications and middleware. The middleware can run centrally on a single server or distributed over different machines, *e.g.*, Bornhövd et al. (2004); Floerkemeier and Lampe (2005); Goyal (2003). Its role is to coordinate a number of RFID readers that are usually located close to each other, for example, within a single plant or production line. The middleware buffers, aggregates and filters data coming in from the readers. The main reason is to reduce the load for the upstream applications. These applications can come from diverse software systems. In manufacturing environments, these are typically MES or ERP systems.

1.3 IT Infrastructures in Manufacturing

Introducing RFID applications into manufacturing plants requires combining RFID software with existing IT environments in this domain. Therefore, this section briefly introduces typical IT infrastructures. One can distinguish between four layers of IT infrastructures depending on the granularity of the controlled operations. Listed top down, the layers are the back-end, edge and device layer. I also match the IT hardware to this layered structure, see Figure 1.1.

The back-end layer comprises the enterprise resource planning (ERP)

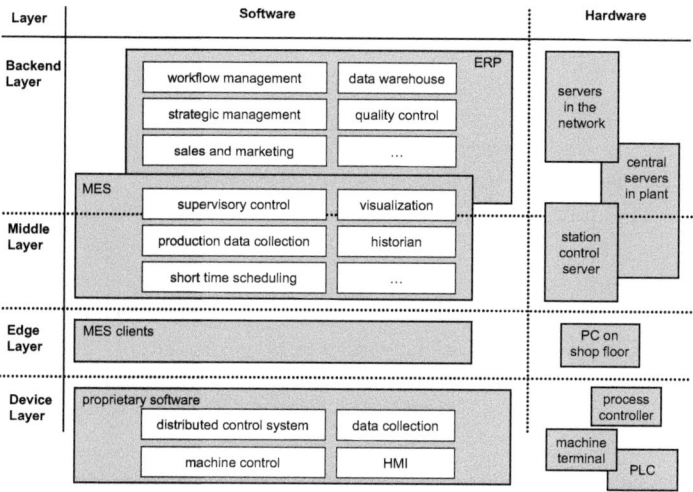

Figure 1.1: General IT infrastructures in manufacturing.

system and can include parts of the manufacturing execution system (MES). Systems in this layer provide coarse-grained control and monitoring of the production, *e.g.*, with a temporal granularity of weeks or months. Most functionality of an MES typically resides in the middle layer. This layer realizes more-fine-grained control of the operations, *e.g.*, the temporal resolution can be days or minutes. The edge layer includes MES clients. The device layer normally comprises distributed control systems (DCS), machine-software interfaces (HMI), and programmable logic controllers (PLC) for machine control. This layer directly realizes the operations on the plant floor.

The hardware can be matched as follows to these four layers. Here I further subdivide the back-end layer into local and remote back-end. The remote back-end comprises hardware that is located outside the plant and accessed via an internet connection. The local back-end comprises hardware that is not located on the plant floor but within the plant's facilities. Hardware in the middle layer is also within the plant and can partially lie on the shop floor. The edge layer comprises PCs on the plant floor. MES clients run on these PCs and serve as control and input devices for workers. The device layer comprises machine controllers (PLC), process controllers, and machine terminals on the plant floor.

The flow of information can generally be described as follows: Sensors on machines generate unfiltered data that are collected by PLCs. The collected data is used for monitoring current operations. The PLCs also control the machine. PLCs may have links to an HMI for transferring data. They can also be connected to a DCS. A DCS is generally used to monitor and control large plants at a single site. HMIs can display job instructions and may also be used for collecting manual inputs from workers. Data from PLCs or DCS are passed to higher layers. In return, they receive machine configurations from there.

The edge layer comprises clients. They display data from the device and middle layer and serve as input device for workers. The middle layer typically hosts an MES or systems with all and additional functionalities of a production data collection system (PDC). The MES collects data acquired by subsystems, filters this according to predefined business rules, and delivers mission-critical information about production activities (Chang et al., 2002, pp. 6). It visualizes, optimizes, and coordinates the entire production process in a time frame between days and minutes. In the MES, data are compressed, filtered, and pushed into databases for later analysis, *i.e.*, a historian. Only a small amount of data is passed on to the upper level, to the ERP.

The ERP system conducts the long-term business plan and manages workflows. It passes customer orders down to the MES. From the MES the ERP receives aggregated status reports and information about the material consumption. The ERP neither directly controls machines on the plant floor nor is it involved in production data acquisition.

Following this general architecture, I allocate RFID tags and readers in the device layer. RFID middleware lies in the middle layer.

1.4 Principal Contributions

This doctoral dissertation analyzes the use of RFID technology in manufacturing. The following is an outline of my five main results.

1. This thesis analyzes potential benefits and manufacturers' motivation of applying RFID technology in manufacturing enterprises. The research approach here was to conduct case studies. This research strategy enables one to gain an in-depth understanding of manufacturers' real-life challenges to preserve a smooth production. Based on the case studies it was possible to evaluate seven use cases for RFID. They are typically either a replacement of bar-code technology or an application that can only be realized using RFID. Five out of six companies' motives for an RFID adoption are purely operational uses within their enterprise. That is, they would like to use this technology for improving processes and productivity on the plant floor. Motivations to use RFID as a strategic enabler and inter-enterprises along the supply chain were found much less frequently.

2. Despite all the potential benefits, RFID technology is not yet widely adopted in production. Therefore, it is valuable to understand why this is the case. Using the case studies it was possible to study the challenges of embedding RFID into manufacturing processes. The contribution of this thesis is to identify and describe which RFID-specific constraints IT infrastructures have to provide.

3. A further contribution is to show how RFID can be embedded into an existing IT infrastructure in manufacturing. For this I first evaluate IT infrastructures at diverse manufacturers by conducting seven more case studies. Only the case study approach enables to investigate IT infrastructures within the real-life context. With the case studies it was possible to evaluate how and where RFID-specific requirements can be deployed in IT infrastructures specific to the manufacturing sector.

4. Another aim of my thesis is to provide guidance for assessing quan-

tifiable and non-quantifiable costs and benefits of an RFID rollout in manufacturing. The analysis is based upon experiences from the RFID case studies. The thesis outlines the most crucial tangible and intangible risks and benefits. It also presents an assessment scheme to assess tangible and intangible aspects, using value-benefit analysis. The approach assures that the most important aspects will be reflected in the decision taken, thus reducing the remaining degree of uncertainty.

5. When looking beyond the shop floor one can see that RFID is also not already widely adopted in the supply chain. The thesis analyzes and answers why; taking the automotive supply chain as an example. The research method here are semi-structured interviews with OEMs and suppliers. The analysis builds on existing inter-organizational system adoption models. It was possible to show that perceived benefits, uncertainty about the technology and directions of the standardization, pressure from powerful partners as well as competitive pressure play an important role in RFID diffusion in the automotive industry.

1.5 Organization

This section gives an overview of the structure of the following chapters and with whom I worked on the different topics. In Chapter 2 I first give technical foundations about recognition systems used in manufacturing. Then the chapter describes and summarizes the findings of six case studies. Each case study comprises an analysis of the production process and (potential) use of RFID technology gained through a series of on-site interviews and observations. I conducted the case studies and their analysis together with Oliver Günther and Holger Ziekow in 2006. We published the results in Günther et al. (2008).

Chapter 3 shows which challenges the manufacturer has to face when applying RFID in shop-floor processes. All challenges are derived from the case studies. I conducted the work of this chapter together with Oliver Günther and Holger Ziekow. We published the results in Ivantysynova et al.

(2008b).

In Chapter 4 I first describe theoretical foundations about IT infrastructures in manufacturing. Then the chapter presents an analysis about the deployed IT infrastructure in seven additional case studies. It also reveals lessons learned. I conducted the case studies together with Holger Ziekow in 2007 and 2008. The case studies and their results are currently under review.

Chapter 5 deals with the question of how to embed RFID into the IT infrastructure at manufacturers. This includes a description about common functionalities, implementation issues and a discussion about how to distribute data and logic within the IT infrastructure. This work was accomplished with Holger Ziekow. We published the results in Ivantysynova and Ziekow (2008).

Chapter 6 addresses costs and benefits for RFID investments in manufacturing. Here I cover quantifiable as well as non-quantifiable aspects. I conducted this work with Oliver Günther, Seckin Kara, Michael Klafft, and Holger Ziekow. Parts of the results have already been published in Ivantysynova et al. (2007). The entire results are currently under review.

Then Chapter 7 identifies important determinants of an RFID adoption decision, taking the automotive supply chain as an example. I conducted this work together with Hanna Krasnova and Lorenz Weser. The results of this chapter have been published in Krasnova et al. (2008). Chapter 8 concludes my thesis.

Chapter 2

Potential Benefits of RFID on the Shop Floor

Applying RFID technologies on the shop floor has recently gained some attention (Chappell et al., 2003; MCBeath, 2006). However, still little experience with such applications exists. Therefore, it is often unclear if and when RFID technology really is a better basis for a solution than alternative technologies such as bar codes.

Thus, this chapter presents an analysis of potential benefits of using RFID for improving production processes. To this end, Holger Ziekow and I conducted case studies at six German manufacturing enterprises to explore possible RFID scenarios. Each case study comprises an analysis of the production process and (potential) use of RFID technology gained through a series of on-site interviews and observations.

RFID is an automatic identification technology (short Auto-ID). Therefore, I will start this chapter with a description of Auto-ID technologies, see Section 2.1. The section focuses the overview of Auto-ID technologies specifically on those used in manufacturing. It gives details about the technologies, and their potentials and drawbacks. RFID distinguishes itself from all other Auto-ID technologies with some specific features. Hence these are discussed in detail. Despite the potential benefits of RFID it also exhibits a number of challenges.

Section 2.2 presents related work on RFID in manufacturing. Section 2.3 then analyzes potential benefits of applying RFID technology in manufacturing enterprises in. Here I present our case studies. Section 2.4 reveals lessons learned from the case studies. This section also discusses manufacturers' motives for considering an RFID rollout.

Five of the six case studies have been carried out in cooperation with the MES software vendor MPDV Mikrolab GmbH. With their support, I approached several of their customers which are interested in applying RFID.

I conducted the case studies together with Holger Ziekow in 2006; Section 2.4 was accomplished together with Oliver Günther and Holger Ziekow. We published the results in Günther et al. (2008). In particular, we published parts of Section 2.1 and the complete Sections 2.3 and 2.4 in Günther et al. (2008), Ivantysynova et al. (2008a) and Ivantysynova et al. (2008b).

2.1 Automatic Identification Technologies

Auto-ID refers to technologies that automatically identify objects, collect data about these objects and map these data into IT systems without human intervention. The aim of Auto-ID systems is to reduce errors in data entries, increase efficiency, and free up personnel to perform more valuable functions (see Auto-ID-Center, 2002, p. 3). Auto-ID entails the following quite heterogeneous technologies: magnetic stripe, smart card, voice recognition, biometrics, machine vision, optical character recognition, bar code, and radio frequency.

Magnetic stripes and smart cards are contact recognition systems. Smart cards are also known as integrated circuit cards (ICC) (Rankl and Effing, 2008). Magnetic stripes contain three independent tracks for storing data. Each track can either contain 7-bit alphanumeric characters or 5-bit numeric characters (ISO/IEC-7813, 2006; ISO/IEC-4909, 2000). Hence magnetic cards have a limited identification depth of 265 byte (210 bits per inch on each track) whereby only the third track is read/write. IC cards can store around 15 kbytes. Both systems have the disadvantage of mechanical wear. The magnetic stripe or the embedded integrated circuit may get scratched or bent, respectively, thereby making future reads impossible. Both technologies are widely used as business or ID cards.

Voice recognition and biometric systems are more complex than magnetic stripes and smart cards, may be more secure but also more expensive. However, all four technologies may be used as access control systems in plants.

Machine vision uses digital cameras and image-processing software for tasks such as counting passing objects, reading serial numbers, or searching for wrongly assembled parts or surface defects (Wiltschi et al., 2000).

Optical character recognition (OCR) identifies information stored in textual formats. Using OCR has the advantage that humans can also read the information, *e.g.*, during system breakdowns. Both machine vision and OCR depend on line of sight. Dirt, reflection, scratches or even vibration interfere with the automatic recognition.

Bar codes belong to optical recognition systems like machine vision and OCR. Therefore, they have the same disadvantage that they depend on a line of sight between object and reader. The length of the encoded data depends on the bar-code specification used. One-dimensional bar codes need more space – especially in the x-axis – to encode the same information as 2D bar codes. Popular 2D bar codes are the PDF417 bar code (ISO/IEC-15438, 2001) or the matrix code (ISO/IEC-16022, 2006).

Bar codes are rather sensitive to disturbances. One non-readable bar is sufficient to make the bar code no longer readable. Therefore, matrix codes have an embedded error correction. By this they can still be read, even if they are partially damaged. However, they require a more sophisticated logic in the evaluating software. Bar codes are the cheapest Auto-ID system; the carriers are merely printed stickers. In recent years the bar code has been established in many areas including manufacturing. To identify goods or objects within manufacturing this code carrier has become indispensable. It requires a careful analysis to see where an existing bar-code solution should be replaced by RFID.

Radio-frequency identification (RFID) is the only identification system that works without any physical contact as well as without a line of sight. In particular, it works over a certain distance and even through non-metallic materials. An antenna emits radio waves generating voltage in the inductor of the passive transponder or triggering the active transponder to send data. The transponder chip operates on the induced energy, uses the inductor as antenna and sends its ID to the reader antenna in bit-serial form. The transponder signal is evaluated in the decoder, checked for errors, and forwarded for further processing.

Low-frequency systems have proved sufficient in many contexts. Successful implementations exist in manufacturing, assembly, logistics, and access control – and this even though their range is limited to 0.5 meters. The transponders are not expensive and also work when embedded in metal. The high-frequency systems reach read ranges of 1-2 meters and may have a memory of up to several megabytes. Anti-collision technology enables them to read several transponders at the same time. However, the transponders are not very resistant to adverse mechanical and thermal conditions and they do not work very well in environments with lots of metal.

UHF transponders also have the highest range, and the additional advantage of combining write/read transponders with anti-collision technology. Due to their increased range, they are particularly suited to tracking pallets and cartons. By means of directional radiation, ranges of up to seven meters can be reached with passive ultra high frequency (UHF) at high transport rates. A popular standard for UHF is the Gen 2 standard of (EPCglobal, 2005). The Gen 2 standard specifies 96 bits for the EPC and an optional user memory. However, these transponders are typically not very robust with respect to adverse mechanical and thermal conditions. Location problems in the presence of metal as well as the relatively high costs for readers constitute other disadvantages.

Active UHF allows read distances of up to 100 meters at high transport rates. In this case, multiple transponders can also be read simultaneously via anti-collision technologies that can manage up to 2000 tags in the reading area. Yet, the high costs for the transponders and readers as well as the limitation of the temperature range due to the battery must be considered as disadvantages. Metal reflections may also prevent the position from being assigned uniquely.

Generally the advantages of RFID can be summed up as follows: The basic technical benefit of RFID in comparison to bar codes or other recognition systems is that the tags may store information, and that this information can be modified, extended, or exchanged automatically, *i.e.*, without requiring any contact. Secondly, RFID allows an item-based tagging. Thirdly, RFID tags have the advantage that they can be covered in protective casings (DeJong, 1998) and may thus work more reliably, especially when dirt can cause false reads. And finally, RFID tags allow bulk reading. Large numbers of objects can be scanned virtually at once. With contact or optical recognition systems scanning only works on an per-object basis.

2.2 RFID Applications

In logistics, RFID is already used for numerous applications. Examples include the autonomous and decentralized management of logistic processes (Scholz-Reiter et al., 2004), tracking and tracing (Fruness, 2006), or the management of perishable goods throughout supply chains (Kärkkäinen, 2003). Table 2.1 shows that companies bought 250 million tags in 2006 for retail apparel and pallet/case applications – both used in logistics operations. This is also because in 2004 and 2005 large retailers such as Wal-Mart and Metro stated that they use RFID in their supply chains and put the demand on their suppliers to use RFID. Since then, RFID has gained increased attention for logistic processes.

The advantages of using RFID in supply chains have been studied broadly. For instance, Wamba and Boeck (2008); Strassner (2005) describe several advantages of using RFID in supply chains. Strassner (2005) gives detailed examples and case studies of how RFID can enhance automotive supply chains. Nevertheless, Table 2.1 shows that smart cards still showed the highest sales of 350 m tags in 2006; whereby 1022.6 m tags were supplied in total.

Table 2.1 also shows that RFID is not yet predominantly used in manufacturing. Less than 1% of the sold tags was used for manufacturing applications. Even tags for animals or car clickers were sold more often (ca. 5% of total). Nevertheless, besides logistic scenarios, RFID also holds potentials

Table 2.1: Number of RFID transponders (millions) sold by application in 2006, see IDTechEx, 2007 (2007).

Tag location	# of tags supplied (millions)	Value of tags (millions USD)
Air baggage	25	5
Animals	70	140
Archiving (documents/samples)	8	2.6
Books	50	17.3
Car clickers	46	46
Consumer goods	10	2.5
Conveyances/other, freight	10	10
Drugs	15	3.5
Other health care	10	5.1
Manufacturing parts, tools	10	4
Military	10	4
Pallet/case	200	34
Passport page	25	100
People	0.5	9.5
Postal	0.5	0.3
Retail apparel	50	10
Smart cards/payment key fobs	350	770
Smart tickets/banknotes/secure doc.	65	13
Tires	0.1	0.1
Vehicles	2.5	23.8
Other tag applications	65	87.1
Total	1022.6	1483.8

for improving manufacturing processes (see MCBeath, 2006; Chappell et al., 2003; Schmitt et al., 2007).

MCBeath (2006), for instance, surveyed 275 companies of different sizes and from diverse manufacturing sectors. They analyzed two drivers of RFID implementations: mandates (34%) and process improvements (41.20%). In the other 24.80%, both factors occurred. In total 2.66% of the surveyed companies had already implemented RFID at the time of the survey. In order to explore the process improvements in more detail they split them into eight major areas. However, the problem with the split beforehand is that the companies had to categorize their RFID application into one of these prescribed groups. Sadly they also do not go into more detail as to why so few companies use RFID. They do not discuss possible hindrances of implementations.

Chappell et al. (2003) give a list of possible impacts of Auto-ID technology in the manufacturing supply chain. This includes tracking and managing spare-parts inventory, reducing cycle time, increasing capacity utilization and yield, and improving product quality – just to name a few. For them Auto-ID are electronic product codes and RFID technologies. They argue that these benefits can directly impact shareholder value levers. Therefore, they also state that RFID applications on the shop floor have gained increasing attention in recent years. In their work they also present a schema of various components of an Auto-ID system rollout and give recommendations for calculating the overall cost.

However, this description is quite cursory and may only be used as a starting point for a profound analysis. In their closing comments the authors name five key areas where manufacturing processes may have opportunities for improvement through Auto-ID. These are equipment effectiveness, asset utilization, product tracking and genealogy, inventory tracking and visibility, and labor productivity. However, the authors do not describe experiences with RFID including hindrances and advantages. Therefore, it is often unclear if and when RFID really is a better solution compared to alternatives like bar-code-based applications.

Besides Chappell et al. (2003) also Automation (2004) name potentials of RFID on the plant floor. These are labor usage, inventory visibility, and plant asset management, and tracking and genealogy. The authors also see that *"RFID has the potential of complementing MES in terms of providing new streams of real-time data that can support existing [...] programs."* However, their discussion is too sketchy to give guidance for companies who are looking to see whether or not RFID would be suitable a choice for them.

Schmitt et al. (2007)'s work is a meta analysis about the adoption and diffusion of RFID in the automotive industry. In their work they list examples of how manufacturing processes specific to the automotive industry can be enhanced. These are improved management of valuable assets, container tracking or inventory management. Besides closed-loop applications the authors also discuss applications along the automotive supply chain. With their meta study they identify significant factors that facilitate adoption of RFID in the automotive industry. The authors analyze the following dominant factors: compatibility (*i.e.*, technological, hardware, software and data standards), costs, complexity of the technology, performance (*i.e.*, technological capability and environmental influences on systems), and top-management support.

Summing up, still little experience with RFID applications in manufacturing exists. None of the work describes detailed experiences with RFID applications. Hindrances of applying RFID are not discussed, nor guidelines given on how to best embed RFID into the manufacturing landscape. It is often unclear if and when RFID really is a better solution compared to alternatives like bar-code-based applications. None of the work provides detailed guidelines for calculating monetary effects, does not address strategic potentials of RFID nor does it propose a corresponding evaluation model. We address these aspects with our case studies.

2.3 Case Studies

This section shows how manufacturing companies can benefit from the above-described advantages of RFID. In order to truly examine the potential of RFID we conducted six case studies at diverse manufacturers. With this qualitative research method we aim at acquiring an in-depth understanding of the situation present in the manufacturing domain. As a result we evaluate RFID potentials that are specific for the manufacturing domain.

We specifically choose the case-study approach as a qualitative-empirical method (see Wilde and Hess, 2007). Case studies have the disadvantage of leading to smaller samples compared to questionnaires. However, the fact of having a much greater depth of the analysis clearly dominates on the positive side (Flyvbjerg, 2006). In our case studies, we have an interpretative research approach. As defined by (Walsham, 1993, p.4-5) interpretative methods of research into information systems are

> aimed at producing an understanding of the context of the information system, and the process whereby the information system influences and is influenced by the context.

In each case study, we analyze the production processes of one specific plant. The participating companies are from the following industries (the company names are not revealed due to non-disclosure agreements):

1. automotive industry: manufacturer of airbags (short AIR),

2. automotive industry: manufacturer of sliding clutches (CLU),

3. automotive industry: manufacturer of engine-cooling modules (COO),

4. steel and mill industry: manufacturer of cast parts (CAS),

5. electronics industry: manufacturer of connectors (CON),

6. packaging industry: manufacturer of packaging (PAC).

All companies are headquartered in Germany. Their size ranges between several hundred and over 65,000 employees. Our reason for choosing these companies is to gain several representatives from first- and second-tier suppliers. Additionally, most of them act as a supplier to OEMs in the automotive industry making them representative for many companies in Germany. The automotive industry is the largest employer in the country (OICA, 2007).

COO is one representative that is already using RFID in production. Two reasons dominate all participating companies' interest in RFID. On the one hand, they expect their customers to demand RFID solutions in the future and they want to be prepared for this scenario. On the other hand, due to specific customers' demands and the need to obtain competitive advantages, the companies aim at improving the tracking of their production processes. All six companies assumed that RFID could either be a solution for cases where bar-code technology is not applicable, or be an advantageous alternative to bar-code technology.

2.3.1 Production of Airbags

I have published extracts of this case study in Ivantysynova and Ziekow (2007). The investigated plant of AIR assembles complete car-airbag modules and produces covers that are part of an airbag. An airbag module consists of a cover, a cushion, and an inflator. The production is divided into seven production steps *injection molding, flash removal, special surface treatment, varnishing, pre-assembly, assembly*, and *shipment* (see Figure 2.1).

The process starts with the *injection molding* of the airbag's cover. Here, plastic is injected into a mold and formed into a cover. At this point a barcode label is applied to the cover which later used for tracing the product in the remaining process steps.

In the second step (*flash removal*), excess plastic at the parting lines of the mold is removed. The following step is a special *surface treatment* which increases the quality of varnishing (this step is not always conducted as some customers do not want this treatment). Subsequently, the covers are sent to *varnishing*. After this step, *pre-* and *assembly* of the airbag start. Here, the emblem of the car brand is mounted on the front side of the cover. Then cover, cushion, and inflator are mounted together. Finally, in the last step *shipment*, airbags are packed into boxes, labeled, and sent to a warehouse.

After each process step, the bar code of the cover has to be scanned. It is of major importance to ensure that all information (executed activity, time *etc.*) is recorded correctly during the production process. This is done because some customers demand tracking of every process step executed during production. Complete information collection is necessary to follow the product's genealogy in case of claims regarding faulty products. For instance, the information is needed to determine who is liable if an airbag did not work in a car accident.

Before each manufacturing operation is begun, a plausibility check is run to verify that the required preceding steps have been finished successfully. These checks help to prevent errors during the production process. For example, before varnishing starts, it is verified that the special surface treatment has been conducted. This check is triggered by the scanning of the bar code

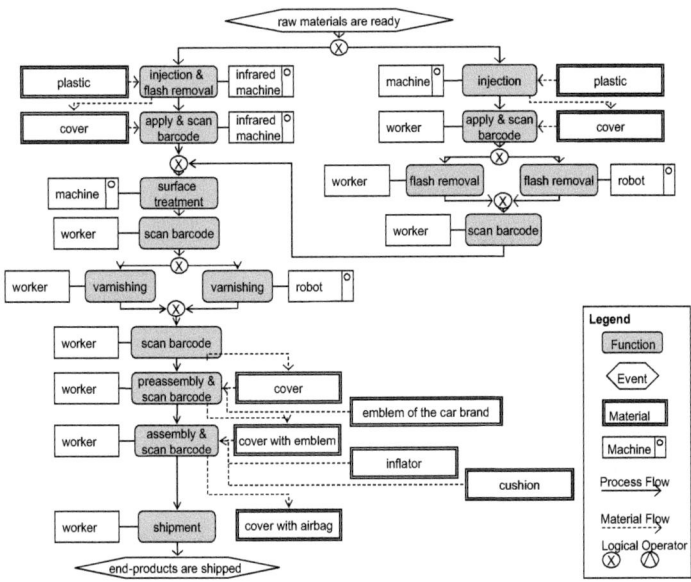

Figure 2.1: Production process for airbags at AIR.

attached to the airbag cover. The bar-code scan triggers a database query in the back-end system and the query results determine whether or not production may proceed.

AIR uses manual as well as automatic bar-code scanning processes. Manual scanning is a relatively time-consuming process. Especially due to the irregular shapes of covers it is cumbersome to establish the line of sight required by bar-code readers. Bar codes are often applied to the inside of the cover and the cover must be turned upside down in order to enable the scan. Furthermore, scanning may fail and may have to be repeated, resulting in extra delay. Within AIR's production process, a manual scan takes four seconds on average. Due to the complicated handling, automating all of the bar-code scanning processes is not a cost-effective option.

Potential Improvements with RFID

AIR currently does not use RFID in its production. Data management and tracking of products is implemented by means of bar codes. Within the case study, we have identified the subsequently described applications for RFID at AIR's plant. They address the following four improvements: reducing communication with the process control system, reducing manual scan transactions in the production process, reducing manual scan transactions in the warehouse, and avoiding bar-code print-quality issues and reducing penalties.

Reducing communication with the process control system: every scan transaction triggers a query in the process control system for getting the required information about the product. The production process must wait for the response to the query in order to ensure the correctness of the production flow. According to the plant manager, response times of more than about half a second are not tolerable. Achieving responses within this time constraint is already challenging with the current infrastructure. Considering that additional scans are planned to be introduced in the future, the load for the process control system will increase further. As a result, the response time may be longer than the tolerable waiting time. According to the production supervisor the scaling of AIR's process control infrastructure is an expensive solution to this problem.

By adopting RFID, the problem of time-consuming communication with the process control system could be overcome. The covers could be labeled with writable RFID tags. The necessary information for the production process could be stored on the tag. As the cover flows through the production process, RFID readers could communicate with the tag on the cover and read the required information from there. Local processing logic could execute the plausibility check (*e.g.,* previous process step has finished successfully). A communication with the process control system would be minimized since most of the required information would be accessible directly from the RFID chip. However, this scenario would require a degree of "local intelligence" which may be provided by a PLC (Programmable Logic Controller) or a PC on the shop floor.

Reducing manual scan transactions in the production process: AIR has implemented scans of the products' bar codes after each production step. Many of these scan transactions are conducted manually and account for a significant percentage of the employees' activities. Furthermore, since the bar codes are applied to the inside of a cover, the cover must be turned upside down before the bar code can be scanned; this takes extra time. Applying RFID would automate the identification process and save valuable employee time. Since automatic scanning could be done in parallel to other tasks, this solution would cause no process delay.

The manual varnishing facility is another point in the production process where an RFID adoption could improve production efficiency. This facility is a separate room with a single entry and exit. After the covers are varnished workers place them on a metal cart that consists of nine shelves. Each shelf carries 200 to 300 covers. Then a worker pushes the cart out of the varnishing facility.

After leaving the room all of the covers on the cart are scanned manually. In this scenario, RFID could be used for scanning whole batches of covers. This would minimize the human intervention and speed up the process. RFID readers could register the covers as they pass through the varnishing facility door. One of the challenges in this scenario is the cart itself, since its metal structure may interfere with the RFID process.

Reducing manual scan transactions in the warehouse: finished products are placed in containers and sent to the warehouse from where they are shipped. At this stage, the management of products is no longer handled at item level but rather at container level. Products that have been placed in a container are booked to the container's account. Booking airbags to a container or booking out an erroneous entry are tasks which are accomplished manually. Therefore, they are time-consuming and possibly error-prone.

RFID readers and tags could provide a more reliable and flexible warehouse and delivery management. RFID readers could be installed at the warehouse door. Then the correctness of the containers' content could be checked automatically. Additionally, realizing this scenario would also allow

AIR's customers to use RFID at their inbound logistics, because the arriving products and containers would already be equipped with RFID tags by AIR. If the customers make use of these tags, cost-sharing models might be feasible. Otherwise, reusing the existing RFID tags at the customer's side can be perceived as a service of AIR and thereby be a competitive advantage.

Avoiding bar-code print-quality issues and reducing penalties: after the production process is completed, new bar codes are applied to airbags formatted according to customer requirements. These bar codes are used for identification and for enabling an information flow between supplier and customer. Bar codes on airbags must be correctly applied and flawless. Scratches or dirt can make the bar code unreadable.

Achieving the printing quality required by the customer creates a considerable technical challenge. The bar-code scanners installed at the customer's location may have problems reading low-quality bar codes. Since many of AIR's customers implement a just-in-sequence delivery each unreadable bar code potentially causes a delay in the customer's production. In such cases AIR has to pay high penalties. To avoid the penalties, AIR puts a great deal of effort into printing high-quality bar-code labels. Nevertheless, this does not prevent dirt and scratches.

If the respective costumer agreed to apply RFID tags instead of bar codes, the possibility of unreadable labels would decrease. The use of RFID would still require a label printer (for printing textual information and applying the tag) but the printing quality (and therefore costs) would not need to be as high. Overall, the burden of printing the labels is eased and penalties due to unreadable labels are less likely.

Costs and Benefits

The main reason for considering RFID technology at AIR is to reduce manual bar-code scanning processes. Manual scanning accounts for a significant proportion of the employees' time. AIR's IT staff estimated that the application of RFID would save up to four seconds at each manual scan point. Applied to all production lines, this would sum up to approximately 26000 hours of work per year (*i.e.*, 24 sec/airbag total saving through the process x 4mio airbags/year).

Additional time could be saved in the outbound shipping processes, where the checkout could be automated. Yet, only a few euro cents could be saved per airbag. Since in this scenario RFID tags remain on the product, the tag cost must be weighed against the savings per airbag. At a price of 20-30 euro cents for low-cost passive RFID labels, this may or may not be cost-effective.

Thus, cost-sharing models with subsequent players in the value chain (who might reuse the tags) should be considered. Also, supply costs and maintenance costs of RFID writers/scanners are likely to be significantly lower than the cost for bar-code scanners, printers and printer/applicators.

Another reason for an RFID adoption is to reduce the load for the process control system. Currently, the infrastructure at AIR is at its limit for processing plausibility checks in the process control system. The planned expansion in the number of scan points would therefore require additional investments in the server infrastructure. If tags with extended writable memory are used, consistency checks could be processed independently from the back-end system. Here, the cost for additional servers must be traded against the running costs for RFID tags with sufficient memory as well the effort for implementing plausibility checks on local PLCs or PCs located on the shop floor.

Further savings may result from avoiding penalties for unreadable bar codes. Currently, AIR pays a few thousand euros per bar code when it is unreadable to the customer. Such penalties could be avoided if RFID is applied. Yet, this requires that the customers agree to switch from bar codes to an RFID-based solution.

Besides these quantifiable effects, the manufacturer may also gain intangible improvements due to an RFID adoption. Strategic benefits that RFID may leverage are improvements in customer service, reputation, and inter-organizational collaboration. With RFID tags on the products, the manufacturer enables its clients to benefit from the technology as well; thereby providing an additional service. Reputation may increase because of the manufacturer's positioning as an innovative company that quickly adapts new technologies. With regards to inter-organizational collaboration RFID may strengthen the manufacturer's position as well.

Labeling each product with an RFID tag makes the manufacturer ready for RFID-based supply chain management and collaboration. In addition to strategic effects the manufacturer may gain non-quantifiable benefits in its operations. That is, RFID could ease the IT management in the medium term by taking away workload from the back-end system.

Summarizing Case AIR

In this case study we discuss the potential benefits of using RFID in AIR's production processes. AIR assembles complete airbag modules and produces covers that are one of the three parts in an airbag module. We analyzed all of the production processes in order to define the potentials of RFID adoption at the investigated plant. We examined whether the use of RFID in this production process could be advantageous compared to the current application of bar codes.

Furthermore, we outline five potential benefits RFID may hold for AIR. These advantages include (i) reducing communication with the back-end system, (ii) reducing manual scan transactions in the production process, (iii) reducing manual scan transactions in the warehouse, (iv) avoiding bar-code print-quality issues and reducing penalties, and (v) avoiding customer-specific bar-code printing. We analyze all advantages with respect to their resulting costs. This covers costs for RFID readers, tags and required software.

In the longer term, a tighter IT-enabled integration of the entire supply chain seems likely for AIR. This would be the case when the tags would remain on the product. At this point, however, the implementation of such integration measures, including related security measures and standards activities, is a costly and possibly risky endeavor. Possible benefits will a priori not be distributed fairly between the different parties in the supply chain. This concerns not only costs for RFID readers, tags and required software, and costs for changing the underlying processes, but also the costs for constructing a more detailed mapping between the shop-floor operations and the IT processes.

2.3.2 Production of Sliding Clutches

The investigated plant of CLU assembles sliding clutches for car drive trains. With the following analysis HU adds to a previous study that was conducted by a consultancy. CLU investigates an RFID implementation due to its aim at narrowing costly product recalls.

The production process at CLU consists of seven operations which are highly automated by machines. These operations are *broaching, milling, cleaning, carburizing, hardening* (combined with *grit blasting*), and *assembly*. An abstract model of this production process is shown in Figure 2.2. Human intervention is limited to loading/unloading, setting up, and maintaining machines as well as recording production data. Workers interact with the IT back-end system via terminals on the plant floor that are controlled by an MES.

CLU's products are assembled from ready-bought parts and diverse metal rings which CLU produces itself. Plastic pallets are used for the internal transportation of ready-bought parts and of the final products. Plastic pallets are also used for outbound shipping. Internally processed metal rings are loaded into metal baskets before they are run through the production process. These baskets are used for loading and unloading the machines as well as for transporting parts to a subsequent operation. At each production step, machines pick up the metal rings from fixed positions in the baskets, process them, and place them back into the baskets. Note that rings are not necessarily put back into the same basket as the one they were taken from.

Potential Improvements with RFID

CLU is currently running tests for a planned RFID implementation. The case study conducted by HU refers to the application which CLU is about to implement as well as to other application scenarios which may be realized in the long term. Altogether, HU identified the following scenarios for the in-

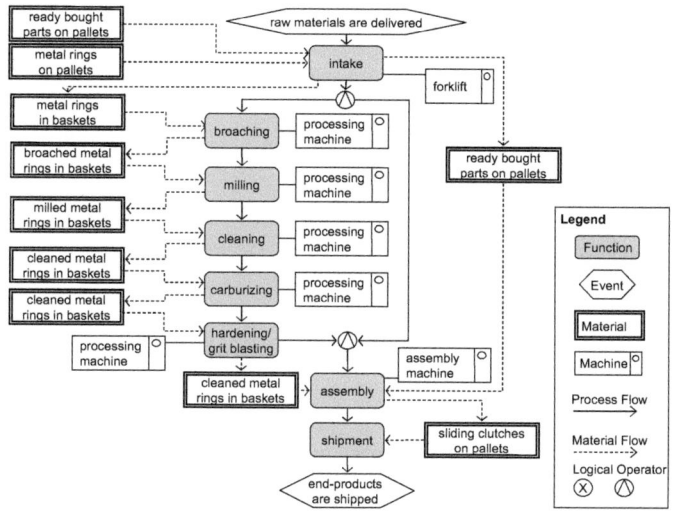

Figure 2.2: Production process for sliding clutches at CLU.

vestigated plant, targeting the following four improvements: narrowing down the scope of recalls, reducing workload for warehouse management, improving quality and timeliness of production tracking, and improving customer services and data exchange.

Narrowing down the scope of recalls: the predominant reason for considering RFID solutions at CLU is to improve the traceability of the production process. The goal is to narrow the scope of possible recalls and to limit resulting financial losses. This is of major importance as recalls account for significant costs at CLU. Using tracking information would help to limit the scope of recalls and manual checks of potentially faulty products. CLU currently plans to equip all plastic pallets carrying material parts with RFID tags. These rewritable tags will store information about the shipment.

Two scan points are planned which monitor three events within the production process. The first event is captured at the gate between the intake and the plant floor. Recording this event allows to track which items get into the current production cycle. Readers at the assembly station register the second event. Here, each plastic pallet of ready-bought parts is scanned at the assembly machine. (Note that only ready-bought parts are transported on pallets at this stage).

The last event is captured when the transportation units pass through the gate between the intake and the plant floor, again indicating that the production process has finished. With the help of these three scans, it can easily be determined which objects are in the production cycle at a particular moment in time.

In the case of malfunctions in the production, the recall can be limited to those items which were in the cycle at the respective time. If pallets were scanned individually, bar-code labels could provide similar functionality. However, since CLU wishes to scan the pallets in bulk at the gate to the plant floor, bar codes are impractical. Through this gate, whole stacks of pallets are transported on a forklift and must be scanned as they pass by.

In the long term, one can also consider mounting RFID tags to the internally used metal baskets. With RFID readers at each machine, the baskets could be traced through the whole production process. As a result, recalls could be narrowed down further. Yet, this application scenario would require an update of the machine/PLC software.

With the current software some parts get moved from one basket to another without documenting this process. The plant IT staff has raised concerns about the effort required and risks involved when changing the software. Changing the proprietary software would require the launching of a software development project with the manufacturers of the machines. The new software would need to undergo extensive testing and fine-tuning in the production environment. Due to these required efforts, changing the machines' software is perceived as costly by the IT staff of CLU.

Reducing workload for warehouse management: realizing the scenario *narrowing down the scope of recalls* leverages other scenarios in which RFID could deliver benefits. Tracking the production process requires the transportation units to be equipped with RFID tags. This includes the transportation units which are also used for shipment processes. RFID tags on these transportation units could be reused at the warehouse. For example, it would be possible to use the RFID tags for managing the warehouse inventory.

Either smart shelves (shelves which are equipped with RFID readers) or mobile RFID readers could be used for quick updates of the whole inventory. Compared with bar-code-based solutions, this would reduce the workload for warehouse management and could improve the accuracy of the inventory list. Furthermore, goods entering and leaving the warehouse could be automatically registered if RFID readers were installed at the warehouse entry.

Improving quality and timeliness of production tracking: currently, CLU uses bar codes to measure the progress of running production tasks. The bar codes are printed on documents that accompany the stacks of metal baskets which carry the materials for processing. Workers are required to scan the bar codes after the corresponding stack has passed a production step.

Thereby, information about the progress of the production is fed into the back-end system and the process is documented. Yet, workers do not always scan the bar codes in a timely manner. Occasionally accompanying documents are even collected and scanned in bulk at the end of a shift. Thus, the status information obtained by scanning bar codes does not always reflect the reality and is of limited use for performance analyses.

Tracking the production progress could be automated if scanning was done automatically with RFID instead of manually with bar codes. This would require equipping every stack of internal transportation units with an RFID tag. Then, readers at each production step could detect if a stack is moved to the next station and the information can be automatically updated in the back-end system. Furthermore, the production process could be monitored in greater detail by implementing additional scan points at the plant floor. For instance, for each stack of metal baskets how long it stays at which operation could be recorded. This would allow to further narrow recalls and to monitor the process in greater detail.

Improving customer services and data exchange: the application of RFID at the production plant may not only improve the production itself but could also improve the information exchange with customers. Here, RFID may serve as both, the medium for information exchange and as the enabler for gathering the information which is provided for the customer. As discussed above, applying RFID in the production process enables the recording of fine-grained process information in real time, assuming that writeable RFID tags were used. This information may be used by CLU but could also be shared with the customers who ordered the products.

Costs and Benefits

Four potential application scenarios for RFID where identified at CLU. Yet, for some it is not possible to calculate monetary benefits without further analysis. For instance, gains due to improved production tracing and improved customer services cannot easily be estimated.

The main driver for implementing RFID at CLU is the expected savings from improving the traceability of products. If a production error is detected, all potentially affected sliding clutches must be checked manually. For faulty and already shipped products, checks must even take place at customers' plants. This results in additional costs for sending engineers to the customers. Costs for recalls are even higher for sliding clutches which were already used in a customer's production, because the manufacturer has to pay penalties in such a case. These penalties sum up to about 7.5% of CLU's revenue.

Thus, improving traceability and thereby narrowing recalls can account for significant savings. The costs for realizing this application scenario depend on the desired level of granularity of tracing. The basic application can be implemented with only one reader gate at the plant floor and reusable tags on the transport units.

Yet, the tracing would still be relatively coarse-grained. To achieve a tracing on the level of individual operations, additional readers on the plant floor would be needed. Furthermore, the software of the machines would need to be updated as the machines move sliding clutches within and between transportation units.

However, when the manufacturer decides to apply RFID technology for expanding traceability, then the technology could also be used for improving other processes in production. For instance, this infrastructure can be used to improve warehouse management and speed up the processes for loading and unloading shipments. In combination with the scenario for improved traceability, only minor additional hardware costs would occur for this application.

Besides these quantifiable aspects one also has to consider intangible aspects of applying RFID. Here we would improve the quality of the manufacturer's services due to more precise recalls. Additionally, a more detailed data capturing may enable data analysts to reveal an unexpected potential for production improvements. With regards to inter-organizational collaboration the RFID adaption would strengthen the manufacturer's strategic position. The planned application would make the manufacturer ready for RFID-based supply chain management and RFID-based information exchange with its partners.

Summarizing Case CLU

In this case study we discuss potentials benefits that CLU may gain from RFID adoption. To specify these possible advantages, we investigate the current situation and production processes. We identify areas that could be improved by using RFID and outlined corresponding application scenarios. This comprises an investigation of whether the use of RFID in this production process could be advantageous compared to the current application of bar codes.

In addition to the outlined RFID potentials in the plant itself, business processes across the supply chain could be improved further to fully exploit the advantages of an RFID-enabled supply chain. Possible measures include the selective communication of RFID data to CLU's customers and business partners. At this point, the production data is simply written into a back-end system.

Strategic issues to be considered are quality and customer relations, because OEMs focus increasingly on traceability. This provides an opportunity for suppliers that are well prepared for such demands. In the longer term, a tighter IT-enabled integration of the entire supply chain is likely. For such

IT-enabled business processes the IT department needs to better map and integrate the information from the shop floor into IT processes.

At this point, however, the implementation of such integration measures, including related security measures and standards activities, is a costly and possibly risky endeavor. Possible benefits will a priori not be distributed fairly between the different parties in the supply chain. This concerns not only costs for RFID readers, tags and required software, and costs for changing the underlying processes, but also the costs for constructing a more detailed mapping between the shop-floor operations and the IT processes.

2.3.3 Production of Engine-Cooling Modules

The investigated plant of COO produces engine-cooling modules and air-conditioning devices. COO is a first-tier automotive supplier. Currently, COO uses RFID technology in two assembly lines for tracking cooling modules along the assembly process. RFID technology was introduced due to a customer's demand for a better process documentation. Figure 2.3 illustrates COO's production process.

The engine-cooling modules are mounted on carriers (one module per carrier) and moved along an assembly line from work station to work station. Coordination of the complete process is done by a PLC and a just-in-sequence (JIS) control system. The JIS software is responsible for the correct sequencing of the engine-cooling modules into the pallets that are later loaded onto the truck to the customer (just-in-sequence delivery).

When the line has assembled all of the modules for the current pallet, its PLC sends a request to the JIS control system. The JIS system then tells the PLC with which modules it has to fill the next pallet. For the subsequent module, the PLC retrieves the new data and produces a data set for each engine-cooling module. The data set includes type information and job parameters and is written to the RFID tag of the carrier for the respective module. As the engine-cooling module moves along the assembly line, the information on the tag is constantly read and updated at each station.

Job instructions are read from the RFID tag and used for local planning purposes at each work station. Once the job has been completed, the relevant information is written back to the tag. About 3000 bytes of data are saved on the RFID tag for each engine-cooling module. This data includes which cooling module was produced, how the production steps were distributed among the active work stations, and whether all tasks were performed accurately. At the end of the production cycle, the complete data set from the RFID tag is stored in the back-end system. This recorded data is made available to the quality assurance and planning department. The RFID tag stays on the carrier and gets reused in the production of the next engine-cooling module.

When a finished engine-cooling module leaves the assembly line, a worker lifts it from the carrier and puts it on the pallet. At this point, all data on the RFID tag (which is attached to the carrier, not to the module) is transferred to the back-end JIS system. Subsequently, a bar-code label with the serial number of the modules is printed and attached to the module. When the pallet is full, the worker checks the position of all modules on the pallet. If the check succeeds, a control label for the forklift operator is printed and attached to the pallet. Finally, the forklift operator scans the bar codes and puts the pallet into the correct position on the truck.

RFID Application and Potential Improvements

COO introduced RFID at the request of one customer who expects improved traceability of the produced parts. Traceability of parts is of increasing importance to OEMs, partly due to legal requirements, and partly in order to improve quality in the long term by identifying faulty components quickly and reliably. In COO's solution, RFID tags are attached to the carriers which are used to move the parts through the assembly line. This allows the tracking of the entire assembly process.

Once a part is separated from the carrier, the information is transferred to the back-end system. The carrier and the RFID tag attached to it can be recycled immediately. Separating the product and the product-related data leads to some challenges regarding data management. In order to obtain accurate data on a given engine-cooling module, the ID of the module must be available and forwarded to a database. This database needs to be maintained to provide the relevant information in the long term. In contrast, having the required data stored with the respective object ensures easy and consistent access.

At the moment, no production data is passed on to the ERP because it is considered to be of operational value only. Production and business processes across the supply chain could possibly be improved further to fully exploit the advantages of an RFID-enabled supply chain. This would require a tighter integration of the RFID data into the existing ERP infrastructure. A closer integration into the ERP system could also facilitate the creation of a data warehouse documenting the production process over a longer period of time. Customers may be interested in obtaining this data. This may even account for new business opportunities. For example, Metro AG, Germany's largest retailer, already realizes substantial revenues offering sales data to its suppliers.

Costs and Benefits

Since the RFID tags are reused, costs for the described application scenario are fixed costs. Thus, the number of RFID tags remains small and tags with extended storage are affordable despite their relatively high costs. In a bar-code-based solution, more functionality in the back-end system would be needed for realizing the same application. By using the RFID-based solution, investments in the back-end system can be reduced. Also, COO's production control system is less complex due to the fact that the data can be written to the tag and updated "in bulk" at the end of the process. Perhaps most importantly, COO has implemented the RFID application due to the demand of an important customer.

Besides this monetary aspect, the manufacturer may achieve positive intangible effects as well. This is because RFID enables an architecture which can positively impact the IT management. Storing data on the tag allows most data management tasks to be pushed to the production lines and reduces the complexity of managing back-end operations. Further intangible benefits are improvements in customer services, the company's reputation, and the inter-organizational collaboration.

Summarizing Case COO

This case study presents an analysis of the productivity and the potential of RFID at COO, a first-tier automotive supplier. This company is already using RFID on the shop floor. Therefore, the key question in this case study was whether RFID is currently used in an efficient manner.

COO installed RFID due to the demand of one customer, who seems to be satisfied with the results. The RFID technology allows recording detailed information about the assembly of each single engine-cooling module, providing a thorough documentation of the production process and thereby a reliable basis for tracing parts in the case of future breakdowns or recalls. However, the advantages of using RFID vs. a classical bar-code solution are limited. Here, we want to point out that business processes across the supply chain could be improved further in order to fully exploit the advantages of an RFID-enabled supply chain. Possible measures include the use of part-specific RFID tags that remain on the part after delivery; a tighter integration of the RFID data into the existing ERP infrastructure; the selective communication of this data to COO's customers and business partners; and the implementation of a production data warehouse.

In the longer term it seems likely that the customer will demand that the tags remain on the product. This would lead to a tighter IT-enabled integration of the entire supply chain. At this point, however, the implementation of such integration measures, including related security measures and standards activities, is a costly and possibly risky endeavor. Possible benefits will a priori not be distributed fairly between the different parties in the supply chain. This not only concerns costs for RFID readers, tags and required software, and costs for changing the underlying processes, but also the costs for constructing a more detailed mapping between the shop-floor operations and the IT processes.

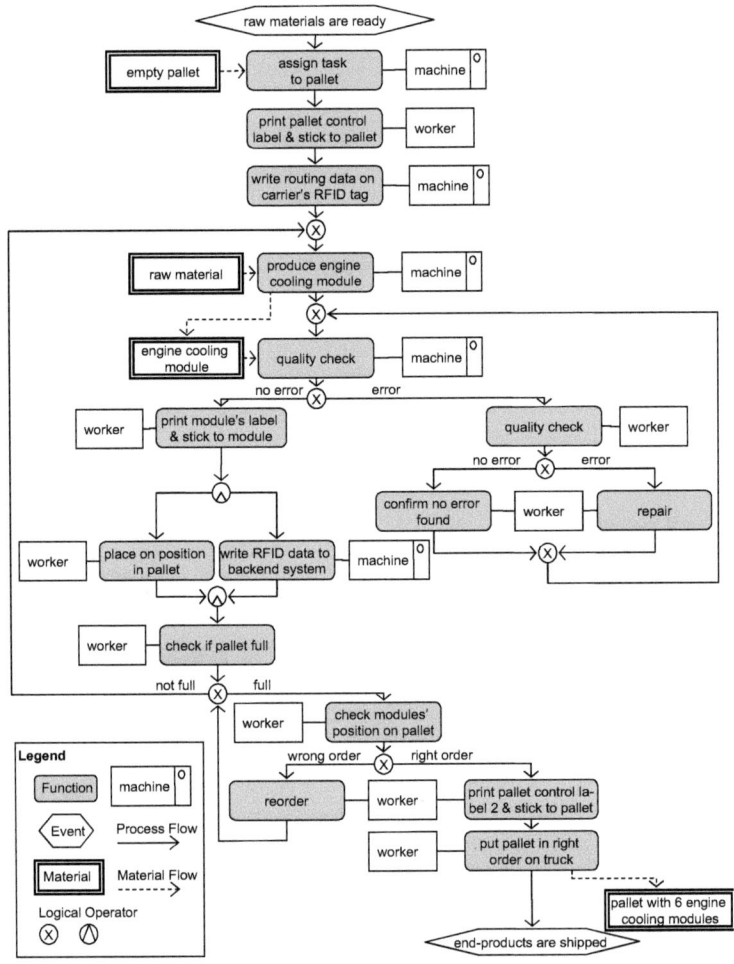

Figure 2.3: Production process for an engine-cooling module at COO.

2.3.4 Production of Cast Parts

The main products of CAS are cast parts in diverse sizes. CAS also designs the models required for casting. Models are the central asset in the production of cast parts. They consist of two model covers and up to 20 core forms. The covers and the cores are stored independently in one of the numerous storage rooms of the plant. Several thousand of these parts are being used. Each part must be fetched in a timely manner before the production can start.

At the beginning of the production, the workers select all needed model parts from the stock. If a location of a part is unknown, workers must search through all of the stocks. Currently, the workers are requested to update the positions of the models in the SAP R/3 system. However, updating the positions is a cumbersome manual task and is therefore not consistently pursued. According to CAS's workers, a consequence is that about 2% of all model parts need to be searched for before they can be used in the production. Reducing search times is of special interest, because the layout of CAS's plant makes searching a very time-consuming task and can possibly delay the production. A model of the production process at CAS is depicted in Figure 2.4.

CAS manages the search problem by planning with time buffers for fetching the required model parts. Currently, production plans are created on a weekly basis and models are fetched the day before they are needed. This allows reacting to situations where models must be searched for. However, CAS is about to switch to planning on a daily basis, leaving less time for searching. Thus, the IT managers of CAS expressed the explicit demand to improve the tracking system for model parts. This would reduce search times and make short-term planning more reliable.

In the production process, model parts are used to create sand molds which are negatives of the final product. Subsequently, melted steel is cast into these sand molds where it cools down. When the cast part is cooled the sand form collapses. Finally, excess metal at parting lines is removed and the product is shipped to the customer.

Potential Improvements with RFID

CAS is currently investigating how to reduce search times for model parts. RFID could be used to automatically keep track of the model parts. Thereby, searching could be avoided and it could be ensured that model parts are provided on time.

For the technical realization, two options have been evaluated: One is based on fixed reader gates while the other employs mobile readers. In both cases, RFID tags would be mounted to model parts. Reader gates could be placed at key points (*e.g.*, doors) on the transport ways. This would allow to keep at least track of the room a certain model part is in.

As an alternative to using reader gates, the workers who transport the model parts could be equipped with mobile readers. In this scenario, certain landmarks on the plant floor would be marked with RFID tags. During transportation, the RFID tags on the model parts as well as position tags on the plant floor or walls would be read by the mobile readers. Evaluating this information would allow to reconstruct the track of each model part. The track's granularity mainly depends on where RFID tags are located at the plant. Thus, tracks with a high spatial resolution could be achieved in this scenario.

Costs and Benefits

CAS considers the application of RFID to overcome its problems in tracking model parts. Fast retrieval of model parts is especially a challenge when CAS realizes its goal to switch from a weekly planning cycle to a daily planning cycle.

Thus, the manufacturer must trade the cost for an improved tracking system against the increasing effort for the search process of needed forms. To determine the hardware cost, two different scenarios must be considered at CAS.

In the first scenario the forms should only be tracked between different production floors and the diverse storage rooms. For this scenario, about ten reader gates would be required at way points on the transportation routes.

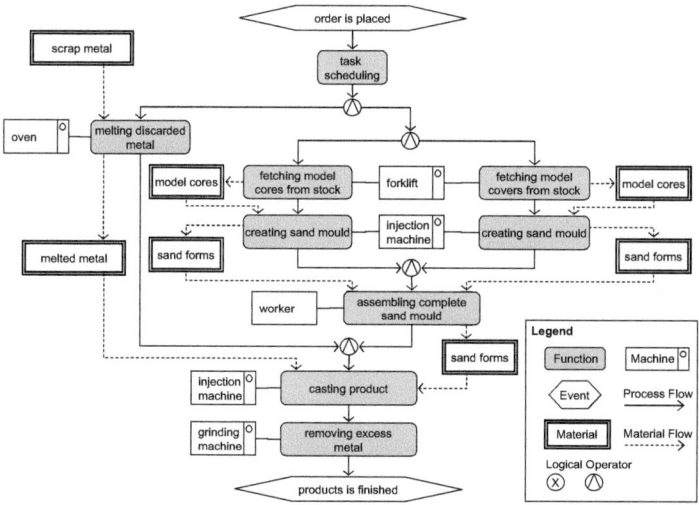

Figure 2.4: Production process at CAS.

Additionally, tens of thousands of RFID tags would be needed to label all of the model parts.

In the other scenario, mobile readers and position tags on the plant floor are required. Two mobile readers would be sufficient to equip each of the two warehouse workers. Compared to the first scenario, the second scenario needs fewer investments in hardware, although additional RFID tags for marking positions on the plant floor are needed. Furthermore, the second scenario would allow tracking with finer granularity.

However, evaluating the reader data is more complex in the mobile reader scenario. Thus, more complex and likely more expensive software would be required. One of the main drivers for RFID was in fact an intangible benefit. That is, the reduced search times would allow the manufacturer to optimize the production planning by switching from weekly to daily planning.

Summarizing Case CAS

In this case study we investigate potential solutions for tracking model parts at CAS. We describe the benefits which CAS may derive from implementing a tracking application and what technological options may be considered for the implementation. We elaborate on different hardware solutions for capturing the tracking data. In particular we discuss potential implementations with mobile readers and fixed reader gates. For these scenarios we point out differences such as the achievable granularity and the related hardware costs. We furthermore describe how data can be captured, evaluated and communicated to the back-end system.

Before CAS implements the mobile-reader or fixed-reader-gates option, hardware tests need to be conducted to determine the read reliability that can be achieved in the different scenarios. Results of these tests have implications not only on the hardware setup but also on the needed software functionality. The achieved reliability and the desired degree of automation determine what inference and filter operations are needed to be performed on the data. Finally, after deciding on these issues, the appropriate architecture and distribution of functionalities can be picked for the tracking application at CAS.

In addition to the outlined RFID potentials in the plant itself, business processes across the supply chain could be improved further to fully exploit the advantages of an RFID-enabled supply chain. At this point, however, the implementation of such integration measures, including related security measures and standards activities, is a costly and possibly risky endeavor. Possible benefits will a priori not be distributed fairly between the different parties in the supply chain. This concerns not only costs for RFID readers, tags and required software, and costs for changing the underlying processes, but also the costs for constructing a more detailed mapping between the shop-floor operations and the IT processes.

2.3.5 Production of Electronic Connectors

CON produces electronic connectors which are used by the automotive industry, telecommunications, and industrial automation. CON processes predominantly two types of input material: plastic granulates and copper straps. Figure 2.5 shows a model of the whole production process. In order to create the pins for the connectors, the copper straps are punched and galvanized. Plastic granulates are molded into the shape of the connector. Finally, pins and plastic parts are joined to create the final product. This is either done in a separate step or in combination with the *molding* (injection molding).

Each production step is documented twice. First, data about the processing steps is manually written onto paper tickets. Second, the documentation of the production is written into the back-end system. At the beginning of a processing step, a worker selects an open task via the workstation's terminal. The worker must book the task back to the back-end system after the task is completed. This is necessary for tracking and controlling the production progress.

The paper tickets are attached to the corresponding materials' transportation units. Plastic parts have boxes as transportation units. Copper straps are transported on coils. Materials are moved from the original to a new transportation unit at each processing step. For instance, copper straps are reeled from a source coil, processed, and reeled to a target coil. The accompanying ticket is then moved from the old to the new coil.

After the production, products must be labeled with the correct information and packed into the right containers for shipment. This is a particular challenge, since every customer requires different formats for the bar-code labels. Consequently, special printers are required that allow handling of multiple formats. Labels are printed at a central location in the plant and distributed to various packing stations. Furthermore, it is required to pick appropriate containers depending on the product and client. Most containers are reusable and cycle in the supply chain. Here, CON faces challenges in locating the transportation units because no detailed tracking system is applied.

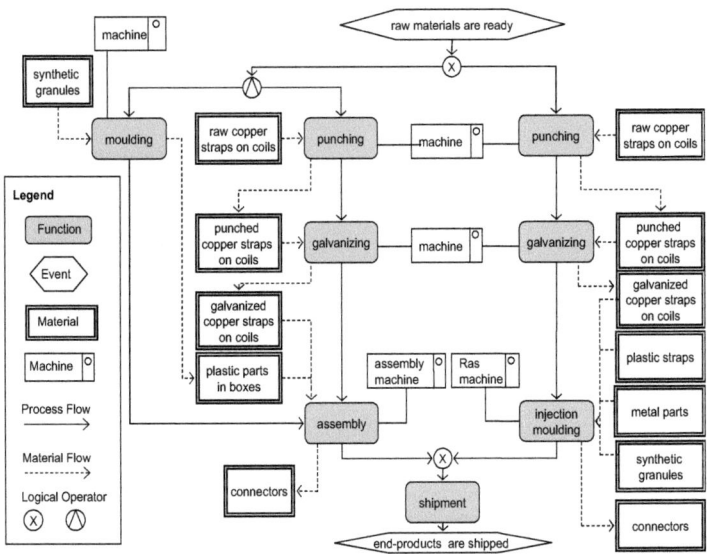

Figure 2.5: Production process of connectors at CON.

Potential Improvements with RFID

CON currently does not yet use RFID technology in its production. However, some processes may be improved through the use of RFID. Within the case study, HU has identified the subsequently described applications at CON's plant. They target the following five improvements: improving quality of production tracking and avoiding interruptions, reducing workload for maintaining process data, improving container localization, reducing effort for printing customer-specific labels, and improving process quality.

Improving quality of production tracking and avoiding interruptions: Before a production step can start, the required material must be transported to the input buffer of the operation. Additionally, the booking of the previous production step must be finished. Currently, transporting and booking are done independently and it is not ensured that both processes are synchronized.

According to CON's employees, occasionally booking is accidentally left out. If a booking is omitted, the worker at the subsequent production step will need to interrupt his task in order to complete the missing booking from the previous operation. The time loss per omitted booking can be as high as 30 minutes according to CON's staff. Instead of correcting such a missing booking, it is also possible to proceed with the production. However, in such a case, the production and the material flow are not accurately tracked and documented.

RFID technology could possibly improve the processes efficiency by ensuring that booking and transporting processes are synchronous. Internal transport units would have to be equipped with RFID tags. Tags could be attached to the coils for the copper straps and to the boxes for the plastic parts. RFID readers would detect when an internal transportation unit is moved to the next production step. Thereby, missing bookings could automatically be detected and the responsible worker could be informed. In a more advanced solution, the booking process itself may be automated. This would make transporting and booking synchronous and ease the maintenance of process data.

Two options exist regarding the installation of RFID readers at the plant floor. One option is to use only a few reader gates which are placed at intersection points of internal routes for material transportation. The installation points must be chosen in a way that materials pass at least one reader when they are transported between subsequent processing steps. This setup could be used to automatically check for missing bookings. An alarm could be triggered if a reader detects material movements which cannot be associated with a corresponding booking. The second option is to have readers at each processing step. Having readers at the machines would enable to control whether or not a processing step has been conducted. Booking could be automated.

Reducing workload for maintaining process data: according to estimates of CON's employees, a worker on the plant floor spends approximately 15%

of their working time on maintaining process data. Up to a third of this time is spent on the maintenance of tickets for the internal transportation. A portion of the data maintenance could be automated if tickets were partly (if not totally) replaced by writable RFID tags. This would increase workers' productivity as well as reduce errors in manual data entries.

Having boxes and coils equipped with RFID tags allows for associating the internal transfer units with data about their content. For example, a machine could automatically identify the transportation unit for the output material. Then, it could link data about the conducted operation with the identified unit. Thereby, manual writing of process information on paper sheets could be avoided or at least reduced.

In general, two options exist for automatically storing data. One is to write the data directly onto an RFID tag attached to the internal transfer units. In this case, a tag with a sufficient amount of memory is needed. Alternatively, the information could be written to a database in the back-end system. This scenario requires internal transfer units to be equipped with an RFID tag holding only an ID. The tag ID could automatically be read and used as a key in the database. Thereby, the RFID technology allows to automatically associate data about processes with the corresponding internal transfer unit. Yet, using a database instead of writing data to RFID tags would increase the number of back-end transactions and may therefore require investments in the back-end system. It must be analyzed carefully which option for storing data is more cost effective.

Improving container localization: numerous types of containers for shipping are used at the plant. Different customers require different packing units for shipping, making container management a challenging task. Containers can be at various locations within the plant and no detailed tracking of containers exists today. Automatic tracking of containers could be realized with the use of RFID technology (see also the previous scenario).

If containers were equipped with RFID tags, readers at different locations could update a database that holds the container's position. Alternatively, mobile readers could be used for a quick update of the inventory. This would reduce time for searching containers, lower the risk of losing containers and reduce costs of renting containers by decreasing the required safety stocks.

For tagging containers, low-cost RFID tags could be utilized to store the container's identifier. If these tags are only used internally, CON could label containers at the inbound. CON's customers could possibly benefit from having RFID tags on these containers as well. In such an arrangement, the partners may agree on the type and format of the data be stored on the tags in order to increase the efficiency of container management across company boundaries.

Reducing effort for printing customer-specific labels: labels on the outbound shipping units vary from customer to customer. The labels differ in terms of which paper is used and which information is printed on the paper. Currently, CON handles this situation by having a central printing station where different labels can be printed on different types of paper. The numerous formats could be handled much more easily if customers agree on replacing paper labels with RFID tags. Different information required on the various labels could then be written on the same type of RFID tags. If readers/writers would be available at the packing station, labels would no longer need to be created at the central location.

Improving process quality: the accuracy of processes at CON currently depends on employees' care and attention. For instance, workers must be careful not to accidentally mix up input materials for a process step or not to mix up labels. If RFID technology were used, correctness could be automatically inferred based on read events and ensured by alerts.

RFID readers at every processing step could be used to identify the materials which are about to be processed. Therefore, internal transfer units had to be equipped with RFID tags. Data about the materials they contain could either be stored on the tag or directly written into the back-end system. However, the latter case would cause additional communication overheads.

Costs and Benefits

The use of RFID technology offers a number of potential benefits for CON. Each application scenario would account for different investment costs and resulting benefits. Not all of the benefits are quantifiable in terms of cost savings. The major investments and savings for the different application scenarios are outlined in the following.

Fixed investment costs are those for readers, RFID tags, training staff and configuring the software system. Tag costs are fixed because the tags cycle in a closed loop. Running costs are those for software licenses and replacements of defect readers and tags. Different requirements for the RFID tags' capabilities exist in the diverse application scenarios. Thus, tag prices may range from about 20 euro cents to several euros. Reader prices range from a few hundred to several thousand euros. Investment costs vary substantially between the scenarios, because of the high variance in required scan points. The same applies to the savings which may be gained within the different applications.

The scenario *improving quality of production tracking and avoiding interruptions* presents two types of cost savings: One is that labor time, required to reconstruct data for missing bookings, can be reduced. Fixing missing bookings can take up to 30 minutes of employee time, according to interviews with the staff. Furthermore, missing bookings can interrupt the production process. The frequency of such incidents and the value generated in the running production process determine the monetary benefit of avoiding these interruptions.

The scenario *reducing workload for maintaining process data* accounts for savings in labor time. Employees on the plant floor spend about 5% of their time on copying data from and to accompanying tickets. This time can be saved if the data is transferred automatically via RFID.

In the scenario for *improving container localization*, RFID can reduce the overall cost for purchasing and renting containers. Tracing containers would allow the reduction of the safety stock for containers and fewer containers would need to be rented. Furthermore, loss of containers could be reduced or external partners could be held accountable for losses at their site.

In the scenario *reducing effort for printing customer-specific labels*, labor time and hardware cost can be saved. This scenario is highly interlinked with other RFID applications. If RFID readers are in place, they can be used to write customer-specific information on tags in the outbound. In this case, expensive, specialized printers for labels would no longer be necessary. This would result in saving hardware cost and increased productivity.

In the scenario *improving process quality*, production waste could be reduced by avoiding false machine settings. The resulting savings of this application scenario depend on the value of the wasted material and the cost of processing it.

Besides these quantifiable aspects, applying RFID might leverage intangible gains. The technology could improve the data tracks on the production processes. This in turn may enable to spot so-far-undetected potentials for improvement.

Summarizing Case CON

This case study presents an analysis of the potentials of adopting RFID at CON. The analysis revealed five areas that hold the potential for improvements at CON's plant. In the case of CON we recommend focusing on closed-loop scenarios within the plant in the short term. This is because CON controls all factors of the setup and can gain experience before negotiating with partners about collaboration. Closed-loop scenarios would address the automatic synchronization of processes with corresponding data tracks, maintenance of process data, and process safety.

In addition to the outlined RFID potentials in the plant itself, business processes across the supply chain – like the container management scenario – could be improved further to fully exploit the advantages of an RFID-enabled supply chain. Possible measures include the selective communication of RFID data to CON's customers and business partners. At this point, all data about the containers are simply written into the ERP system.

However, for such IT-enabled business processes the IT department needs to better map and integrate the information from the shop floor into the IT processes. Today, CON cannot fully map the container tracking into the IT systems. This results in repeated container shortages.

At this point, however, the implementation of such integration measures, including related security measures and standards activities, is a costly and possibly risky endeavor. Possible benefits will a priori not be distributed fairly between the different parties in the supply chain. This concerns not only costs for RFID readers, tags and required software, and costs for changing the underlying processes, but also the costs for constructing a more detailed mapping between the shop-floor operations and the IT processes.

2.3.6 Production of Aluminum Foils for Packaging

PAC produces printed aluminum foils for packaging. Its customers belong primarily to the food industry and the pharmaceutical industry. The production is subdivided into two sections: The first section is used to mill aluminum foils into the desired thickness and then cut into a specific length and width. Between the milling steps, the foils are also annealed in an oven which heats up to about 400°C (750 F). This section is referred to as *pre-processing*.

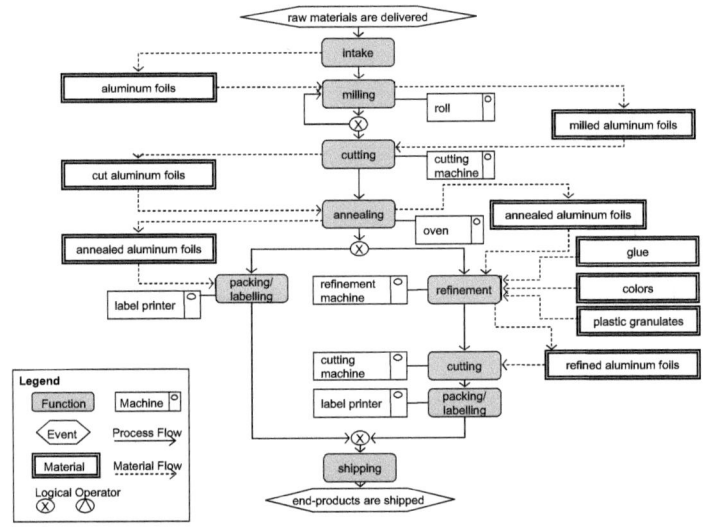

Figure 2.6: Production process of aluminum foils at PAC.

In the second section, the foil is colored and coated with cellulose films. This section is referred to as the *refining section*. Figure 2.6 shows the general workflow of a production step for pre-processing along with the related activities for data management.

At the beginning of a production step, the required material is fetched according to the production plan. Rolls with aluminum foils carry accompanying paper tickets which are used to identify the materials. After the required material has been fetched, the machine is configured and the milling (or cutting) is started. Subsequently, the completed processing step is documented on the accompanying ticket and booked to the MES. Processed rolls are moved on to the next production step or to a material buffer on the plant floor.

At the refinement section a production step starts with loading materials into the machines. Additional input materials are varnish and glue which are filled into the machines. All of these processing tasks are conducted within the same machine. In the final step, the foils can be cut into smaller parts and reeled on rolls for shipment.

Within the production, all foils are transported on rolls. Each processing machine winds off the input foils from the source roll. After processing, the foil is reeled back to a new target roll. In a cutting process, a foil from one roll can be split up into several foils and reeled to so-called child rolls. Also, multiple foils can be reeled in several layers of one roll. This material flow must be tracked during the whole production process. An accurate track is necessary for picking the correct materials at each step and for documenting the production.

Due to the larger number of input materials, configuring the machines in the second section is more complex than during the first one. Like during the pre-processing, each input material and machine setting must be documented in case the information is required for later recalls. A special challenge in the refining section is that input materials may be subject to changes during the processing. An example is refilling glue or varnish. Here it must be tracked which parts of the resulting foil were created under which conditions with which input materials (*e.g.*, the first 100 meters where produced with glue A, and the rest with glue B). Additionally, temporary production errors can affect the foil, at least in parts. These parts must be marked and cut out later. Figure 2.6 provides an overview of how refining is conducted and documented.

In the final step, foils are packed and labeled for shipment. Different customers require different bar-code labels on the packed rolls. Also, labels may change for different orders. Thus, each roll has individual bar codes that are printed right before packing. Labeling information is associated with each roll and retrieved from the back-end system right before printing.

Potential Improvements with RFID

PAC does not yet use RFID technology in its production. Instead, data management is realized with bar codes and paper documents. However, PAC is currently investigating whether RFID technology could improve the data management. Within the case study, HU has identified the subsequently described applications for the investigated plant. They target the following three improvements: better process reliability by realizing an emergency backup system, more detailed location tracking of rolls, and better quality of production tracking.

Better process reliability by realizing emergency backup system: realizing an emergency system was explicitly demanded by the IT staff of PAC. The issue is of high importance because currently the production at the investigated plant will stop in cases of a back-end failure. Such incidents have repeatedly occurred in the past and caused downtimes of several days with associated financial losses. Consequently, it is highly desired to decouple critical functionality from the back-end system and to ensure at least partial operation if the back-end systems fail.

RFID can be used as an enabler for an emergency system which can operate without the back-end. This is due to the ability of RFID tags to store data. In the desired application, rolls would be equipped with writable RFID tags. Using the memory on the tags, product and process information related to the associated foils can be stored directly at the rolls. Thus, required information must no longer be queried in the back-end system but could rather be retrieved from the tags directly. However, some of the manufacturing steps such as the heating may cause challenges for the selection of appropriate RFID tags.

More detailed location tracking of rolls: the IT staff expressed the demand to improve the granularity of tracking the rolls' locations on the plant floor. In particular, the process of annealing was the focus of this demand. Here, the rolls are moved into a chamber for heating where they must remain for a specific period of time. Workers document the time when they loaded and unloaded the chamber. However, as tracking is done on the level of batches, it is unknown how long a particular roll was in the chamber. In general, it is not documented where exactly the rolls are located. Before and after each processing step, the aluminum foils are stored in material buffers. Currently, workers must keep track of the rolls without any technical support.

RFID can be used to establish an automatic tracking system for rolls. For this scenario, rolls could be marked with RFID tags. This would enable the automatic registration of the rolls' position at checkpoints on the plant floor. Together with the back-end system, the solution would allow the recording of detailed tracks of the rolls' positions, and the monitoring of the production progress. Thereby, searching for rolls would be avoided and it would be ensured that all rolls are transported as planned. Furthermore, each roll could be tracked individually in the process of annealing (given that RFID tags were used that can resist the heat). This would enable the exact time of heat exposure to be recorded in detail. This could help to address quality issues.

Better quality of production tracking: at PAC, management of process data on the plant floor is currently done with tickets which accompany the rolls during the process. Information on these tickets is used by the workers to identify the materials on the plant floor and to choose the appropriate machine settings. Here, the manual data maintenance is a potential source of errors. For instance, if multiple foils are reeled in layers on one roll, the workers determine the order of layers via the tickets. Mixing up these positions results in false processing of the material. Another issue is that tickets can fall off and get mixed up.

These problems may be solved by an application which uses writable RFID tags for maintaining process data. In this application scenario, RFID tags could be permanently attached to the rolls. Thereby, information would be directly coupled with the corresponding object and could not be mixed up or get lost. Data about the conducted operations could be copied electronically from the machines or from the back-end system to the RFID tag's memory. Thereby, errors in manual data management could be avoided. For instance, information about the order of multiple layers on a roll could be copied from the machine which reeled the foils on the roll.

Costs and Benefits

The main reason for the manufacturer to investigate the usage of RFID is the decentralization of the IT system. The manufacturer suffered from breakdowns of the back-end system in the past. This resulted in production stops of several days, causing a loss of revenue and reputation. A fail-over solution for the central database has been discussed, but decentralized data management via RFID is currently favored by the company's production supervisor.

RFID would provide a simple solution for managing production data in an emergency case. This would require writable RFID tags with a few kilobytes of memory as well as one reader per workstation. Additionally, RFID may help to reduce production errors and improve the product quality. This could be achieved by automating the data management and thereby avoiding errors in manual data maintenance. The frequency of errors and the related costs determine the potential savings for this application scenario. Furthermore, improvements in the data accuracy may help to better analyze and streamline the processes. Altogether, applying RFID would enable more reliable production planning, ease the IT management, improve the reliability of the production, as well as increase the manufacturers' reputation. Yet, the monetary effects of these applications are difficult to estimate.

Summarizing Case PAC

In this case study we present an analysis of the potentials of adopting RFID at PAC. We identified three main scenarios of how RFID can improve PAC's operations. The first scenario is to realize an application for tracking foils. Here, the ability of RFID to be read out without line of sight and the possibility to provide protective casings for RFID tags are the major arguments for considering RFID instead of bar codes.

The second scenario targets the maintenance of production data. Here, RFID could be used to ensure that production information is associated with the right object. In the third scenario, RFID would be used to realize an emergency system. This system should ensure at least partial operation of the production even if the back-end system fails. Here, the possibility to write information onto the RFID tags is exploited ("data-on-tag"). This allows to decentralize the business logic and to decouple it from the back-end system. All three scenarios require a detailed mapping of the shop-floor processes into the IT systems.

In addition to the outlined RFID potentials in the plant itself, business processes across the supply chain could be improved further to fully exploit the advantages of an RFID-enabled supply chain. Possible measures include the selective communication of RFID data to PAC's customers and business partners. At this point, however, the implementation of such integration measures, including related security measures and standards activities, is a costly and possibly risky endeavor. Possible benefits will a priori not be distributed fairly between the different parties in the supply chain. This concerns not only costs for RFID readers, tags and required software, and costs for changing the underlying processes, but also the costs for constructing a more detailed mapping between the shop-floor operations and the IT processes.

2.4 Lessons Learned

This section summarizes the key findings of the conducted case studies regarding evaluated RFID potentials. First we present typical use cases of RFID which we derive from the case studies. Then in 2.4.2 we portray for each use case whether and why other Auto-ID technologies, especially bar code, are not as suitable as RFID. Finally in Section 2.4.3 we describe current motives and open potentials for using RFID.

2.4.1 Evaluating Potential Benefits

Based on the experiences drawn from the case studies we now describe several general use cases for RFID. They are typically either a replacement of barcode technology or an application that can *only* be realized using RFID. Our findings are in line with Chappell et al. (2003) and show the practical relevance of RFID in manufacturing. We found that most of the relevant issues came up repeatedly in the case studies. The most common motivations for planning RFID introduction were:

1. accelerating scan processes,
2. extending scan processes for quality and efficiency,
3. extending scan processes for narrowing recalls,
4. reducing paper-based data management,
5. automating asset tracking,
6. reducing back-end interactions,
7. unifying labels.

In Table 2.2 I summarize in which case studies we identify these seven objectives for using RFID. We describe each use case in detail. This includes a discussion of which RFID tags work best for a certain use case. Here, technological properties of tags must be considered as well as standards, tag costs and expected future developments.

Table 2.2: Identified use cases for RFID in manufacturing.

| Case Study | \multicolumn{7}{c}{The Seven RFID use cases} |

Case Study	1	2	3	4	5	6	7
AIR	√	√				√	√
CLU	√	√	√				
COO					√		
CAS		√		√			
CON	√	√		√			√
PAC			√	√	√	√	√

Accelerating Scan Processes

Currently, many companies monitor their production processes by scanning bar codes or manually registering objects at certain check points. These approaches may have several drawbacks, depending on the particular process. Manual data recording is generally error prone and time consuming. Scanning bar codes can be automated in some cases, but must be conducted manually if a line of sight cannot be ensured. Thus, scanning bar codes may also require time-consuming, manual intervention. Depending on the particular process, manual scanning may account for a significant proportion of the employees' workload. Consequently, manufacturers aim at reducing the time for manual scans or to automate the process.

RFID enables to automatically read information from the tag without a line of sight. This property can significantly speed up the scanning of identifiers due to the following three advantages of RFID technology: First, some objects in the manufacturing plant are shaped in a way that bar codes must be applied at places which are difficult to scan (see case studies 2.3.1, 2.3.5). In such cases, RFID can help to speed up manual scan processes (García et al., 2003). This property may also allow the automation of manual scan processes – a second major advantage of RFID technology.

The third advantage occurs when whole batches of objects must be identified (see case studies 2.3.1 2.3.2). With RFID, all of the objects in these batches can be captured at once. Scanning without line of sight and capturing whole batches of objects reduces the need for manual labor (Chappell et al., 2003). In cases in which line of sight for traditional identification methods is hard to achieve, RFID allows the time workers spend on scanning to be reduced. This in turn enables labor costs to be reduced and productivity to be improved.

Extending Scan Processes for Quality and Efficiency

Manufacturers have a high interest in getting more insight into the operations on the plant floor. Analyzing information about activities in the production and measurements of environmental conditions can help to identify causes of quality problems and point out potentials for improvements. Furthermore, analyzing live data can enable fast reactions to exceptions in the process. In general, a larger data set allows better insights into the process. Thus, many companies aim at extending data recording on the plant floor.

With RFID technology, activities in production are often much easier to monitor in detail. With the help of RFID technology, new scan points can be introduced without increasing the workload of the staff. Furthermore, RFID labels are typically more robust to hostile conditions that may occur in the production environment. For example, bar codes can become unreadable due to exposure to dirt, heat, or mechanical influence.

RFID tags have the advantage that they can be covered in protective casings (DeJong, 1998). Thus, in some production environments, RFID tags may work more reliably than bar codes do (2.3.1, 2.3.4, 2.3.6). On the other hand, there are environments where bar codes still beat RFID by a margin. This is especially true if a substantial quantity of metal is present.

Some of the investigated companies have stringent requirements on process reliability and process documentation (*e.g.*, consistency checks must ensure that no process step is skipped). In one example from the case studies, the investigated company scanned the WIP parts after every operation to be compliant with customers' demands (2.3.1). RFID can help to meet such demands by simplifying the process of scanning items. Thereby the technology also makes it easier to comply with regulations for process documentation.

The exact information about which object was manufactured from which components and materials is required to identify all of the products which include potentially flawed parts. Additionally, fine-grained and reliable data records can be important in legal disputes (2.3.1). A company may be held liable if malfunctioning products cause damage. In this case, data records are important to be able to prove that the production was conducted in a way consistent with the state of the art. Here, sensor data can help to detect the cause of failure and further narrow the scope of potentially affected products. Evaluating this data can provide additional insights into performance measures like cycle times. It can even help to identify the cause of quality changes.

RFID technology can also be used to ensure accurate and real-time reporting about the production status. Typically, a production step is reported back to the MES after processing has been completed. This information may also be required in future consistency checks and for later process analysis. As the case studies have shown, it is not uncommon that manual reporting is sometimes forgotten or not conducted in a timely manner (2.3.2, 2.3.5). Occasionally, production process information is even reported in a wrong order. Possible consequences are inaccurate data tracks, incorrect status information, or even interruptions in the production process. These problems may be overcome if RFID tags are applied to the materials or to the transportation units. In such setups, RFID readers could automatically detect if materials are transported to the next process step. Thereby consistency would be guaranteed.

Extending Scan Processes for Narrowing Recalls

Narrowing the scope of recalls was a major concern for many of the investigated plants. Manufacturers may have to pay high penalties for each object that is called back. Recalls can significantly reduce companies' revenue and their reputation with customers. It is therefore a major concern to limit recalls and their effects to the largest degree possible.

To narrow recalls it is first necessary to locate the cause of failure as specifically as possible. Commonly, a faulty material or malfunctioning machine has to be identified. In the second step, all potentially affected products must be located. This requires a detailed track of which materials and intermediate products are assembled in which finalized products, as well as information about these products' locations. If the cause of failure was a malfunctioning machine, it is important to know the exact period of time in which the machine did not work properly and which products were processed during this period.

In order to limit recalls to the maximum extent, companies aim at creating fine-grained tracks of their internal material flow. Yet, manual tracking or tracking by using bar-code technologies may not always be feasible. Time-consuming scans or the inability to create line of sight or hostile conditions can pose a limit on the number of possible checks and thereby the granularity of data tracks.

RFID can help to introduce additional scan points into the production processes. This is partly because RFID tags can automatically be read out in more situations than bar-code labels. Additionally, RFID tags can handle hostile conditions such as exposure to dirt. Furthermore, RFID tags with sensing capabilities can help to determine the cause of failure and to rate the damage. All these properties of RFID render the technology helpful to narrow recalls in cases where more traditional approaches fail (2.3.2, 2.3.6).

Reducing Paper Based Data Management

Paper documents that accompany the WIP are currently a common method for recording and maintaining data throughout the production process. These paper documents are transported along with their corresponding materials and are used to record data about the production process. Additionally, these documents can hold information about how to conduct subsequent operations. The accompanying documents are usually only loosely coupled with the objects they belong to. That is, documents move along with the corresponding objects but are physically separated from them while data is written on the paper. This may cause a mix up of documents and incorrect data maintenance. Furthermore, handwritten notes occasionally cannot be deciphered, which effectively constitutes an information loss.

A correct data track of the production is crucial in many cases. Customers may demand high-quality data tracks or the company itself needs those tracks for recalls and legal disputes about liability. Furthermore, the data is used for steering and controlling production itself. Thus, mixed-up documents can lead to production errors and loss. Consequently, companies seek a way to ensure that data are recorded correctly and are permanently associated with the right object.

RFID tags with writable memory can be used to store data from accompanying documents right at the corresponding object. Thus, information cannot get lost on the shop floor or accidentally get mixed up with other documents, like can be the case with paper documents. Loosing information would only occur, when the tags get damaged or the RFID reader had a read or write error.

Using RFID may also leverage the automation of some of the manual data maintenance. For instance, records of the conducted operations can automatically be written from machines to tags. Automatic data maintenance would account for time savings and a reduction of errors.

Alternatively, information about an object can be stored in the back-end system. In these cases an identifier for the corresponding object is needed. Depending on particularities in the targeted application environment, bar codes can be a suitable alternative to RFID. As mentioned, however, the application of bar codes may be infeasible, *e.g.*, in dirty environments. Furthermore, applying bar codes may reduce the degree of automation in cases where line of sight cannot be created automatically.

Other trade-offs concern the required adaptations of the back-end system. In order to guarantee fast response times and high availability, an appropriate network infrastructure and software system for the back-end is required. The investment in such an infrastructure must be traded against the investment in RFID tags and readers and the resulting network load must be considered carefully. However, even when data is stored locally on an RFID tag, the back-end system typically keeps a copy of this information, which may cause problems regarding data synchronization.

Automating Asset Tracking

Knowing the spatial location of assets can be crucial to ensure the production processes. All materials for an operation and the required tools need to be at the designated machine in time. If timely fetching of required materials cannot be ensured, the production process may be interrupted and result in a reduction of productivity.

In general, companies follow two strategies to avoid downtimes due to missing assets: One is to fetch the required materials and tools with a long time buffer before production starts. This allows reacting to situations where the assets cannot be found and must be searched for (2.3.4). Yet, in this approach it is necessary to schedule the production in the long term to have the work plan ready for asset fetching. Consequently, this strategy is infeasible for companies that seek high flexibility and reactivity in using their production lines.

Another way to reduce fetching times for assets is to keep a detailed track of their positions. This reduces search times and makes planning of the fetching time more reliable. Yet, keeping an accurate and updated track of assets typically requires – often manual – interference. A special challenge is to track materials in material buffers on the plant floor. These material buffers are often only loosely structured and their content is changed dynamically. However, tracking objects in wide-spread stocks can be challenging and time consuming as well.

RFID technology has the potential to facilitate the recording of assets' positions. For instance, assets can be equipped with RFID tags and registered by stationary readers at key points. Alternatively, mobile readers can be used to quickly register items at certain locations. Thereby, the RFID technology leverages detailed asset tracking and can help to avoid search times for materials and tools (Lampe and Strassner, 2003).

Furthermore, companies also demanded better container tracking, 2.3.5, 2.3.2. It is often attractive to use low-cost RFID tags for container-tracking scenarios. UHF Gen 2 tags may be an option. The Gen 2 standard is well established and designed for logistic processes. Applying this standard would leverage the utilization of these tags by customers and other supply chain partners and may allow the investment costs to be shared. Furthermore, tags for this standard are already produced in large quantities and are relatively cheap.

Reducing Back-end Interactions

Some of the investigated companies expressed the demand for reducing interaction with the back-end IT system. In one case, the network infrastructure and the back-end database were perceived as unreliable (2.3.6). Consequently, production IT systems should also work during temporary disconnections from the back-end servers.

In another case, the company's network and back-end computers were barely able to serve the demanded response time (2.3.1). Its IT staff predicted significant bottlenecks when data volumes increase in the future. In both cases, RFID tags with writable memory ("data-on-tag") could help to decouple processing of business logic from the back-end system and to distribute the workload.

Currently, interaction with databases in the back-end system is needed to retrieve task-related data at each operation. In 2.3.3 the company decided in advance to build their production line to be independent from back-end interactions. The production line can work autarkically because all routing data is stored on writable RFID tags.

With the help of RFID the workload of the back-end system as well as the communication with back-end databases can be reduced significantly. The capability of RFID tags to store up to several megabytes of data enables a novel distribution of data and business logic. Data needed for consistency checks and process control can be stored directly on the RFID tag of the corresponding objects. Usually that comprises tasks descriptions of the referring order and history data about the conducted operations. For instance, consistency checks that verify if all needed steps were conducted can be performed solely on the basis of the history data stored on the tag.

Moreover, using the memory on RFID tags, the business logic for checks and process control can be moved close to the point of operation. For instance, the business logic can be run on PCs that are connected to RFID readers and machines on the plant floor.

Higher-class RFID tags could enable more distribution of business logic. Programmable readers can perform check operations locally and even independently of PCs on the shop floor. Furthermore, smart sensor tags can process business logic on the items themselves. Early examples for such applications are investigated, for instance, in the CoBIs project (Spiess, 2005). This EU-funded project deals with distributing business logic to smart sensor nodes. Prototypes have been construed with partners like BP and Infineon.

Moving the business logic closer to the point of action on the plant floor helps to ensure fast responses of the system without tuning the back-end databases and the network infrastructure. It also helps to increase system reliability because in a distributed system device failures only affect small parts of the infrastructure.

By storing information on the tags, investments in the back-end system could be avoided. The used database would need to be adjusted if the manufacturer decides to use tags that only hold an ID. Which option is most cost efficient depends on the tag prices and the cost of extending the back-end system.

Unifying Labels

The case studies showed that manufacturers face challenges in handling labels at the outbound shipment. Different customers typically demand different bar-code solutions for labeling transportation units and packages (2.3.1, 2.3.5). These differences can be in the demanded label format, coding scheme and the information on the label. Thus, manufacturers have to manage and print a wide range of different labels for their shipment processes.

Another challenge is that customers may claim financial compensation from the manufacturer if bar-code labels are unreadable. In the case study in 2.3.1, a customer's production line stops if a bar code is unreadable. Resulting costs for unreadable bar codes must be reimbursed. Consequently, the manufacturer checks each created label to make sure they can be read.

This demand for high-quality labels that hold diverse information in various formats poses challenges in managing and printing bar-code labels. Often, special printers are used to achieve the desired print quality and to handle different label formats. Since these printers are expensive devices, some manufacturers create labels at a central location to reduce the number of printers needed. Yet, printing at a central location has the drawback that labels must be transported to the respective packing stations. This causes extra time and bears the risk that labels will get mixed up.

RFID technology can be used for unified labels that abstract from the physical representation of data. Radio-frequency protocols such as defined in the ISO 18000 or EPCglobalTM standards (ISO/IEC-18000, 2004a; EPCglobal, 2005) provide well-defined ways to access data on RFID tags. For instance, the Gen 2 standard specifies an optional user memory that can be used for arbitrary purposes. Using such standards, customer-specific information can be written on the same kind of label in a standardized way. This holds even if customers require individual coding schemes for the data.

Abstracting from the physical representation of data allows for using standard RFID readers to create customer-specific labels. Thus, one kind of reader can be used for all labels and specialized printing stations are no longer necessary. Note that RFID readers may be available at packing stations for scanning logistic applications. In contrast to bar-code scanners, RFID readers also have the ability to write on tags. Thus, only one device for reading and writing is needed.

Yet, to achieve this abstraction, the supply chain partners need to agree on applying RFID in general and on the frequency to be used in particular. Within a given RF spectrum, the readers' software can support different communication protocols and thereby abstract from different tag versions.

RFID can help to increase the reliability of labels. This accounts especially for environments where dirt or mechanical influence can affect the bar code. It is generally easier to protect RFID tags from mechanical damage like scratches or loss. This is because RFID tags do not need to be applied to the outside of an object where they are visible. Instead, they can be built into the product during the manufacturing process, applied inside the product's casing or be protected by a special casing for the tag's inlay.

Note that the discussed cases for label handling not only affect operations at the manufacturers, but also at their customers (OEMs *etc.*) down the supply chain. Using RFID tags as uniform labels therefore implies a close coordination across the whole supply chain (or at least significant parts of it). Customers would at least need to equip their intakes with RFID readers. Having incoming items labeled with RFID tags would leverage an extended use of this technology within customers' processes and may lead to significant productivity gains there as well.

2.4.2 Comparing RFID with other Auto-ID Technologies

In this section we discuss if and how the previously described use cases could also be realized using other Auto-ID technologies. Voice recognition and biometrics are useful systems for access control. However we do not focus on access control. Magnetic stripes and smart cards suffer from mechanical wear. Additionally they need physical contact to the reader while read.

Machine vision, bar codes or RFID do not have this disadvantage. Therefore, these systems are used in manufacturing. Machine vision and bar code need a line of sight to work. Manufacturers are likely to use machine-vision technologies when products have to be compared to pictures stored in a database (2.3.3). In cases where bar codes would get damaged due to hostile conditions machine-vision or OCR technologies are used as well. Nevertheless, machine-vision technologies are more complex and thereby more expensive than bar-code technology. However both systems do not allow data to be stored right at the object.

Today bar codes are predominantly used in manufacturing. All inspected companies rely on this technology in one case or the other. The comparison between RFID and bar code is an important part of our evaluation as labels and readers for RFID require higher investments than corresponding bar-code equipment. Consequently, technical arguments or process requirements must account for the economic feasibility of an RFID adoption.

Accelerating Scan Processes

This use case exploits the property of RFID that no line of sight is needed. Thereby it allows for automatic reading of tags. Thus, tags can be read without workers' intervention and the booking process can be automated and thereby speeded up (2.3.1). If a line of sight does not affect the speed of the process, then bar codes could be used as well. Only when this use case relies on the capability of RFID to detect tags without a line of sight is it not possible to use any other Auto-ID technology.

Extending Scan Processes for Quality and Efficiency

Additional consistency checks are often added to the production steps for process safety (see 2.3.1, 2.3.2, 2.3.6, 2.3.5). Information about the content of internal transfer units as well as configurations from terminals and the production planning are required to perform consistency checks.

At least an ID must be read to retrieve information about the internal transfer units. This can be done using passive ID tags without user memory or bar codes. Yet, in both cases additional database lookups are necessary to retrieve the required information. If the manufacturer uses bar codes, then he may also need a manual intervention to ensure a line of sight for the read process. This may cause additional workload and thereby additional cost. In contrast, RFID tags with sufficient memory could enable automatic consistency checks without additional database queries and manual intervention.

Extending Scan Processes for Narrowing Recalls

Often the same degree of automation can be achieved with bar codes (2.3.1, 2.3.5, 2.3.3). Yet, this would require modifications of the production process ensuring line of sight read outs after each step. For instance, this could be achieved by using conveyors for transportation. However, such an investment renders a bar-code-based approach infeasible. However, in many other cases bar codes cannot be used, because of the hostile conditions on the plant floor

(2.3.6, 2.3.4, 2.3.2). And even at 2.3.1 and 2.3.3 – here the conditions allow the usage of bar codes – RFID is more feasible due to the use case *reducing back-end interactions*.

Reducing Paper Based Data Management

This use case comprises the idea to automatically communicate process data between different operations, rather than using manually written papers. The data can be communicated on tags or via back-end systems.

Bar-code labels can theoretically be used in the same way as RFID tags without user memory. Yet, if process data is not manually written on paper anymore, workers must identify internal transfer units by their labels. Unlike RFID, bar-code labels would require time-consuming, manual scanning with line of sight.

Automating Asset Tracking

Besides asset tracking this use case can also include container management. Assets are usually managed only within the boundaries of the company. However, in one case study assets were also shipped between the manufacturer and its customers (2.3.4).

RFID technology could be applied to keep track of assets' movements. Scanning without a line of sight allows for an easy observation of their positions. Any RFID tag capable of holding an ID could be used for this application. Yet, the tag price plays an important role, even though tags can possibly be reused. One reason for that is the relatively high number of assets and containers. Another reason is that assets may, and containers nearly always do, leave the plant. Consequently, manufacturers cannot always ensure that they are returned in due time.

However, using bar codes as identifiers would also be an option. Yet, a line of sight must be ensured for the scanning process. This would cause several manual interventions and additional costs, *i.e.*, workers' time. Moreover, bar codes are less robust than RFID tags and may be rendered illegible or get lost. Thus, applying bar codes for asset management and container tracking is possible but may not be cost effective.

Reducing Back-end Interactions

With RFID it is possible to decentralize data storage and reduce the bottleneck to central databases. This scenario cannot be conducted with any Auto-ID technology other than RFID. This is because one can store information on the object, *e.g.*, routing data for the production.

Unifying Labels

This use case targets the challenge of handling labels for the shipment process. Different customers require different information and different label formats for shipment. These different formats could be realized on the same kind of RIFD label if the customers agree on using RFID in the shipment process. Information for each customer can then be encoded in the desired format and written to the RFID tags.

For this use case, tags with sufficient storage such as active tags or passive tags with user memory are required. Yet, labeling packing units with active RFID tags is cost intensive. Thus, passive tags with user memory should be preferred. Using bar codes is possible but has several disadvantages. The manufacturer then needs high-quality printers and checks whether bar codes are readable (2.3.1). Printers need to be adjusted, with new labels added. And last but not least, bar codes can be ripped off or destroyed.

Summary

In Table 2.3 I summarize the use cases with regard to the possible utilization of RFID and bar code. Bar code is predominantly used in manufacturing today. And during the case studies we repeatedly found that RFID should replace the used bar-code technology. In Table 2.3 I further divide RFID into active tags (a. tag) and passive tags (p. tag). Regarding passive tags, we distinguish between tags that only hold an ID (only ID) and tags that are equipped with additional user memory (mem.). Note that we consider active tags to have an ID plus additional user memory, as this is usually the case. This table shows that when RFID is being used in closed-loop applications within the boundaries of the company, advanced tags are also feasible. However, already when considering closed loop within the own supply chain, the costs of more advanced tags tend to increase drastically, because often more tags and more scan points are needed.

2.4.3 Evaluating Current Motives and Open Potentials

The RFID application areas discussed above can be categorized along two dimensions as visualized in Figure 2.7.We distinguish between operational use and strategic use, on the one hand, and between intra-enterprise and inter-enterprise applications, on the other.

The term operational use refers to improvements that impact processes and productivity directly. That is, the RFID technology is applied to make processes faster, more secure *etc.* Furthermore, improved planning of activities and better resource allocation due to RFID falls into this category. The term strategic use refers to use cases where RFID is introduced for longterm strategic purposes. For instance, RFID may allow providing additional services or quality guarantees to customers, thus changing the market positioning of the enterprise as a whole. Strategic decisions have a long-term impact whereas operational decisions focus on immediate results.

Use cases for RFID in which the technology as well as the captured data are only used within one organization fall into the category intra-enterprise applications. However, RFID holds the potential of applications that span several steps in the supply chain. For instance, enterprises may exchange data that is obtained using RFID. Also, RFID labels may remain on products and could be reused by several companies downstream in the supply chain. We categorize these use cases as inter-enterprise applications. Figure 2.8 depicts how the cases fit into this taxonomy. The motives to use RFID determine the position in the taxonomy chart for each case.

The manufacturer of airbags (AIR) aims to apply RFID for several reasons. One driver is the operational improvement of accelerating scan processes and thereby raising productivity. However, another argument was that

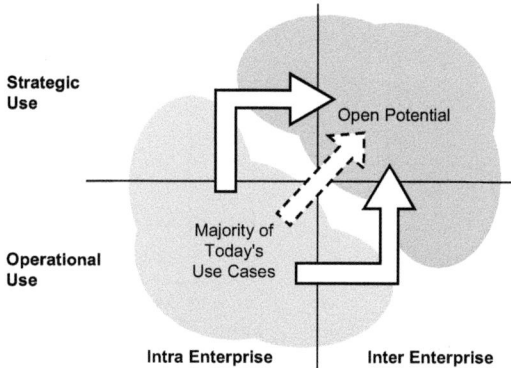

Figure 2.7: Taxonomy of motives for RFID adoption.

AIR expects some of its costumers to demand RFID adoption in the near future and wants to be prepared. At this point AIR can potentially gain strategic advantages by being ready for an RFID-enabled value chain. This could be a distinguishing factor and competitive advantage to competitors.

AIR was also interested in using RFID for product labeling. Keeping RFID labels on the products would enable to improve operations at the customers' side as well. This way AIR could provide additional services to its customers which may account for further strategic advantages. Because the main driver for RFID at AIR is to increase productivity on the plant floor, this case belongs to the cluster of operational use within one enterprise. However, we also found aspects of strategic use for the enterprise as well as inter-enterprise operational use. Consequently the case of AIR overlaps with these clusters in Figure 2.8.

For the manufacturer of sliding clutches (CLU) the main driver of its RFID efforts is to improve product tracking in order to narrow recalls. A minor reason was to obtain more accurate reports about the production status. Consequently, the case of CLU is clearly motivated by operational intra-enterprise use. However, narrowed recalls may have the positive side effect of a better reception of CLU by customers. Therefore, it includes some strate-

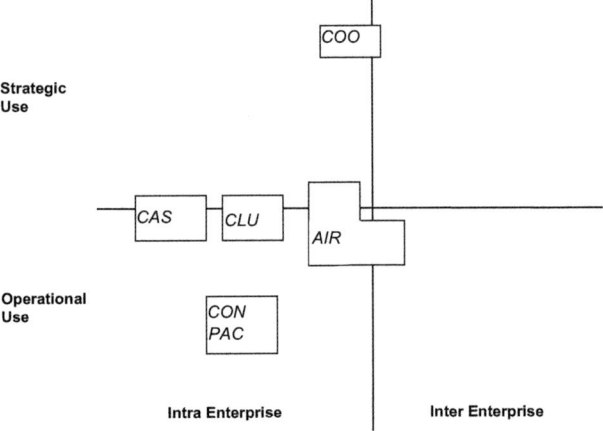

Figure 2.8: Motives for RFID adoption depending on the company.

gic aspects as well. Another effect is that efficient handling of recalls reduces the risk of disturbances in the production at the customers' side. These side effects are reflected in the positioning of CLU in Figure 2.8.

The manufacturer of packaging (PAC) aims to use RFID to improve material tracking in the plant as well as to reduce the dependency on its IT back-end layer. Thus, the targeted improvements are operation and intra-enterprise. Similarly, the motives of the manufacturer of connectors (CON) are also merely for operational improvements within the company. In this case the main goal was to improve the material tracking on the plant floor and to create more accurate production reports. Since in the cases of CON and PAC only operational use within the enterprise is targeted, these cases build a group in Figure 2.8.

The motive for the RFID efforts at the manufacturer of cast pasts (CAS) is to improve asset tracking within the plant. This application is mainly of local and operational use. However, reducing search times for assets allows CAS to produce more flexibly and at shorter notice which can lead to a strategic advantage (see Figure 2.8).

The RFID application at the manufacturer of engine-cooling modules (COO) is solely motivated by strategic issues. In this case no apparent operational benefits result from the use of RFID. Instead, RFID was introduced on a customer's demand. Meeting this requirement is a strategic decision of COO. Additionally the case has some aspect of inter-enterprise collaboration, because COO provides the captured RFID data to the respective customers. However, the option is currently rarely used. In Figure 2.8, the case of COO is placed accordingly.

As visualized in Fig 2.8 the motives for RFID applications in the investigated cases are dominated by local operational improvements. That is, the technology helps to improve processes and productivity on the plant floor. With regards to planning, RFID-enabled decisions are also mainly of local scope. In most cases only locally obtained RFID data are used and decisions are made for local processes. Using RFID for strategic issues or across company boundaries is rarely targeted.

This focus on operational, intra-enterprise applications neglects the potential of RFID technology to be used in many steps of the supply chain. Companies may collaborate on the operational level to use RFID in several steps of the value chain (Günther et al., 2006). Operational use across enterprises can be enabled due to the reuse of RFID tags. One option is to permanently leave RFID tags on the products as they move through the supply chain.

Another option is to reuse the tags in a closed loop but extending the loop across several enterprises. This does not only supports seamless integration of processes but also enables cost-sharing models for hardware expenses (Ivantysynova and Ziekow, 2007). Beyond this, RFID use across enterprises may strengthen the strategic position of the supply chain as a whole. For instance, cooperating partners can use the technology to provide fine-grained product traceability and quality assurances across the whole supply chain. Moving towards this opportunity may become a distinguishing factor and competitive advantage for innovative manufacturers in the near future.

A problem when considering RFID introduction in a supply chain is that costs and benefits are not always correlated. Some participating companies may incur considerable costs that outweigh the local benefits, and vice versa. This can lead to a classical prisoner's dilemma: It could well be possible that an existing supply chain could gain considerably from introducing RFID technology. These gains, however, are never realized because some participants would need to incur costs that are not justifiable in comparison to their local benefits.

As a result, they decide – for completely rational reasons – not to adopt the new technology. One way to break this deadlock is to negotiate compensation payments between different participants in the supply chain with the objective of distributing the global benefit fairly among the participants. These compensation payments do not have to be monetary – in the retail domain, certain types of data (*e.g.*, sales data about one's own products or the products of one's competitors) are also common currency.

2.5 Conclusion

Generally, the case studies show that RFID technology holds many promises for improving manufacturing processes while also exhibiting new challenges. The automation of object identification processes through RFID can help to increase the efficiency by reducing scan times and manual work, reduce errors due to manual data entry and analysis, and improve product tracking and tracing. Detailed data tracks can help increasing product quality and narrowing the extent of necessary product recalls.

In comparison to bar-code technology, RFID does not require a line of sight for scanning, enables simultaneous batch scanning, does not require the technological effort for high-quality printing, and is more resistant to physical influences such as dirt or scratches. Avoiding problems related to unreadable bar codes may help to reduce the number returns and penalties and increase customer satisfaction, especially in supply chains operating according to the just-in-sequence paradigm.

Five out of six companies' motives for an RFID adoption are purely operational uses within their enterprise. That is, they would like to use this technology to improve processes and productivity on the plant floor. Motivations to use RFID as a strategic enabler of data exchange between enterprises along the supply chain were found much less frequently. However, this focus on operational, intra-enterprise applications fails to exploit the full potential of RFID technology.

Despite the high potential of RFID technology, the manufacturer has to consider a number of issues before starting an implementation. The next chapter analyzes these challenges.

Table 2.3: Applicability of RFID and Bar code Technologies

Use Case	Active Tag	Passive Tag with Memory	Passive Tag no Memory	Bar Code
1: Accelerating scan processes	√ feasible because closed loop manufacturer	√	√	X
2: Extending scan processes for quality and efficiency	√ feasible because closed loop manufacturer	√	√ and additional database	√ and additional database and workload for manual scanning
3: Extending scan processes for narrowing recalls	√ feasible because closed loop manufacturer	√	√	X
4: Reducing paper-based data management	√ feasible because closed loop manufacturer	√	√ and additional database	√ and additional database and workload for manual scanning
5: Automating asset tracking	√ but cost intensive because closed loop supply chain	√	√	√ and additional workload for manual scanning
6: Reducing back-end interactions	√ feasible because closed loop manufacturer	X	X	X
7: Unifying labels	√ but cost intensive because closed loop supply chain	√	X	X

Chapter 3

Challenges of Embedding RFID into Shop-Floor Processes

This chapter evaluates which challenges the manufacturer has to face when applying RFID in shop-floor processes. All challenges are derived from the case studies described in Chapter 2. These challenges include software as well as hardware issues. Section 3.1 presents a reference model for production processes and the management of the corresponding production data. The model enables me later to better describe required RFID functionalities and constraints for IT infrastructures. I conducted the work for this chapter together with Oliver Günther and Holger Ziekow. We published the results in Ivantysynova et al. (2008b).

Section 3.2 discusses diverse difficulties and impediments of using RFID hardware in hostile conditions on the shop floor. Then Section 3.3 describes the functional requirements of RFID infrastructures. In the subsequent Section 3.4 we discuss constraints for IT infrastructures when integrating RFID in manufacturing. This goes along with an overview of upcoming paradigms for data processing that are useful in the context of RFID and manufacturing. Section 3.5 concludes this chapter.

3.1 Reference Model for Production Processes

The reference model for production captures typical activities on the plant floor and the corresponding data management issues. We derive this model because it will later enable us later to describe required RFID functionalities and constraints for IT infrastructures along this model. The model focuses on activities that may be affected by the introduction of RFID.

We derive this model from the analysis of the case studies presented in 2.3. Although the production processes differ significantly among the companies, it is possible to identify common patterns in manufacturing and the associated information management. Moreover, it is important to keep in mind that process steps are not always optimally accomplished. Loss of materials, inefficient manual data management and a low degree of data digitalization are only some of the problems we observed during the field studies. On one hand, the model shows what data need to be provided by the IT infrastructure at each production step and, on the other hand, it also illustrates which data the IT infrastructure gets for further processing from each production step.

Generally a production process consists of a sequence of operations. An operation can generally be subdivided into the following ten activities: selection, material fetching, tool exchanging, machine configuration, consistency checks, processing, documenting, booking, loading into transportation units, and transporting, see 3.1.

The first step is to *select the correct operation* from the routing (*e.g.*, bill of operations). The second activity is to *fetch needed materials* for the operation. These materials must be retrieved from stock or a material input buffer near the resource and loaded into the machine. Materials are usually identified via transportation units in which they are packed. However, in some cases, materials may also be marked directly with an identifier. When the materials are ready to be used, the machines need to be configured. *Configuring a machine* may include *mounting special tools on the machine*. These tools must be retrieved from the tools inventory. Due to quality issues and tracking, it may be required to maintain a history of all utilized tools.

Consistency checks may be conducted before processing starts. Such checks verify that the correct materials are used and that the materials have passed all required previous operations. When *processing* is completed, the conducted work is *documented*. Recorded information may include machine settings and reports about production errors. Thereby a track of the production is kept. It can later be used for process analysis and to help to narrow recalls. One challenge in tracking is that materials may be *packed into transportation units*. This must be taken into account if materials are identified by their transportation units. Another challenge is that materials may be split up into several parts or combined into one part during assembly. This impacts how data tracks have to be recorded and retrieved.

An operation usually ends with *booking* the finished tasks into the MES in the middle layer. The data may be required for consistency checks in the following operations. Then, the processed parts or WIP are *transported* to the next operation, the stock, or a material buffer on the plant floor. Information about the materials' locations may need to be recorded in some inventory list or may be derived from their current status in the production.

After the production has been completed, the finished products are transferred to a shipping area where they are packed and labeled for shipment. A special challenge is that different customers may demand different labels and different information on the labels. This may comprise different numbering and coding schemes for identification- and product-related data.

Note that a particular production process may only implement a subset of the described activities. For instance, in many cases it may not be necessary to exchange tools on the machines. Thus, apart from the *processing* itself, each activity is optional in the reference model. Not all actions necessarily occur in every case and others may be added. Still, the reference model may serve as a general pattern which approximates most production processes. All activities in the derived model may be supported by RFID or can influence RFID adoption. A software system supporting RFID in manufacturing should certainly take the steps of this reference model into account.

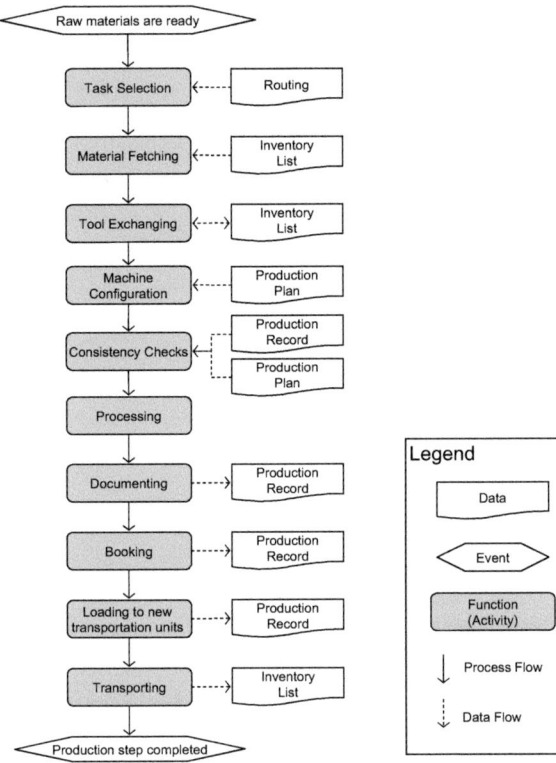

Figure 3.1: Reference model for production.

3.2 Hindrances on the Shop Floor

As the case studies in the previous Chapter 2 show, plant floors of manufacturing companies are often hostile environments with extreme conditions, *e.g.*, 2.3.1, 2.3.4, 2.3.6. Challenging factors include dirt, heat, presence of metal, limited space and others. RFID solutions for manufacturing must be able to cope with such conditions. Yet, no standard solutions can serve the requirements of all production environments. Instead, an individual solution must be found for each case. In this section we discuss general hardware issues for RFID implementations in manufacturing. In particular we focus on the following: hostile physical conditions, presence of metal, demand for wireless communication, and processes in close spatial proximity.

3.2.1 Hostile Physical Conditions

In many of the studied companies, products are exposed to extreme conditions, of which heat occurred most frequently 2.3.1, 2.3.6. Special casings or foils can protect RFID tags from external influences. Protection against heat ensures slow heat conduction from the environment to the tag. Thereby, the temperature at the tag can be kept below its tolerance threshold if the exposure is only temporary. For Gen 2 tags the maximal tolerance for heat is 85°C and correct operation is ensured up to 65°C. Consequently, a protection is needed for temperatures above 85°C. Some RFID tags are already shipped in protection cases. Others can be wrapped in protective materials by so-called converters (converters add materials to RFID inlays and produce complete labels).

3.2.2 Presence of Metal

Many metal objects are present on the plant floor of the investigated plants, *e.g.*, 2.3.2 – 2.3.4, 2.3.6. For instance, transportation units, machines or even the products themselves can be made out of metal. The presence of metal can influence communication with RFID tags due to signal attenuation, reflection, detuning, and eddy currents. How the communication is influenced depends on the communication technology of the physical layer.

Ultra-high-frequency tags communicate using a backscatter technology (Finkenzeller, 2003). High-frequency and low-frequency tags communicate by inductive coupling in the near field. In general, ultra-high-frequency tags suffer less form detuning effects and distortions due to eddy currents than low-frequency and high-frequency tags do. By contrast, near-field-communicating tags face fewer problems caused by reflected waves. Such waves may cancel out a signal totally. Also, ultra-high-frequency signals are more actuated when passing materials. This holds especially for materials containing water. Yet, all frequencies are shielded by metal.

Problems caused by detuning and eddy currents can be overcome by applying an isolation layer between the metal object and the tag. Reflections by metal objects in the near can be blocked by RF absorbers. Also, reflections may even be beneficial to direct signals around metal object which would otherwise block the communication. Which effects have the most influence depends on the particularities of the application environment. Thus, only field tests can fully clarify which hardware setup is most suitable.

3.2.3 Demand for Wireless Communication

Introducing new scan points and sensor devices on the plant floor requires the establishment of new communication channels. This can either be an extension of existing channels or the introduction of new communication means. Fixed wires may be sufficient for stationary scan points. However, wireless communication is necessary if mobile hand readers are applied, see 2.3.4. Furthermore, the number of devices may render wired communication channels infeasible. This is especially the case if large numbers of sensor tags are installed on the plant floor. For easy deployment in the target setting, sensor tags are designed to work independently of fixed infrastructures and facilitate establishments of wireless ad-hoc networks.

The wireless medium poses numerous challenges which are already known from other application domains. Security problems, bandwidth changes and energy issues of battery-powered devices are just some of them. Furthermore, the diversity on the physical layer must be considered in the system design. Devices with different operation frequencies and communication protocols must be integrated via gateways and hubs which bridge channels with different communication technologies.

3.2.4 Processes in Close Spatial Proximity

At some plant floors, different production steps take place in close physical proximity. In one of the investigated plants, different assembly steps have been conducted within a one-meter distance (2.3.1). Associating an RFID read event with the correct process step may be challenging if several steps are performed within the range of a reader. The read range for tags that communicate in the near field is generally easier to control than for backscatter tags.

For tags which use inductive coupling the read range is limited to the size of the near field. High-frequency tags can typically be read out within about a one-meter distance. The relative long range of seven meters and the possibility of reflections may cause ultra-high-frequency tags to be read from unexpected positions. In general, this makes ultra-high-frequency tags more difficult to handle than low-frequency and high-frequency tags if items in different process steps are physically close. However, directional antennas and limitations in the signal strength can help to restrict read outs of ultra-high-frequency tags to the point of interest.

3.3 Required RFID Functionalities

In this section we describe functional building blocks which are needed for IT infrastructures supporting RFID. Prominent middleware solutions like Bornhövd et al. (2004) provide modules that support these functionalities to a certain extent. Note that in this section, we discuss the software functionality independently of our use cases. We address generic building blocks that are typically required in RFID infrastructures. Therefore, this section applies to RFID setups in logistics as well as in manufacturing, or in other applications.

Special requirements for RFID systems in manufacturing are discussed in the next Section 3.4. IT infrastructures supporting RFID need the following functional components: filtering and enriching RFID data, storing RFID data, exchanging RFID data (sharing information along the supply chain), and detecting events in RFID data. We now describe each component in detail.

3.3.1 Filtering and Enriching RFID Data

Several operations must be applied to make use of RFID data. These are filtering of events, enriching RFID data with process semantics and additional information, as well as inference on the data and reactions to events. Filtering RFID data takes place on the edge or middle layer, *e.g.*, during pre-processing or complex pre-processing. Read errors like double reads are filtered during pre-processing, see Figure 3.2. This is usually done by the device controller which provides the software interface to the readers. RFID readers communicate via proprietary protocols with the device controller. If pre-processing and complex pre-processing are in different software modules, data can be exchanged via the PML standard (Floerkemeier et al., 2003). During the complex pre-processing RFID data must be filtered with regard to the events of interest. At a gate, for instance, *appearance* and *disappearance* events may be dropped and replaced by one aggregate *passing* event.

If additional information for an RFID tag is available, this information must be associated with the read event. This can be, for example, information in the user memory of a tag or corresponding sensor measures. On higher levels the read events must be enriched with process semantics. That is, for each event which aspect of the production process is reflected needs to be inferred.

For implementing business logic based on RFID data, we further evaluate the event data after it has been filtered and enriched. This is done by rules that define actions to be conducted when certain observations have been made. Such rules can operate on an intermediate storage holding RFID data that were collected during a certain period. Alternatively, the rules could

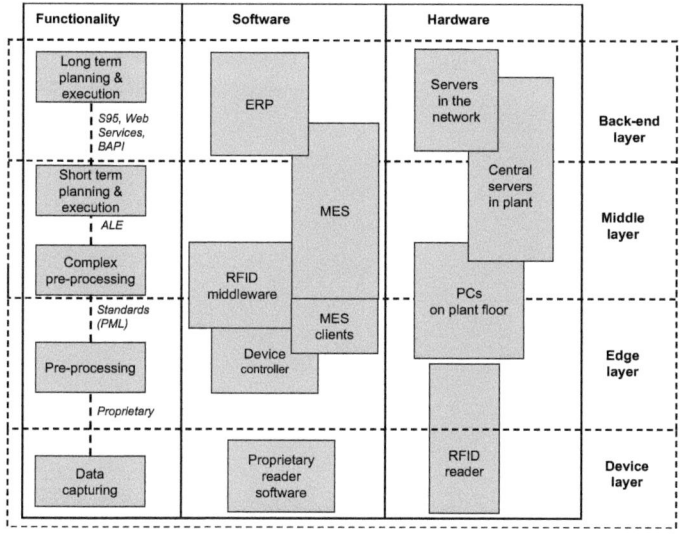

Figure 3.2: Software functionalities on different levels.

run directly on the input stream of the read events. Any other system could be informed via application-level events (short ALE EPCglobal, 2005) and actions could be triggered if certain predefined conditions occur.

The ALE standard describes how client applications can access middleware in order to read data from various sources. The ALE interface allows client applications to be completely agnostic of the reader infrastructure, *e.g.*, the number of readers or their make and model. In addition, it provides means for client applications to specify what to do with EPC data, *e.g.*, how to filter or aggregate the data.

3.3.2 Storing RFID Data

To decide on the overall architecture, one needs to determine how and where to store collected RFID data. This decision is affected by three major aspects: First, one must be clear about where in the IT system the data should be evaluated. Second, one must determine which degree of data aggregation is suitable for the intended use. Third, a policy about how to handle data in the long term has to be devised. This policy must specify how long the data are to be kept on a specific medium and if data can be deleted after a certain time. For instance, the US Tread Act mandates OEMs to report and log detailed production information for three years.

Evaluation of RFID-based information can be done with two distinct purposes. One is to control and monitor business processes. The other is to allow long-term analysis of the monitored activities and to document production. These two objectives lead to different storage requirements. Data for the control of business processes must be available very fast and usually comprises only recent information. For instance, automatic booking at the intake would only require the RFID data currently read and recent advanced shipping notices. Consequently, the required data should be kept in a storage that may be relatively small but must be fast.

Long-term data analysis and business intelligence require different features. Typical tasks can be, for example, an investigation of how overall performance developed over time. Such tasks do not have demands for realtime data. Instead, a database is needed to store the data in the long term. Data historians are tailored to store large amounts of time-stamped data. Using a data historian would allow to store information from every RFID read out. Such fine-grained information could be useful in detailed analysis of the production processes. Mining tools could use the rich data source to search for patterns in the data and for identifying potential improvements in production.

Another way of data analysis is provided by data warehouses. Such software systems support data analysis by advanced tools for reporting and visualization (*e.g.*, OLAP cubes). However, reports in data warehouses do not display raw data. Instead, the data is aggregated and evaluated to show key performance parameters. The raw read events must be mapped to the corresponding process step and enriched with context information in order to reflect the process semantics. Thus, data warehouses work on an excerpt of the complete data set.

In case of recalls, detailed information from the history is needed. Depending on the type of possible recalls perhaps no aggregation is suitable. For instance, the US Tread Act mandates OEMs to report and log detailed production information for three years. Then fine-grained event data must be kept in a database (*e.g.*, data historian) at least for the time a recall can occur. That is, the stored data must provide all information about the production process of parts which could be called back.

3.3.3 Exchanging RFID Data

Fully exploiting the potential of RFID may involve the exchange of captured RFID data with business partners, *i.e.,* sharing information along the supply chain. For instance, since January 2005 the regulation on consumer protection (EC) No. 178/2002 of the European Parliament and of the Council has forced food companies to ensure a seamless traceability for all food and their ingredients – from the producer to the wholesalers and retailers (Cox and Camps, 2002). Increasing the transparency across organizational borders allows for optimizing the collaboration. EPCglobalTM is developing the EPC Network for this purpose (EPCglobal, 2005). The network will contain services for discovering and accessing information.

Several issues need careful consideration before RFID data can be exchanged with business partners. First, it must be decided which information should be available to whom. This requires management of roles and rights for all partners. Also, it is not sufficient to just provide the captured RFID data. The information must be aggregated and semantically enriched to be reasonably interpretable for the business partners.

Furthermore, the exchange format and the communication model must be determined. EPCglobalTM has proposed the Physical Markup Language (PML) for exchanging RFID related data (Floerkemeier et al., 2003). This XML-based language allows to associate RFID reads with additional data such as sensor measures. It is used to encode the output of RFID readers in existing middleware solutions (Bornhövd et al., 2004). However, data exchange on enterprise level may go beyond using pure PML or may be realized based on different standards.

With the specification of EPC Information Services (EPCIS), EPCglobalTM has released another standard that is relevant for exchanging RFID data (EPCglobal, 2007). EPCIS leverage exchange of data that is related to Electronic Product Codes (EPC) (EPCglobal, 2006). The standard specifies data types as well as query interfaces and describes the use of an EPCIS in a framework for exchanging RFID data.

EPCIS supports both, interfaces for ad-hoc queries, and a callback interface for standing queries. It needs to be decided whether information should be pushed via callback functions to the recipient once they are available or if data should be queried on demand via ad-hoc requests. This trade off can be decided on the frequencies in which data would be requested and pushed. Pushing information can reduce network traffic in case of high information demand, while the opposite is the case when demand is low.

Another important aspect is security. If trusted partners are getting insight into business operations, competitors may try to spy on the transferred information. Thus, it is highly recommendable to conduct a detailed security analysis before deciding on a concrete information-sharing arrangement.

3.3.4 Detecting Events in RFID Data

It is necessary to evaluate the semantics of RFID read events in order to use the data for monitoring and controlling production processes. Evaluating these semantics is generally straightforward in logistics applications. For instance, the semantics of reading an object at the inbound gate is that the object has been taken in; an object which is read repeatedly by a smart shelf is stored in this shelf.

Processes on the shop floor can add complexity to the evaluation of the semantic. To be more precise: Observing an object at a certain point may not be sufficient for determining its status in the process. For example, registering a certain process step may involve detecting an object at the machine, registering a disappearance as it is loaded to the machine, checking that the machine is running, and observing the object to appear again.

Evaluating such complex events requires explicit domain knowledge. That is, a model of how a series of read events adds up to a complex event and how this is mapped to certain steps in the production process is needed. Modeling and evaluating such domain knowledge should be supported by software systems for embedding RFID in manufacturing applications. This comprises a language for expressing evaluation rules and software components to execute these rules. Technologies of complex event processing (CEP) are suitable for processing such rules (Luckham, 2001).

A complex event rule comprises three parts: a pattern, a constraint, and an action part. The pattern part and the constraint part together describe the complex event that should be detected. The action part defines how the system must react when the defined event occurs. In that sense, CEP rules are similar to Event Condition Action rules (ECA) in active data bases (Paton et al., 1998). However, active databases focus on in-database events and do not support temporal constraints in RFID-specific queries well (Wang et al., 2006; Wu et al., 2006).

Dedicated approaches for detecting complex events often use finite-state automata (*e.g.*, Gehani et al., 1992; Coral8, 2006) or Petri Nets (*e.g.*, Gatziu and Dirtrich, 1994). Particularities of RFID-specific applications for CEP have been targeted in recent research (Wang et al., 2006; Wu et al., 2006; Gyllstrom et al., 2007). For RFID solutions in manufacturing it must be determined what kind of events the software system should detect and what event-detection technology is implemented in the software system.

The streaming nature of RFID data must be considered as well. Read events float into the back-end layer as continuous data streams. Read outs which belong to one complex event are usually distributed over time. Thus, modeling processing rules requires a windowed operation on event streams. Research projects like STREAM (Arasu et al., 2003) and AURORA (Abadi et al., 2003) have targeted the issue of modeling and executing stream queries. Even though they lack expressiveness for complex events, results may be adopted to RFID in manufacturing.

In Jaroszewicz et al. (2007) we developed an algorithm that correctly matches imperfectly documented incoming data streams to large databases without seeing the whole steam. By this it is possible to identify likely correspondences between attributes of the stream and the database. However, exact calculation of these similarities requires processing of all database records, which is infeasible for data streams. Therefore we devise a fast matching algorithm that uses only a small sample of records, and is yet guaranteed to find a matching that is a close approximation of the matching that would be obtained if the entire stream were processed. The method can be applied to any given (combination of) similarity metrics that can be estimated from a sample with bounded error. This procedure enables us to detect occurring events in RFID-data streams.

3.4 Constraints for IT Infrastructures

Large-scale RFID applications are already in use, for instance, in logistics. Such applications are supported by existing middleware solutions for capturing and processing RFID data. The typical use cases in manufacturing described above pose new requirements for the IT infrastructure. In this section we summarize technological issues which must be respected by software systems for a successful RFID integration in the manufacturing context. This comprises middleware issues that are important for any RFID integration in the business context.

Additionally, we focus on the particular requirements of RFID applications on the plant floor. This covers aspects of integration with other systems, paradigms for data processing as well as architectural and functional requirements. In particular the following six issues for IT systems were derived: distributing business logic and data, supporting heterogeneous data sources, dealing with noise and uncertainty, supporting process analysis, supporting asset tracking, and providing RFID data to components of ISA-95 Level 3.

They all aim to support RFID integration on the plant floor. In the following we describe each in detail.

3.4.1 Distributing Business Logic and Data

Distributing business logic and decoupling it from the back-end layer was an explicit demand in some of the investigated enterprises (2.3.1, 2.3.6). One reason was the aim to improve reliability of the IT infrastructure by decentralization. For decentralized processes, the back-end layer would no longer be a single point of failure and the overall reliability would be improved. For instance, production control and consistency checks could be conducted independently of the back-end layer on PCs on the shop floor. In this setup, a failure of the back-end database or the communication network would have a smaller impact on the production. Besides pushing business logic to the edge layer on the shop-floor PCs, it is even possible to push queries on the RFID-data streams into the device layer. This is possible when the data is gathered using networked devices, (Ziekow and Ivantysynova, 2006).

Another reason for decentralizing business logic is reducing the load on the back-end layer and the communication network. Interviews with the IT staff of the visited companies revealed that retrieving data from the back-end system often reveals bottlenecks in the system performance. Processing and retrieving data locally at the shop-floor PCs could reduce the network load and speed up the system.

In order to decentralize the business logic, the required input data must be distributed as well. For instance, consistency checks usually need data about the planned process. Additionally, information about the input materials is required. This can comprise static information about the input materials as well as history data about past operations that were performed on them.

Required data from the production plan could be pushed to workers' PCs right after the plan has been created. Therefore, the IT infrastructure must support identification of shop-floor PCs which will be in charge of certain parts in a production plan, extracting the corresponding information from the production plan and pushing the data to the shop-floor PC's hard drive. History data about production steps could be stored directly at the manufactured product. This would require applying RFID tags with sufficient writable memory which move along with the product as it is processed.

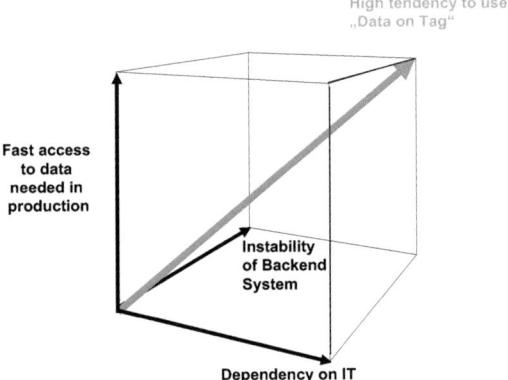

Figure 3.3: Incentives for storing data on tag.

From these observations we derive two degrees of freedom concerning the distribution of data and logic. One is about the question where to store the data – on the tag or in the network. The other is about the question of where to place the business logic: near the production floor or on the edge. Factors affecting the first degree of freedom – data on tag vs. data in network – are visualized in Figure 3.3. One factor captures the need for fast access to data. This is when the IT infrastructure must meet real-time requirements and lookups in the middle or even back-end layer are bottlenecks (*e.g.*, 2.3.1). For such cases data on tag may help to ensure fast access to required information.

Another factor concerns the dependency of the production on the middle and back-end layer. High dependency means that the production cannot run if components situated in on of these layers are down due to system failures. Storing production data on tag can help to establish emergency solutions that – at least temporarily – allow the production to be kept up without having a connection to higher layers (*e.g.*, 2.3.6).

The third factor refers to the reliability of the middle and back-end layer. Storing data on tag facilitates decentralization and helps to avoid single points of failures. This can be relevant if the existing IT infrastructure is

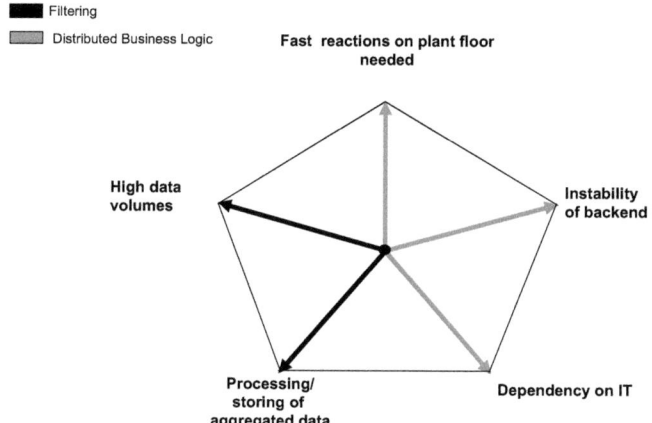

Figure 3.4: Incentives for processing in the middle or edge layer.

not optimized for reliability (*e.g.*, no redundant systems are in place). Figure 3.4 visualizes the second degree of freedom, which is about processing the business logic locally vs. at the edge.

We identified five factors of influence, each reflected in a dimension of the pentagon in Figure 3.4. Three of these factors are identical to the factors in the cube described above. This is because identified use cases for data on tag often coincide with the deployment of business logic in the middle layer. For instance, decentralization by means of data on tag is only beneficial if the processing is decentralized as well.

The remaining two factors are high data volumes and processing/storing of aggregated data. These factors refer to issues of data pre-processing in terms of filtering and aggregation. Reducing the amount of data by means of filtering and aggregation is a necessity if data volumes are high. Pushing these operations to the edge layer can help to avoid bottlenecks and improve scalability of the system. The higher the data volumes are, the higher the incentive to push pre-processing to the edge or even device layer.

Another reason for pre-processing and aggregation is that raw data are often not of interest. Instead, semantically enriched and meaningful information must be extracted from the stream of input data. Performing related operations in the middle layer, avoids forwarding unnecessary information to the back-end layer and reduces the overall system load.

Altogether five factors support the tendency toward pushing processing to lower layers. These are depicted in the pentagon in Figure 3.4. Properties of a given production environment span a surface in this pentagon. The bigger this surface is, the higher the motivation of pushing business logic toward lower layers.

3.4.2 Supporting Heterogeneous Data Sources

One driver for adopting RFID in manufacturing is the demand for getting better insights into production processes (2.3.2, 2.3.6). For instance, the demand for applications which help to address quality issues was mentioned in several of the case studies (2.3.6). Such applications need to keep track of each object in the production along with corresponding machine settings and sensor measurements of environmental conditions. Furthermore, control applications that evaluate production data in real time would have access to these information sources as well. For instance, the investigated manufacturer of cooling frames uses optical sensors to automatically route faulty products to a separate control station.

To enable such applications, RFID and sensor data must be correlated with information from different data sources. Therefore, a software module is needed that supports numerous ways of data acquisition and provides an integrated view on the collected information. Besides interfaces for RFID and bar-code readers, interfaces for sensor networks, relational databases, XML databases and machines on the plant floor are relevant as well.

3.4.3 Dealing with Noise and Uncertainty

Using RFID and sensor data to monitor processes on the plant floor requires advanced evaluation of the raw input data. Sensor data are inherently overlaid with noise and distorted by measurement errors. Thus, software for using sensor data in business processes must take the imperfect nature of the input data into account. This can be done by various filtering algorithms. A simple example would be to apply low-pass filtering over a set of input data or to build the average over multiple measurements in order to suppress noise.

Like sensor measurements, data from RFID readers also include errors. These errors are usually not corrupted read outs of RFID tags, since those errors are filtered out by checksums in the communication protocol in the reader. However, readers can miss RFID tags within their read range. This results in the false observation that the respective tag is absent (false negative).

3.4.4 Supporting Process Analysis

In several investigated plants, the predominant reason for considering RFID adoption was to be able to better narrow recalls, see 2.4.1. This is because RFID eases scan processes and makes data capturing in more situations feasible than other Auto-ID technologies do. Fine-grained data tracks would enable to determine faulty products. Due to the importance of narrowing recalls, software systems that support RFID applications in manufacturing must provide special analysis tools.

Another major potential of applying RFID on the plant floor is to gain more insight into the processes. The collected data may help to detect inefficiencies and reasons for quality problems in the production. Yet, analysis tools are needed to extract this knowledge from the data. These tools should be tailored to the application domain to extract performance measures in correspondence to the respective manufacturing processes as well as data from sensors and machines. For instance, identifying an unexpected quality problem due to humidity on the plant floor requires detecting a correlation between data from quality checks and sensor data taken during the processing of the respective products.

3.4.5 Supporting Asset Tracking

Using RFID for tracking crucial assets was a targeted application in several of the plants. This was desired to improve planning of the production schedule and to direct employees who fetch the assets. In order to meet this demand, tracking software must be integrated with RFID data and the planning application.

For integrating RFID data, the tracking application must be able to associate RFID readers or RFID position tags with spatial positions. Furthermore, the software must be capable of inferring relocation of assets from the captured RFID read events. In some technical setups, this may be realized by simple rules that associate objects registered by certain readers with the respective positions. For instance, this can be suitable for assets in smart shelves that are equipped with RFID readers.

However, inferring the position of assets may be more complex in other situations. For instance, if assets are registered by mobile readers, asset tracking requires determining the reader's position first and then inferring the position of registered objects. Such particularities of the planned application setup pose requirements to the tracking software of choice. Here it is of special interest how object positions can be obtained and analyzed by the software system.

3.4.6 Providing RFID Data to Components of the Middle Layer

In our case studies, we observed similarities in the IT infrastructures that are used at the investigated plants. The used software systems support a set of typical functionalities such as planning, controlling and monitoring production processes.

A complete RFID solution always spans multiple layers from the IT infrastructure. We put RFID readers, plant-local control devices such as a PLC or PCs on the shop floor into the device layer. PCs on the shop floor with RFID device controller aggregate RFID read events and provide the interface to higher-layer control systems such as an MES or an ERP system. MES lie in the middle layer. They are responsible for orchestrating the manufacturing processes in the factory. This includes responsibilities such as operations scheduling, production control, or labor management. In many use cases monitoring components in the device layer will be based on RFID technology, see Section 2.3. Thus, data from RFID readers must be fed into the middle layer components in order to support the workflow management. Yet, it is infeasible to directly link reader interfaces to components of the middle layer. Instead, RFID data must be pre-processed to extract information which is of relevance for this system level. To be more precise, at least noise in the form of double reads or false disappearance events should be filtered. Furthermore, RFID reads should be aggregated to meaningful events; *e.g.*, the completion of a certain production step.

Thus, interfaces to pre-processing components must be defined for the components in the middle layer. These interfaces should support push-based communication paradigms to account for the event character of RFID read outs. Furthermore, a coding scheme for data exchange must be defined. This coding scheme should allow associating identification numbers of RFID tags with related data and information about the read event.

Notice that the distinction of clearly separated layers often does not correspond to reality. The functionality of certain layers may be combined into an integrated system. For example, an ERP system may include an RFID integration component, such as SAP's Auto-ID Infrastructure, which enables it to directly communicate with manufacturing or logistics processes. In the future, the strict separation into layers and system boundaries is likely to disappear in favor of a more modular and flexible service-oriented architecture, see (Günther et al., 2008, Chapt.3).

3.5 Conclusion

This chapter shows that despite the high potential of RFID technology, manufacturers have to consider a number of issues before starting an implementation. Environmental conditions, such as heat, the presence of metal or water, or the plant layout may impact the applicability of RFID. Furthermore, the effort for creating and maintaining an infrastructure of RFID readers, shop-floor PCs communication networks as well as the costs for the tags must be weighed against the benefits. This is because tag costs will become significant in high-volume, low-value products that are individually tagged. Apart from the hardware, robust and scalable software is needed to handle the processing of RFID data streams.

When implementing RFID, the company needs to integrate it into its existing IT infrastructure. A tight integration with existing ERP and MES systems facilitates that RFID leads to concrete and local productivity improvements in the short and medium term. Then the company can use the full potential of this technology. This is because RFID can be used for data collection in cases in which other Auto-ID technologies are impractical. Integrating these data into IT-enabled business processes would result in a more precise match of the shop floor with the company's IT processes. This leads to more visibility about production processes; permitting faster adaptations to production variations.

Such improvements – especially if they are purely intra-enterprise, *i.e.*, independent of any coordination with supply chain partners – facilitate the adoption decision considerably. Therefore, I will focus on how to integrate RFID into existing IT infrastructures in the next two chapters, starting with a detailed analysis of deployed IT infrastructures.

Chapter 4

IT Infrastructures Deployed in Manufacturing

Before embedding RFID into IT infrastructures one needs to evaluate where the resulting RFID data should be integrated and which applied software components would be affected. Furthermore, it is important to know how RFID data could be passed to these software components.

In order to be able to give well-founded design guidelines for embedding RFID into shop-floor applications and the company's IT infrastructure it is necessary to conduct an in-depth analysis of the state-of-the-art in manufacturing IT infrastructures. I completed this analysis together with Holger Ziekow in 2007 and 2008. Our research method was the case-study approach. We plant to publish the results of the case studies.

Manufacturing operations can be generally classified as discrete, continuous, or batch processes. Continuous and batch can be summed up into the process industry. Discrete and process industry are likely to have heterogeneous software requirements. Therefore, for our case studies we explicitly chose manufacturers from both industry sectors.

For a profound understanding of the state-of the-art in manufacturing it is essential to evaluate technical fundamentals beforehand. This includes applied standards and software systems. This part of the chapter was conducted with Oliver Günther and Holger Ziekow. Parts of it are published in

Günther et al. (2008).

The chapter starts with a discussion of these technical foundations. Section 4.2 presents the conducted case studies with an analysis of actual industrial implementations. Section 4.3 reveals lessons learned. Section 4.4 concludes this chapter.

4.1 Flow of Information between Shop Floor and Top Floor

In general, today's flow of information in the producing industry can be described as follows: Sensors on machines generate unfiltered data that are collected through so-called distributed control systems (DCS). The tasks of the DCS are to monitor the actual processes and to provide a human-machine interface for control of the machines. They also pass the collected data on to the next level, to the manufacturing execution system (MES). The MES collects and filters the data for analysis, and coordinates the entire production process. Here, all data that could be needed can be accessed in a time frame between days and minutes, compared to a time frame between hours and seconds in a DCS. In the MES, data are compressed, and passed to historians for later analysis. Only a few data for long-term analysis are passed on to the upper level. This level is the enterprise resource planning software (ERP). The ERP deals with data in the range of months and weeks. It manages the long-term production and passes customer orders down to the MES.

In order to make development and, even more importantly, maintenance of software easier, several consortia are devising standards that define and normalize the flow of information. Together these standards give a detailed description of every level, define what tasks have to be completed and which information has to be kept on every level. They also characterize the exchange between these levels. With the use of the standards, replacing and adjusting installed software promises to be easier.

In the following I describe these standards. I begin with the description of the Purdue reference model for computer-integrated manufacturing (PRM).

The goal of this standard is to create a general design about the operations of any production plant. The second standard family that we consider is the ISA-S95 family. This is a standard family for plant-to-business (P2B) integration with a special focus on manufacturing. The ISA-S95 standard builds on the PRM.

Besides the ISA-S95 P2B standard there are two other P2B integration standards: RosettaNet (Malakooty, 2005), and OAGIS (OAGIS, 2007). In contrast to these standards, ISA-S95 focuses solely on the integration of ERP and MES. Both, RosettaNet and OAGIS go far beyond P2B integration in an attempt to model every class of B2B (Business-to-Business) transaction. The cost of this approach is the lack of depth for P2B integration.

The section closes with the outline of the OLE for process control standard (OPC). It is a standard for exchanging messages on the shop floor.

4.1.1 The Purdue Reference Model for Computer-Integrated Manufacturing

The Purdue reference model (PRM) for computer-integrated manufacturing (CIM) Williams (1992) was prepared by the CIM reference model committee at the international Purdue workshop on industrial computer systems in 1989. The goal was to create a general design about the operations of any production plant. It divides the manufacturing domain into six levels of computing functionality, which are based on the hierarchy of the manufacturing enterprise. These six levels are considered to be sufficient for the purpose of identifying necessary integration standards. The levels in their hierarchical structure are shown in Figure 4.1. Besides the detailed description of the six levels and their functions for a generic manufacturing facility, the PRM provides definitions for the flow of data.

In level 1 are the actual processes on the equipment-machines and robots. It represents the realization of level 2 commands. Because of the wide differences of equipment and functions between different industries, the detailed descriptions of the functions in this level are not included in the PRM. The scope of the PRM lies between levels 2 and 5.

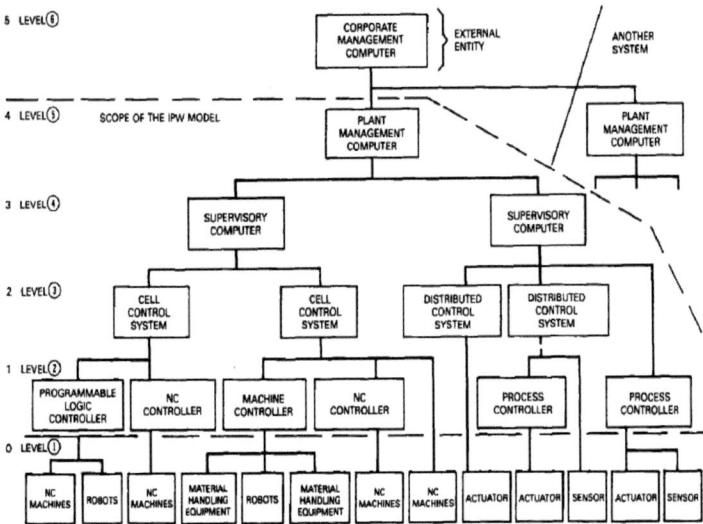

Figure 4.1: Purdue reference model showing connectivity from shop floor to top floor for adaptive manufacturing; source Williams (1992).

Level 2 maintains the direct control of the plant units, the whole of the equipment and coordinates the activities of the shop floor. It detects and responds to emergency conditions which may occur in the plant units. Another task is the collection of information on production, raw material and energy use and the transmission of this information to the next level. Also, diagnostics and updates on any standby systems belong to the tasks performed here. Programmable logic controllers (PLC) and human-machine interfaces (HMI) lie in this level.

Level 3 coordinates multiple machines and operations. The responsibility here is the sequencing and supervision of the jobs at the shop floor and support of various services. It responds to any emergency condition which may exist in its region of the plant. The second control task is the optimization of units within the limits of the established production schedule. For system coordination and operational data reporting it collects and maintains data queues of production, inventory, raw material and energy usage information for the units under its control. Levels 2 and 3 carry out necessary control and optimization functions for individual production units to enforce the production schedule, which is defined in the upper levels and communicated down.

Level 4 deals with an area of a plant. It handles the detailed production scheduling and area coordination for one plant subdivision. This level controls the allocation and supervision of materials and resources, coordinates the production and supports the jobs and obtains needed resources. Another task is caring out the production schedule that has been created by the upper level. Together with the upper level it also modifies the production schedules in order to compensate interruptions of the production, which may occur in the area of its responsibility. Operational reports, including variable manufacturing costs, are generated here. The data for offline analysis are collected. As on the lower levels, this level also diagnoses itself and the underlying functions of the other levels.

Level 5 is the last level which lies in the scope of the PRM. It deals with the planning of the production for the whole plant. It coordinates the implementation of the enterprise functions and plans and also modifies the basic schedule of the production for all units. Other basic functions include the product design and production engineering and the upper-level production management, procurement, resource and maintenance management. It is the main interface with the plant for company management, sales and shipping personnel, accounting and supply production. All status information is collected and is supplied in the form of regular production and status reports. In coordination with the actual schedule it develops the optimal inventory levels of raw material and energy sources. Another function on this level is the collection and maintenance of all goods in process. There is also a function for the maintenance of the used equipment. This level does not include any control functions. It only deals with the production scheduling and overall plant data functions. It is used as an upper-management and staff-level interface.

Level 6 is not included due to the fact that it is considered as an external entity. This level represents the corporate management, the task of which is to achieve the mission of the enterprise. Basic functions include finance, marketing and sales, and research and development.

4.1.2 ISA-S95

ANSI/ISA-S95 (internationally standardized under ISO/IEC-62246) is a prominent plant-to-business (P2B) integration standard relevant for manufacturing (Brandl, 2000, 2001, 2005). This standard builds on the Purdue reference model for computer-integrated manufacturing to define a multi-level functional reference model for manufacturing systems.

This standard defines a terminology and concepts to structure manufacturing systems and operations. Figure 4.2 illustrates how the functionality within a manufacturing system is distributed across four different levels. Each of these comprises manufacturing functionality on a particular level of abstraction. In particular, the following areas are addressed:

- Level 0: Physical processes (machines). Location of the actual production processes.

- Level 1: Sensing and manipulating physical processes (sensors, actuators, RFID readers).

- Level 2: Monitoring and controlling physical processes (PLC, HMI).

- Level 3: Manufacturing operations & control: dispatching production, detailed production, scheduling, reliability assurance, etc. Maintaining records and optimizing the production process. Relevant time frame: seconds to days.

- Level 4: Business planning & logistics: plant production scheduling, production, material use, delivery and shipping, inventory management. Relevant time frame: days to months.

Nevertheless, the functionalities on the different levels should not convey a false impression of accuracy. For many functionalities, one has several

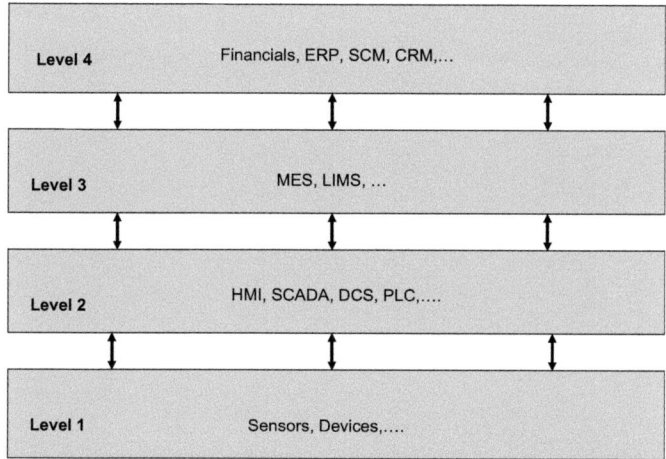

Figure 4.2: ISA-S95 functional reference model showing connectivity from shop floor to top floor for adaptive manufacturing.

choices regarding how to assign them to the levels. The border between hardware controllers (level 2) and MES (level 3) is equally fuzzy, as is the border between MES and ERP (level 4), see Figure 4.3.

A complete RFID solution always spans multiple of the levels defined in ISA-S95. RFID tags are typically attached to material or material containers that are being tracked through the process. Machine tools, inventory locations, or even workers may also be identified through RFID tags. The RFID tags themselves correspond to ISA-S95 level 0. Hardware, such as RFID readers offer level 1 functionality by reading from or writing information to RFID tags. Plant-local control devices such as a PLC or PCs with RFID device controller aggregate RFID read events and provide the interface to higher-level control systems such as an MES or an ERP system. MES are classified as level 3 systems and are responsible for orchestrating the manufacturing processes in the factory. This includes responsibilities such as operations scheduling, production control, or labor management. Level

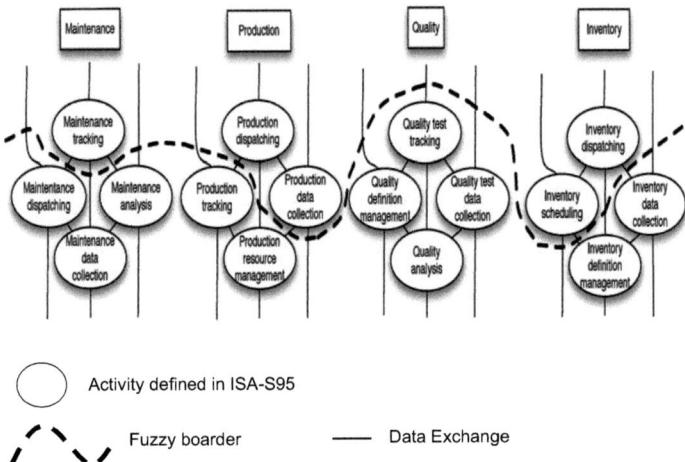

Figure 4.3: Fuzzy borders between level 3 and 4 of the ISA-S95 standard, source Brandl (2005).

4 functionality is typically provided by ERP systems such as SAP mySAP ERP.

The distinction of clearly separated levels constitutes a reference model but often does not correspond to reality. The functionality of certain levels may be combined into an integrated system. For example, an ERP system may include an RFID integration component, such as SAP's Auto-ID Infrastructure, which enables it to directly communicate with manufacturing or logistics processes. In the future, the strict separation into levels and system boundaries is likely to disappear in favor of a more modular and flexible service-oriented architecture.

ISA-S95 addresses the interfaces between level 3 and 4 describing the information that is being communicated between the MES and the back-end ERP system. In part 2, the standard provides abstract definitions of information models describing a production order, the equipment to be used for the execution, personnel, material and other production-related entities. The ISA-S95 standard defines these information models but does not offer an implementation or syntax. The B2MML (Business-to-Manufacturing Markup Language) fills that void and fully implements ISA-S95 as a set of XML schemas, one schema per information model.

A recently started cooperation between ISA and OAGIS is likely to further harmonize the currently competing standards. ISA-S95, although still far from being mainstream, has already been deployed successfully by a number of businesses and is currently the leading standard for plant-to-business data exchange.

RFID itself is not explicitly considered within ISA-95. However, many of the ISA-S95 information models include identification information such as data to identify a particular material or personnel. These data may be contained on an RFID tag attached to a material or carried by plant-floor personnel.

4.1.3 OPC

OPC is a family of different standards. The goal is to ensure the interoperability of different shop-floor devices among each other as well as providing a standardized way for applications to communicate with shop-floor devices, e.g., sensors, PLCs, or Historians. The OPC Foundation is responsible for the OPC standards. It offers free tools for its members to test OPC compliance. Initiated in 1996 by a task force of a handful of companies from the automation industry the organization today has more than 300 members. Originally the OPC standard was based on Microsoft Object Linking and Embedding (Distributed) Component Object Model technology (short OLE COM/DCOM technology) and, therefore, the name was OLE for Production Control. In the meantime the OPC standards are no longer restricted to COM/DCOM technology and therefore the name has been changed to Openness, Productivity and Collaboration.

The OPC architecture is based upon the client/server computer model as depicted in Figure 4.4. In this model an OPC server is a data source.

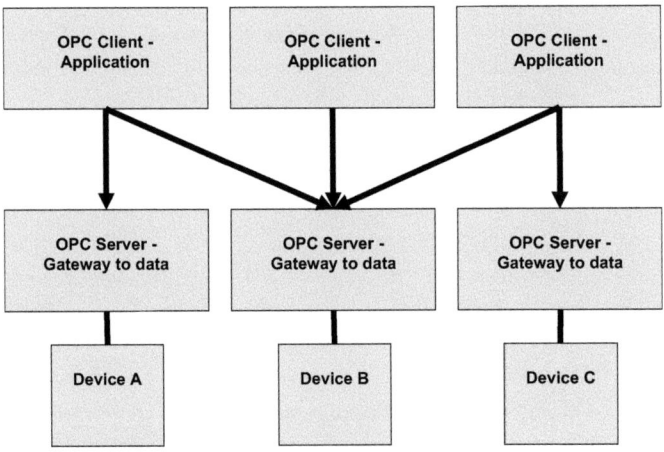

Figure 4.4: Accessing devices via OPC.

It receives requests for data from an OPC client, obtains the data from the device - often the proprietary system - and serves the data to the OPC client.

The first standard in the OPC family was the OPC Data Access Specification. It is still the most important standard within the family and rules the acquisition of data from shop-floor devices through production control stations, manufacturing execution systems or even ERP systems. A so-called OPC server running on a shop-floor device or industrial PC close to the shop floor communicates via field buses with the data sources and exposes the data in a standardized way to higher-level applications, the OPC clients. With the new OPC XML-DA standard a web-service-based data access standard is provided. It allows OPC components to be run on non-Microsoft systems.

The OPC Alarm & Events Specification provides a means to OPC clients for registering certain events or alarm conditions. Thereby, the clients only receive messages when something of interest to them happens instead of having to read data streams continuously as would be necessary if OPC Data Access was used.

OPC Batch specifies interfaces for the exchange of information about equipment capabilities and operating conditions with a special focus on batch processes. OPC Data eXchange specifies the communication between OPC servers via field buses. In contrast to the OPC Data Access standard that deals with real-time data only, the OPC Historical Data Access standard specifies how data that is already stored in some system, *e.g.*, a plant historian, can be accessed. OPC Security defines how the sensitive data on OPC servers can be protected against accidental or intentional manipulation.

The OPC Unified Architecture (OPC-UA) is the latest specification from the OPC foundation. The first parts of this new specification were finalized in June 2006. OPC-UA provides a uniform web-service-based access to the various formerly separated functionalities like OPC DA, A&E, HDA. It also overcomes the dependability on Microsoft COM/DCOM with the specification of an own communication stack. This allows OPC-UA to be run on non-Microsoft systems including embedded systems that get more and more important as OPC servers.

The OPC standard primarily addresses communications with systems close to the shop floor like PLCs or plant historians. In an RFID scenario, OPC/OPC-UA would be most suitable for the communication between the middleware and the readers. As of today, OPC is not broadly accepted for this purpose. However, it is an important standard for shop-floor integration with IT systems in general and is used in cases where RFID readers and shop-floor equipment have to be used in combination.

4.2 Case Studies

In this section we show how manufacturing companies apply information technology for their production processes. In order to truly examine the use of IT, we conducted several case studies at diverse manufacturers. This qualitative research method enables us to acquire an in-depth understanding of the situation present. As is true for any case-based analysis we cannot claim that our insights are representative for the whole manufacturing domain. However, the fact of having more depth in the analysis dominates on the positive side (Flyvbjerg, 2006). In the case studies we have an interpretive research approach.

I conducted the case studies together with Holger Ziekow in the period from August 2007 to August 2008. The participating companies are from the following industries (the company names are not revealed due to non-disclosure agreements):

1. batch production: manufacturer of milk products (short MIP),

2. discrete production: manufacturer of engine cooling modules (COO),

3. discrete production: manufacturer of refractories (REF),

4. discrete production: manufacturer of engines (ENG),

5. batch production: manufacturer of chemicals (CHE),

6. discrete production: manufacturer of power plants (POW),

7. discrete production: manufacturer of tires (TIR).

All seven companies are headquartered in Germany. Their size ranges between several hundred and over 100,000 employees. Four out of seven are listed in the DAX or MDAX, respectively. Our reason for choosing these companies was to gain several representatives from diverse industrial sectors.

4.2.1 Production of Milk Products

The production at the manufacturer of milk products (short MIP) is organized in several divisions producing diverse products. For this case study we analyzed two departments. Dep1 produces plastic cups and blank shapes for bottles. Dep2 produces and processes perishable products. The production processes in Dep1 are highly automated. Manual intervention is limited to: configuring machine settings, loading and unloading the machines, and taking samples for quality checks.

The set-up time for a machine depends on how much the settings from the previous production task differ from the subsequent one. Furthermore, machines need to be cleaned in periodical intervals and after processing of specific ingredients. Therefore, the setup times range between 30 minutes and 4 hours. A production step itself runs for about half a day to one day in the same configuration.

The production processes at Dep1 differ slightly depending on the produced product. The department produces blank shapes for bottles, colored plastic cups and cups which are decorated with paper sleeves. Blank shapes for bottles are directly transported to another department for filling or are directly sold. In contrast, plastic cups are decorated before they leave the department. The processes for producing cups vary with respect to how cups are decorated. The cups can either be colored or decorated with paper. Figure 4.5 shows the production process for colored plastic cups.

In the first step, plastic granules are melted and molded to a reel. Subsequently, the same machine punches plastic cups out of the molded reel. A different machine is used to color these cups with the desired imprint. Input materials for the coloring steps are a range of colors and blank plastic cups. The output of this step is the finished cups that leave Dep1. The cups are subsequently filled with food and sealed at another department.

In the production at Dep2 milk and yogurt is processed and bottled. Figure 4.6 shows the exemplary process of processing and filling flavored milk at Dep2. Each process step is conducted by a different machine. Therefore, we omit machines in the process model in Figure 4.6.

The first steps of the production process in Dep2 run in parallel. In one part milk is processed while bottles are prepared in the other part. Processing milk covers heating the milk and enriching it with flavors. Processing of bottles starts with blowing blank shapes from Dep1 into the desired bottle shape. In the following step the bottles are cleaned with acid. Subsequently, the bottles are filled with the flavored milk and closed with a lid. After that, the blank bottles are decorated with plastic foils which are shrink-fitted onto the bottle's body. Finally the bottles are packed. Like all the other steps, the packing is fully automated and manual intervention is limited to configuring and controlling the machines and taking samples for quality checks.

The described process is an example of the production at Dep2. Other

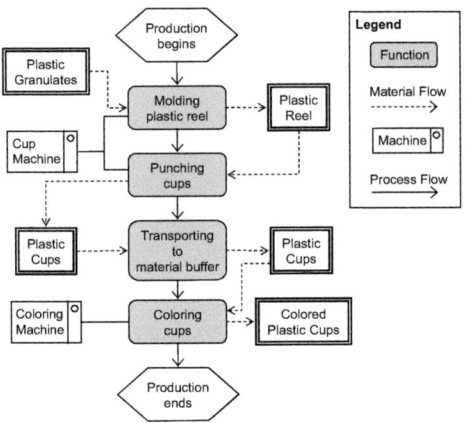

Figure 4.5: Production process for producing cups at MIP in Dept1.

processes for processing and filling yogurt are conducted in this department as well. However, these processes are similar to the one described above and are therefore not addressed in detail.

IT Infrastructure

We describe the IT Infrastructure of MIP with regards to production data management. This covers a description of the main system components and their interaction. In addition we delineate the physical deployment of the software and discuss details of how the IT infrastructure is used along the production activities.

Regarding the management of production data, the IT infrastructure at MIP differs throughout the company. All departments are managed using the central ERP system SAP R/3. A dedicated PDC system is only used in three departments among which are the investigated departments Dep1 and Dep2. For the remaining departments it is planned to introduce a PDC

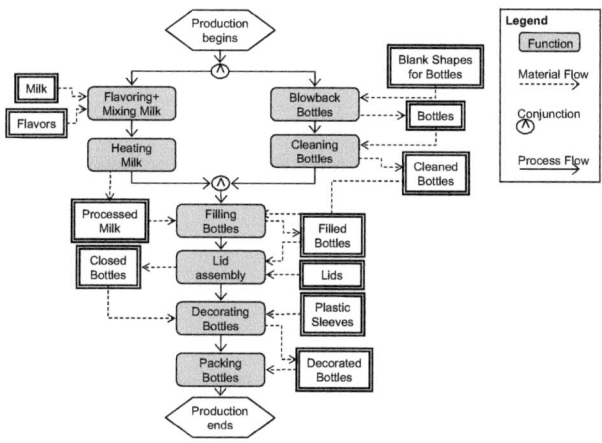

Figure 4.6: Processing and filling milk at MIP in Dept2.

system in the future. In the flowing we focus on those departments that have a PDC system in place. Figure 4.7 visualizes the deployment of the system components across the four different system layers.

The device layer consists of PLCs, machines, and machine terminals. MIP uses mainly Siemens S5 and S7 controllers as PLCs. The PLCs are connected with scan nodes that host OPC servers. These servers in turn are linked to the PDC system. Data from machine sensors, machine settings, production tasks as well as programs for machine control are communicated along this connection. Note that all machine data are read via OPC. For communicating settings to the machines OPC is used in approx. 80% of the cases. In the remaining 20% proprietary interfaces (*e.g.* based on XML) are used.

Many machines on the shop floor have a terminal through which communication with the PLCs of the machine is enabled. Workers use these terminals for machine configuration, data monitoring, and data entry. Here, the machine terminal serves as interface to the PLCs. The settings for a

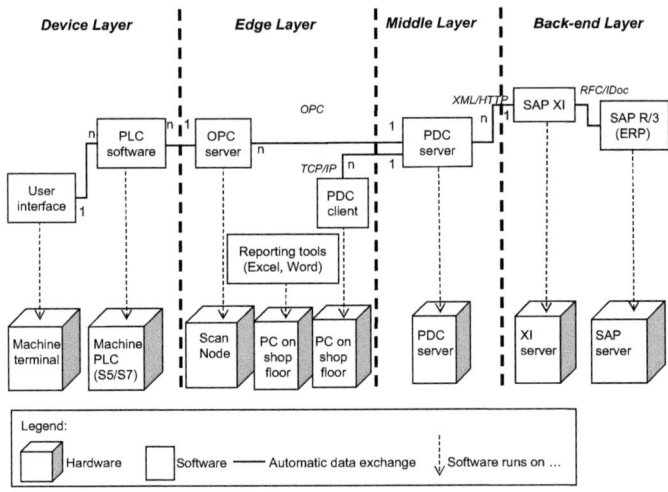

Figure 4.7: Deployment diagram of the software and hardware at MIP.

machine can be provided via OPC from the middle layer, entered manually or both.

The functionalities for data monitoring allow the workers to observe important machine parameters while the production is running. In the case of aberrations the worker can react by changing machine settings. If any major disturbances occur, the machine software may enforce an error report. For such reports the worker must manually select predefined error categories at the machine terminal. The policies about when reports are enforced as well as the error categories are in most cases a static part of the machine software and not configurable.

Terminals are also used for managing production tasks of the machine. Therefore, production tasks that are approved in the middle layer (*i.e.* the MES or PDC) and are displayed at the respective machine. Workers can select from the range of approved tasks and thereby determine the schedule on the lowest level of granularity. Log data about this activity are automatically created and then communicated via PDC or MES clients to higher system layers.

The edge layer comprises PCs for accessing the PDC system and scan nodes for communicating with the device layer. Scan nodes host OPC servers and are connected to several PLCs on the plant floor. Thereby scan nodes serve as a communication hub that converts both, communication protocols and physical connections. Theoretically whole production departments could be served by one scan node. However, to ease maintenance and reduce the risk of failure only about 15-30 PLCs are connected to one scan node.

PCs on the edge layer are used for accessing data in the PDC system. Shift foreman and workers use such PCs for obtaining statistics about the performance of production lines and machines. Therefore, these PCs run PDC clients. However, most access is done via dedicated reporting tools that MIPs IT staff implemented on request. In parts of the production, terminal PCs are used for manually created reports. In such cases workers fill out Microsoft Excel sheets or Word documents to report about details of the conducted production processes. In addition to these electronic notes, some data are handwritten on paper forms, *e.g.*, to document quality checks.

The middle layer comprises the PDC system installations. For communicating machine events to the ERP system, the PDC system creates notifications that are passed through a Notification Monitor to the SAP XI. The SAP XI then passes the data on to the ERP via RFC calls. A part of the PDC system solution is an Order Monitor. This component is used to manage production tasks at specific process steps. From the Order Monitor the production tasks are communicated to the PLC of the respective machine.

Machine data are captured by the PDC system via OPC. Overall 10,000 measuring points are recorded, of which about 7,000 are located at the investigated departments (approx. 2,500 at Dep1 and approx. 4,500 at Dep2). The machine data are regularly polled at a frequency of typically 1Hz (up to 10Hz). For saving and reporting, the information is aggregated whereby redundant information is omitted. That is, identical measurements are not recorded in the database.

Furthermore, only an extract of information is reported to the SAP system. This includes key information such as the produced quantities and finished production tasks. This information accounts for about 20% of the evaluated production data. Thus, most of the data evaluation is done with the PDC system's visualization tools that use the PDC database. Here, potentials for improving the production are identified based on analysis of the recorded machine data. Along with improved data safety, these analyses are one major reason for MIP to use a PDC system. According to the staff at MIP, these analyses have already enabled major improvements in the production.

Another functionality of the middle layer is the management of alerts and notification. Notifications about abbreviations in the production process are generated if the deviation between the recorded data and the corresponding product recipe exceeds a specific threshold. However, many abbreviations are due to necessary adjustments and should not result in a notification. Overall, only 60% of the created notifications reflect real errors. Therefore, each notification is manually checked using the notification monitor of the PDC system before it is reported to the SAP system.

Generally abbreviations in the production process can result in alerts for workers. Such alerts are created if a disturbance in the process needs immediate reaction by a worker. The IT staff of MIP has extended the PDC system with functionality to send alters via SMS to the cell phones of shop-floor workers. This is realized using active database technology in the database of the PDC system. In the future it is planned to extend these alerts for ensuring timely reaction in critical situations.

The back-end layer comprises the ERP system. MIP is currently using the SAP R/3 ERP system. Communication from the ERP system to lower system layers is enabled via SAP XI. Data exchange between the ERP system and SAP XI is realized using iDocs, specifically -ZSM_Loipro and -ZSM_MatMas. The communication between SAP XI and the PDC system is done by means of XML documents which are transmitted via HTTP.

Summarizing Case MIP

The case of MIP shows how a manufacturer can benefit from the application of a PDC system. The tasks of the PDC system can be grouped into the categories of capturing machine data, aggregating data, recoding history information, managing notifications and alerts, generating status reports, controlling machine settings, and data evaluation. In this case RFID data would be fed into the PDC system, rather than directly to the ERP.

4.2.2 Production of Cooling Engines

Including intermediate products, about 1000 different products are produced in COOs plants. The specification for these products is usually provided by the clients and production lines are individually established for particular contracts. A contract usually runs for several years - basically as long as the respective car is produced and spare parts are needed. Overall, the demand for a certain product changes only slowly. This allows COO to produce with a small buffer of about two days in advance. The supply for the customer is generally pulled using a Kanban system. For a small proportion of the production lines COO realizes just-in-sequence delivery (JIS). However, it is believed that this proportion will increase in the future.

Coarse-grained planning at COO addresses the assignment of orders to plants. This is a long-term decision that is made by a planning committee without particular software support. Fine-grained planning is conducted locally at the different plants. The employed planning techniques are isolated applications that vary from plant to plant. Generally the planning is done several days ahead and on the granularity of shifts (approx. 6-8 hours). Plans for the lines with JIS are made when the sequence specification is stated by the customer. This is about two days ahead of the delivery date.

Figure 4.8 shows an exemplary process of the production at COO that is used to assemble and check coolers. In the fist process step several metal parts are squeezed and combined into a cooler. At this stage the parts of the cooler are only loosely attached to each other and moistened with solder. In the subsequent step the parts are soldered together in an oven. After this

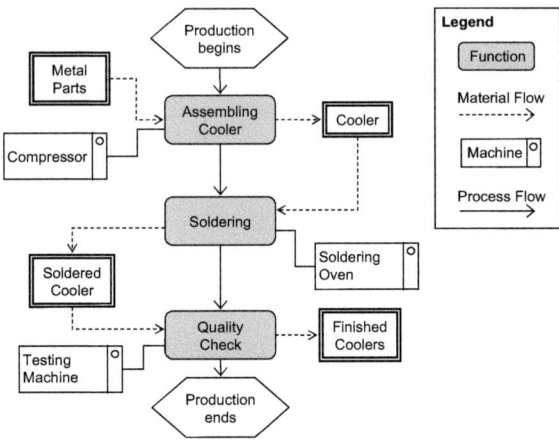

Figure 4.8: Production process for coolers.

the product is ready but still needs to undergo an intensive quality check. In this last step the cooler is filled with air under different pressure. This allows leaks to be discovered and faulty products to be sorted out.

IT Infrastructure

COO uses SAP as ERP system. However, no consistent solution for production data acquisition is currently in place. We describe aspects of the IT infrastructure that are relevant to the acquisition and processing of production data. We introduce this description with a discussion of functional requirements for the infrastructure. This is followed by an outline of the common data flow from the plant floor through the system. Subsequent to this general overview of the data flow we discuss details of the data acquisition. This is done along the sample process which was introduced in the previous section.

Production data at COO is used for three general purposes: analyzing and eliminating production errors, performance control of production lines, and benchmarking between production plants. Analyzing and eliminating production errors is the primary use of the production data. Due to the nature of the contracts with clients, COO is obligated to ensure process safety. If a production error occurs, COO must be able to identify the cause and exclude future repetition of the problem. The second utilization of the data is for performance control of the production line. Performance indicators are used by shift foremen and maintenance staff for detecting declines in productivity. Here, the collection of production data allows anomalies to be spotted and helps to prioritize maintenance activities. Beyond this, performance indicators impact the workers' salaries.

At COO the salary has a variable component. It depends on the amount of products the worker produces during his/her shifts and is calculated from the production data. The third use of the collected data is benchmarking. Benchmarking between production plants is important on the management level. In order to make investment decisions and to assign production tasks the performance of different locations must be considered. For this purpose the management demands regular reports on key performance parameters from each plant. These parameters are aggregates from production data that are acquired on the plant floor.

The IT solutions at COO's plants are not unified. This is due to the fact that the management of log files is within the responsibility of each plant. Consequently the particular solutions differ across the facilities. However, some similarities can be identified throughout the isolated solutions. We outline these similarities in Figure 4.9, which gives an overview of the IT system.

Device layer: Commonly, production data is recorded by programmable logic controllers (PLCs) on the machines. Depending on its purpose the data is then forwarded from the PLCs through different channels to the higher-edge layer for reporting. These machine data are also displayed on machine terminals. This allows workers to monitor the machine activity and to intervene in cases of aberrations. Moreover, workers use the displayed data for writing production reports on paper. These reports differ from plant

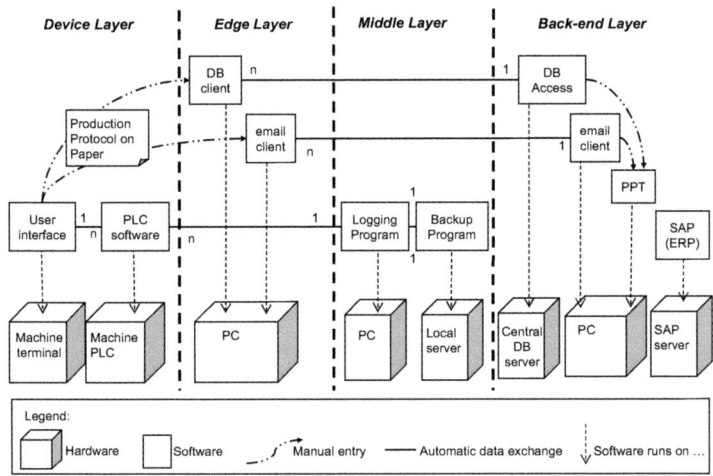

Figure 4.9: Deployment diagram of the software and hardware at COO.

to plant. However, the reports include some attributes which are common throughout the whole company. For instance, COO records the amount of finished products and defective goods in all plants.

The edge layer: For monitoring the performance of plants and production lines each plant of COO has to generate reports at monthly intervals. The staff creates all reports based on the above-mentioned paper documents from the plant floor. Here again, some particularities of how the reports are created vary among the plants. Yet, a significant proportion of COO's plants apply the same solution: Via MS Access clients in the plants, workers enter data into the database from the manually written paper reports. For plants which do not use the MS Access database the key performance parameters are communicated via email

The middle layer is used for logging all data from the PLCs. This covers machine settings, sensor data, and user input. These log files are recorded on the machines and copied to PCs as well as local servers for archiving. The middle layer is neither directly connected with the edge layer nor with the back-end layer.

In the first production step – the assembly – several constraints on machine parameters are set. These constraints are defined as upper and lower bounds. For instance, during the testing step machines pump gas into the coolers. Here, upper and lower bounds define the allowed gas pressure for the test. The machines measure these parameters during production and check whether they are within the defined bounds. In addition, the machines record these parameters with the corresponding upper and lower bounds into log files. An example is the power consumption which is measured at different parts of the machine.

Overall eight measurements are logged along with their bounds. In addition six bytes with Boolean values are recorded. Each bit in these values corresponds to a Boolean measurement of checkpoints. These bits may be aggregates of several measurements that indicate success or failure of a check. In addition to these values each data record keeps the machine identifier, a timestamp, and a running counter value as identifier. Overall these data fields add up to about 300 bytes. Within a year each machine stores about 250,000 records, creating log files of approx. 72 MB.

Further data records are created at the process step quality check. At this step the machine fills the coolers with gas under a certain pressure to check for leaks and conducts mechanical checks. Again, upper and lower bounds are defined for certain sensor values and are logged along with the measured data. The most important attributes from the quality check are depicted in Table 4.1. This table includes attributes that were defined for improving the acquisition of production data.

In the back-end layer COO hosts the MS Access database on a central server for maintaining the production data. This MS Access database was developed in house for one plant and was subsequently introduced at other production sites. The IT department uses this data source for generating regular reports on performance data. Shift foremen revise monthly performance statistics about production lines under their responsibility. The IT department also generates reports of key performance parameters for the whole plant. The management receives this information via Microsoft Power

Table 4.1: Attributes for quality checks

Number	Description
1	Equipment data
2	Employee identity
3	Article code of the product
4	Maximal admissible gas concentration
5	Minimal admissible gas concentration
6	Measured gas concentration
7	Maximal admissible measuring pressure
8	Minimal admissible measuring pressure
9	Measured measuring pressure
10	Configured maximal testing time
11	Actual testing time
12	Minimal admissible pressure after testing time
13	Measured pressure after testing time
14	Mechanical check at checkpoint 1
15	Mechanical check at checkpoint 2
16	Mechanical check at checkpoint 3
17	Mechanical check at checkpoint 4
18	Mechanical check at checkpoint 5

Point slides that summarize the overall and relative performance. For plants which do not use the MS Access database the key performance parameters are communicated via email and added to the presentations for the management.

Summarizing Case COO

COO does not employ a dedicated system for production data acquisition. Instead, numerous isolated solutions are installed at different plants. The low degree of vertical integration accounts for significant manual intervention in the data acquisition and poses the risk of data errors. Furthermore, the current solution limits the room for in-depth data analysis. Due to this COO has started to analyze the option of using a dedicated software solution for production data acquisition. The reasons are improvements in the data accuracy, data availability and enhanced options for in-depth data analysis.

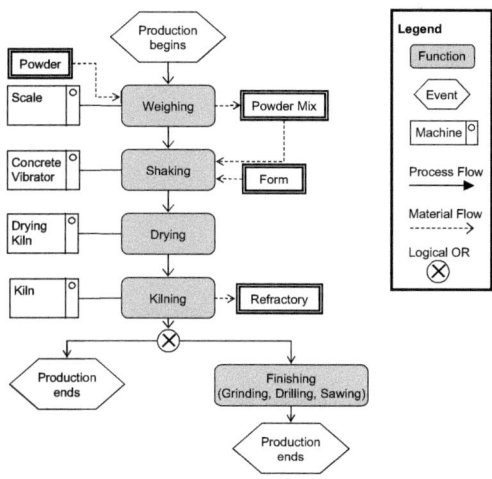

Figure 4.10: Production process for refractories.

In addition, having one consistent solution for production data acquisition and evaluation in place would bring positive scale effects.

4.2.3 Production of Refractories

REF is a globally operating company producing refractories for diverse industrial sectors. Customer orders require between 8 weeks and approx. 8 months. Each order is subdivided into several detailed planning units. They span between one day and approx. 15 weeks. Each unit specifies the production of a given amount of refractories. Each refractory unit has an accompanying ticket with the following data: order number, amount to be produced, sort, customer order, delivery date, net weight, and kilning / drying °C. We describe the production of a refractory in detail. Figure 4.10 depicts an abstracted exemplary process model for producing a certain refractory. The process comprises five steps: weighing, shaking, drying, kilning and finishing.

REF produces refractories either via compression or via casting. The mode depends on the amount of produced refractories; REF uses casting only for orders under 300 pieces. Each refractory is made out of a specific mix of cementitious materials. The mix is always approved with the customer and should therefore be exactly as specified in the recipe. Consequently each production starts with weighing the used cementitious substitutes for the powder mix.

In the second step workers mix the powder with water and pour it into forms. This is done manually if it is an order under 300 pieces. Subsequently a concrete vibrator shakes the forms, so that excess air can get out. In the third step the mixed compound dries. REF uses special drying kilns for the drying process. The temperature in the drying kilns depends on the selected program; the maximal temperature is 200°C. Which program the workers select depends on the thickness of the material. The foreman in charge advises each worker orally about which program is to select.

After the material is dry, workers move it out of the drying kiln, check it for cracks, and move it to the entrepot for the kiln. REF has three kilns which run 24/7/365. The temperature is up to 1800°C. These kilns are the production's bottleneck. Workers load all kiln cars with as much material as possible. How much fits on a car strongly depends on the form and thickness of each dry form.

After the kilning step some refractories undergo a finishing process. Here workers may grind, drill or saw excess material of the refractory. Approx. 3500 different refractory types undergo this last processing step. Finished refractories may then be put to stock or directly shipped to the customer. This depends on the type of the refractory.

REF produces frequently ordered refractories for stock when the production has the capacity to handle this. Additionally REF can have produced more refractories than was ordered. This is because during each process step the material undergoes a quality check and cracked material is sorted out. REF calculates with these losses. 3% of the production cracks on average. However, sometimes less material gets sorted out than was calculated. These then go to stock as well. At the beginning of each day the foreman reports the production progress of the previous day. The report includes a complete

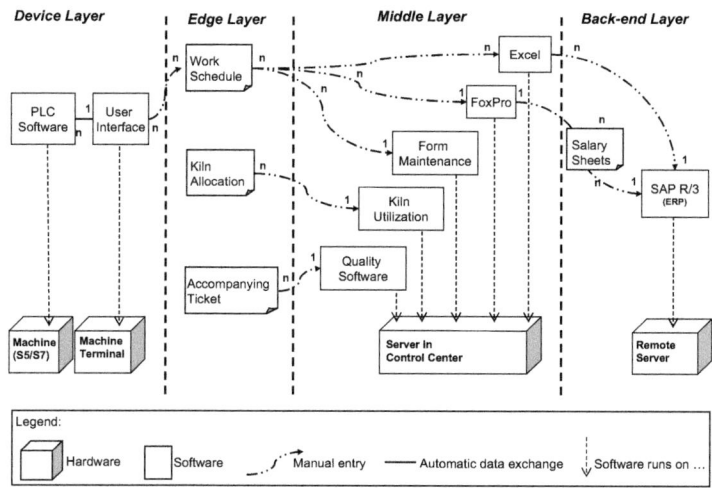

Figure 4.11: Deployment diagram of the software and hardware at REF.

list of all materials and about the production step which there are in, *e.g.*, drying. The report also has a notification about the broken materials.

IT Infrastructure

We identified eight software solutions (or classes of solutions) at REF that are relevant for production activities and the related data management. These are an ERP system (SAP R/3), Excel for the detailed planning, a salary control system (FoxPro), a form maintenance and kiln utilization system, a quality check system, user interfaces on machine terminals, and programmable logic controller (PLC) software for machine control. Figure 4.11 depicts how these systems are associated with the four logical layers. For each layer we discuss the corresponding functionality and data exchange.

The back-end layer consists of the ERP system SAP R/3. REF has used an SAP system since 2004. The company hosts the SAP system remotely in a different town in Germany. They use the SAP system for salary, order, purchase, and production plant management. When a new order comes in, the system automatically creates a production plan including new material requests. The staff takes these data and generates a monthly diagram of the ordered and used material in Excel in the middle layer.

The SAP system is not updated with intermediate reports on the production process. Thus, it is not possible to notice delays in the production via the SAP system. Therefore, the inventory has regularly discrepancies of approx. 5% between targeted and actually produced products; *i.e.*, due to deficient products.

The middle layer comprises all systems that have a central task for the plant. These are Excel, FoxPro, the form maintenance and kiln utilization system, and the quality check system. The IT staff constructs the detailed production plan in Excel based on the plan from the SAP system. The reason for conducting the fine-granular plan outside the SAP system is that it is not possible to generate a volume flow of the materials with their current SAP modules. In the fine planning the staff subsumes orders from diverse customers to one production unit if the orders contain identical refractories. They create the fine-granular plans once a month, generating four weekly plans in advance. These plans are printed out and given to the foremen as the work schedule.

FoxPro is used for calculating the exact salary for the workers, which has a variable factor depending on the overall productivity. The IT staff only insert working hours into the FoxPro system. The FoxPro data is manually entered into the SAP system at the end of each month.

The middle layer also comprises a software tool for the management of used refractory forms. Herewith, REF records the wear out of its forms that they use with the compression machines. As described in the previous section after each production step there can be a quality check. Especially the check at the end of the production includes an optical, chemical and a size accuracy check. These checks are recorded in a specific quality software package.

Last but not least, the middle layer also includes software, where the kiln utilization is recorded. They use this software for controlling which refractories are in the kiln. From this they can calculate when the refractories will be ready for delivery.

In the edge layer all production data is recorded on paper documents. Workers write all collected production data into the work schedule, or the accompanying ticket. The foremen and workers fill them out while producing the products and return them after completion. They include the exact amount of produced products and the time the workers spent on the production. Foremen create summaries on extra work sheets for reporting data back to the planning system. This information from the paper documents is manually written into the software components from the middle layer. However, workers do not conduct this task by themselves. It is a task of the IT staff.

The device layer comprises only the user interface of the machine terminals and the PLCs of machines and robots on the plant floor. Workers select specific configurations from the user interfaces. For instance, the drying kilns have 20 diverse drying programs; which one to choose is communicated via the paper work schedule in the edge layer.

Summarizing Case REF

REF does not employ a dedicated system for production data collection. Instead, data is recoded manually on paper. Integration with the ERP system is realized manually. All production operations are managed in the SAP system and self-created Excel tools. REF uses paper documents for communicating production tasks to the plant floor and for recording production data.

4.2.4 Production of Engines

ENG assembles, checks, and varnishes engines. Located on the plant floor are several production units for different production tasks. A unit for one task may have several production stations that can be physically distributed across the shop floor. For example, ENG has three stations for post assembly. These stations are identical in terms of the tasks that they can conduct and are subdivided into several production cells.

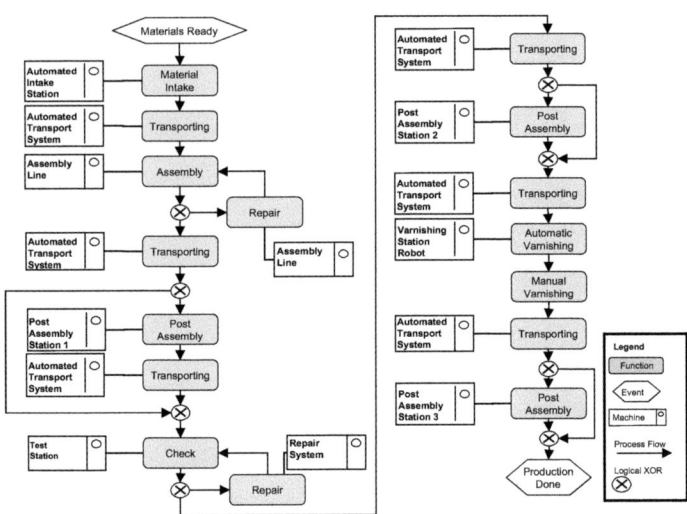

Figure 4.12: Production process for engines.

Figure 4.12 depicts an abstracted exemplary process model for producing a certain engine type. The process starts with the material intake which is conducted by a completely automated transport system. Robots autonomously unload and load incoming trucks and transport the material to its destination in the shop floor. Therefore, the incoming trucks are all labeled with HF RFID tags. The gates at the material intake read the content of the truck with an RFID reader and trigger an unloading conveyor if a truck with the correct load is present. The load is then piled up and an automated transport system (ATS) with driverless forklifts moves the materials to their destination on the plant floor. This central transport system also controls all further transportation of materials throughout the production. It calculates a globally efficient transportation using all forklifts in the shop floor.

After the material has been transported to the right assembly line, the assembly of an engine starts. An engine can consist of up to about 550 production steps including approx. 400 different parts. The assembly begins with mounting parts to the crankcase in one of the two assembly lines. Each assembly line includes about 80 sequential assembly steps. At these steps workers and robots mount different engine parts to the crankcase. The used materials and machine settings for these tasks can vary from engine to engine. Yet, the variability in the assembly lines is relatively low compared to later post-assembly steps (the line can construct several different variants of an engine).

Workers and machines control the assembly process as the engines move through the line. Workers detect visible aberrations and control their own operations on the engine. Additionally, machines check their sensor information against reference parameters for their respective production task.

At the test station workers conduct a comprehensive check of the engines. Each engine requires different tests and has different setpoint values associated with it. Predefined values determine if an engine can proceed to the subsequent production step painting or requires repair. Legal regulations or customer requirements determine some of the setpoint values. It is mandatory to meet these values in the tests.

When the engines successfully pass the tests, the automated transport system moves them into a painting facility. Some engines require an additional post assembly at post assembly station 2 before painting. The painting facility comprises two painting steps: In the first step a robot paints the engines. In the second step a worker checks the varnished engine and manually adds paint where necessary. Depending on the engine's shape the robot must use different control programs. A standard program exists which they use if no other program is available. However, the standard program generally yields suboptimal results. This increases the workload in the second painting step and reduces the throughput of the painting facility. To avoid this, it is possible to adjust the robots' CNC programs and associate them with specific engine types.

A final post assembly step at assembly station 3 follows the painting. Like the other post assembly step the assembly at assembly station 3 is optional and conducted dependent on the engine type. The production of engines is accomplished after painting or the optional last assembly step.

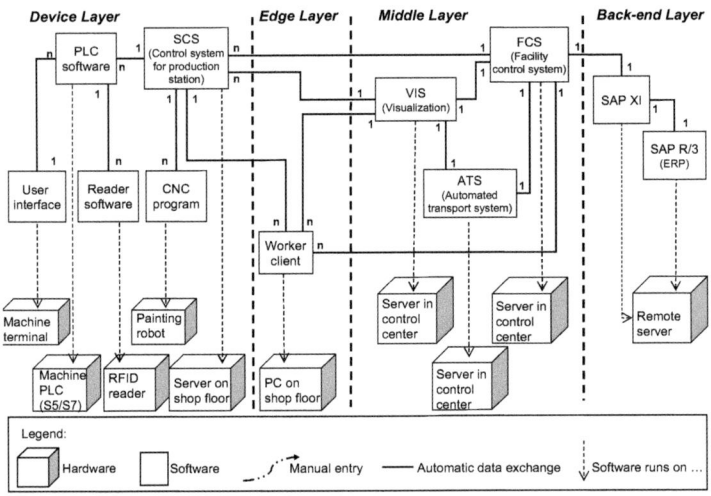

Figure 4.13: Deployment diagram of the software and hardware at ENG.

IT Infrastructure

We identified nine software solutions (or classes of solutions) at ENG that are relevant for production activities and the related data management. These are an ERP system (SAP R/3), an integration software (SAP XI), a facility control system (FCS), a visualization system (VIS), a control system for automated transports (ATS), worker clients for plant-floor workers, station control systems for production facilities (SCS), programmable logic controller (PLC) software for machine control, and CNC programs for robot control. Table 4.2 lists all of these systems with their abbreviations. Figure 4.13 shows the deployment of these systems at ENG along with logical communication links.

Figure 4.14 shows the physical network that realizes the described communication links. The investigated plant has a 10/100 MBit Ethernet connection. Via this connection the FCS interacts with the ERP and an external application at a logistic partner of ENG. In the local area network ENG uses

Table 4.2: Software solutions at ENG

System Component	Description
ERP -> SAP R/3	Enterprise resource planning
SAP XI	Integration software
FCS	Facility control system – similar to an MES
VIS	Visualization system
ATS	Automated transport system
PLC and CNC	Programmable logic and numeric controller
SCS	Station control system for production facilities
Worker Client	SCS client with interface for workers

a 10/100 MBit Ethernet connection which interlinks PCs, servers, and PLCs in the plant. Overall this local network has about 500 network nodes of which approx. 70 are PLCs. All machines are controlled either by an S5 or S7 PLC.

An exception is the control of driverless forklifts by the automated transport system. Here, the communication between the SCS and the forklifts is realized by an infrared network. Further important system components that are not directly accessible via Ethernet are RFID readers and tags. The RFID solutions are part of autonomous subsystems which provide PLC interfaces that abstract from the RFID-specific functionality. Together, these listed devices and networks build the physical infrastructure of ENG's IT. Each part of the system plays a different role in one of the three system layers. In the following we describe the functionality in each system layer and the information flow between layers in more detail.

The device layer comprises PLCs, CNC programs, user interfaces to the machines, and SCSs. Servers on the plant floor run SCSs for controlling operations at different production facilities. A facility can include several production stations with different devices (*e.g.,* several stations at an assembly line). SCSs communicate with PLCs of the respective stations, CNC programs and worker clients in the edge layer. They receive measured data from the PLCs and manual entries from worker clients.

Via the SCSs the PLCs exchange data with the VIS and the FCS in the middle layer. That is, an SCS serves as a gateway to the middle layer.

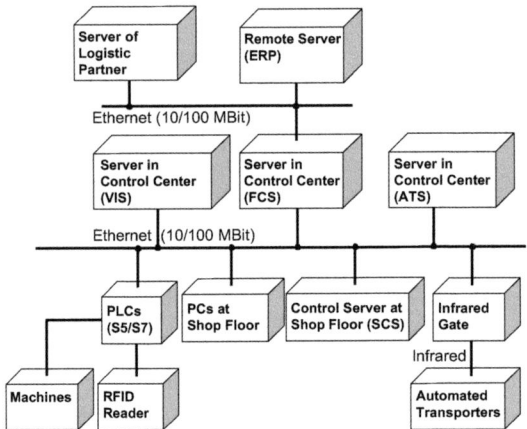

Figure 4.14: Communication infrastructure at ENG.

The data exchange includes status reports on the production, alerts, and engine-specific documentation of the conducted tasks. These are measurements related to the production of a certain engine. This information is communicated to the FCS along with engine-specific status reports. Overall ENG records values from about 60 measurement points per engine. Status reports and log data are forwarded to the FCS for documenting. However, the VIS receives alerts and status reports for immediate visualization of the plant's operational status.

The painting robots download CNC programs for painting different engines from the respective SCS. Other machines have fixed programs but receive configuration parameters along with the routing data for a task. For example, testing stations get parameters that determine what to measure during the tests and what value ranges are expected. Thus, no manual configuration of machines is required.

Furthermore, ENG caches the data for the upcoming productions tasks beforehand in the SCS. That is, the FCS loads all necessary information to the SCS. It does this one hour in advance. Thereby ENG is able to seamlessly continue the production in cases of temporary downtimes of the middle layer. The two assembly lines are special cases. Here, ENG also uses RFID technology to store routing data directly at the material carriers.

This RFID application serves two purposes: One is to support the autarky of the assembly lines from the SCS. The other purpose is to ease the linkage of carriers with the corresponding engine and routing information. PLCs at each assembly step read the routing information and write logging data to the RFID tags. At the last step on the assembly lines all data from the tags are read and forwarded to the SCS of the assembly line.

The logic in the PLC programs controls the operations of the machine as well as the reporting of sensor data and status events. ENG solely uses Siemens S5 and S7 for machine control. Other sensors monitor the operations of the machines. Based on these sensors the PLCs generate alerts and status information which they submit via an SCS to VIS for visualization. However, the sensor data can also directly impact the production process. For example, the assembly lines can route engines to repair steps if the sensors indicate errors in an assembly step. Overall ENG has specified about 15,000 event types that the PLCs can use for reporting about machine states. The control center processes about 100,000 status messages a day.

The edge layer comprises PCs which host client software for directing workers on the plant floor. These clients typically receive the assembly specifications from the SCS. These clients do not exchange data with the PLCs on the machines. Yet, in a few cases there is no SCS at a station. Then the worker client exchanges messages directly with the FCS. In such cases, worker clients also directly notify the VIS about status changes.

The role of worker clients is to support the shop-floor workers during their tasks. Each post-assembly cell has a PC with installed worker clients. The hosted client is a software solution that was designed and implemented according to ENG's specifications. Workers use the client for displaying information about their upcoming assembly tasks. This includes data items such as illustrative pictures and texts. For the next ten scheduled production tasks the clients proactively request and cache the associated texts and pictures. Cached data remain at the client until the FCS notifies the PCs about a new version of the data. The PCs on the shop floor display production information, and serve as input devices for manual data entries. Here, workers can report finished production tasks. Furthermore, workers can detect and report errors.

The middle layer includes soft- and hardware that is not located on the plant floor but within the plant's facilities. These are the FCS, the VIS, the ATS and hosting servers for these systems. The production control system FCS organizes the production tasks and manages the corresponding information exchange. The FCS runs on a server in the plant's control center. The system VIS and ATS run in the same control center but on different servers.

Production tasks coming from the ERP system describe production steps and production units where these steps can be conducted. Yet, several work places within a station may be a candidate for a certain production step on the plant floor. The FCS forwards the production task to the appropriate SCS. The SCS then autonomously decides at which work place the task will be conducted. When the SCS receives a task it sends a request for material to the FCS. The FCS is in charge of ordering the required materials for the upcoming production tasks in advance. The FCS sends orders to an external logistic service provider directly via an Ethernet connection to a server of the logistic service provider. The FCS then receives status reports about the delivery via the same connection.

The central transport system at ENG identifies arriving shipments and notifies the FCS. The FCS triggers the coordination of the material transport to the production stations. Therefore, the FCS issues transportation tasks to the ATS. The ATS in turn coordinates the autonomous forklifts on the plant floor and reports conducted transports back to the FCS. That is, additionally to coordinating the ordering of material at the logistic service provider, the FCS similarly triggers the internal transport of the engines between the production stations.

Besides planning and control, the middle layer also includes functionalities for monitoring and visualizing the operations on the plant floor. The software that implements this functionality is the VIS. It is hosted in the control center of the plant where the responsible employees have permanent access to visualization terminals. The visualization interface is designed according to specifications of ENG. Via this interface the employees get a live view of the plant and the operational status of each facility. This includes display of operational machine statuses in the color code of traffic lights.

The employees can also see detailed machine-specific reports if needed. That is, they can display charts on how certain performance indicators have developed over time. Overall, the VIS is a sink for alerts and performance measures which help to spot problems in the operation. Employees in the control center detect curtail aberrations. Via an internal phone system they can directly contact workers on the plant floor and advise them to take care of the detected problems.

The back-end layer comprises soft- and hardware that is located outside the plant. In the ENG's case this is the ERP system SAP R/3 and the integration software SAP XI which are on a remote server. SAP XI facilitates the interaction between the back-end and the middle layer (the FCS in the plant).

ENG employs a wide range of SAP modules. Within the ERP, ENG keeps different assembly specification for producing each engine type. These specifications include information about the engine parts, associated production and testing steps, machine parameters, machine programs, as well as illustrative texts and pictures. Note that binary data such as pictures and machine programs are not always directly stored in the ERP. Instead some assembly specifications hold pointers to files in the FCS. This has historical reasons: it was not possible to store binary data in ENG's former ERP version.

All data for the assembly specification is organized in a tree-like data structure. The job descriptions can be derived from this tree structure. In addition ENG extended the SAP system table to reflect relations between elements in the specifications. These relations encode knowledge on how elements of the specification can be combined in a job description and which combinations are feasible.

The ERP system uses two interfaces for the communication with the FCS: one is order related and the other not. Through the first interface the ERP sends all orders to the FCS. The second interface is used for transmitting PLC parameters and texts and pictures for the worker clients. The FCS stores these data. The SCS or worker client pulls these data from the FCS if they are required for an order.

The information management for a production task starts in the backend. Orders from the sales and distribution module trigger the process of planning in the ERP system. At this point quantity, type, delivery dates and technical specifications for the order are already defined. In the subsequent step the information from the assembly specifications is resolved to create an assembly task. This task defines which production steps must be conducted with which materials and when the task has to be completed. To estimate the total production time of a task, the time of each sub-step is added up. Based on this a task plan with the granularity of days is created.

The ERP system then forwards the created task plan to the FCS. The FCS forwards the assembly plan to the right SCS in the plant and sends permanent status reports about the production's progress to the ERP. One exception is the test station. Here the FCS reports only about the completion of an order. Generally when the ERP system receives the message "order is accomplished" it calculates the used material for this order. The information is then used for calculating the processing time, which is needed for planning and inventory updates. As a side effect this information may also be used by the sales department to check the status of orders. This data is communicated via SAP XI to the ERP system. ENG uses for this a self-designed data structure that is wrapped in iDOCs.

ENG uses the reported data for planning and inventory updates. Additionally, they also archive the data in the ERP. For this purpose ENG especially extended the SAP system with additional tables. This serves as their historian for archiving engine-specific production data. In the history tables ENG stores all measurements of machine sensors that are associated with a specific engine and the corresponding assembly specification. With the assembly specification they also store the texts for the worker clients in their history. However, ENG does not directly store the used pictures for the worker clients in the history. Here they use pointers to the directories in the

FCS.

Summarizing Case ENG

The IT infrastructure was built from scratch along with the production hall. Major components like the FCS and worker clients were developed under the guidance and with the involvement of ENG's IT staff. The IT infrastructure is therefore very well tailored to ENG's needs, both in terms of functionality and architecture.

From the functional point of view ENG has implemented most functionalities of a manufacturing execution system. This includes, for instance, visualization and archiving of production data as well as dedicated modules for fine-grained production planning. The solution yields some remarkable particularities. One notable aspect is that not all functionalities are embedded in the same system. In particular visualization and control are completely decoupled. Thus, workers in the control center use different systems for detecting and reacting to aberrations in the production.

Another particularity of the IT at ENG is the solution for storing history data. This is a self-designed extension of the SAP system. Engine-specific reports from the plant floor are stored in supplementary added tables. An advantage of this solution is the integration in one system. Future improvements could address the coupling with the FCS and the integrity of history information. The coupling with the FCS is currently realized via a tunnel through SAP XI.

Of further note is the high degree of automation in the plant floor. ENG realized a completely paperless data management on the plant floor and also avoids manual configuration of machines. In addition, ENG uses an automated transport system for material movements on the plant floor. Together with the direct coupling of machines to the back-end this allows ENG to get an accurate and detailed view on the production in real time.

From the architectural point of view two aspects of ENG's infrastructure are remarkable: One is the pronounced decentralization of data and logic and the other is the consequent implementation of event-driven communication. Decentralization and autarky of system components was a design requirement that ENG emphasized during the planning of the plant. This is reflected in the distribution of routing data and processing logic close to the corresponding operations. Due to proactive caching ENG is able to continue the production in cases of back-end downtimes for up to four hours. In addition, caching at the point of operation enables ENG to realize fast response times of the systems easily.

The event-driven communication of production data further improves the reactivity of the system and increases the scalability. By employing this communication scheme, ENG is able to reduce load on the local network and completely avoids bottlenecks in the managing of the 180 production stations.

4.2.5 Production of Chemicals

CHE is a globally operating company producing various chemicals. We categorize the production into batch production. In total CHE produces around 5000 products. CHE produces in a 7/24 time frame and has a delivery reliability of 99%. The company gets orders typically 1–2 months in advance. However, JIT orders can come in at very short notice; starting production two days later. Nevertheless a lead time of one week is the usual practice.

Generally the production of chemicals consists of the following steps: dosing of diverse chemicals, heating up the chemical mix, letting it react, performing quality checks, optional distilling, cooling down and finally pumping the chemical mix into tanks and shipping it to the customer. Figure 4.15 depicts an abstracted exemplary process model for producing a certain chemical mix in one production facility.

Before the production starts, a worker constructs the fine-granular production planning from the orders deposited in the ERP system. This happens one day in advance. Along with planning, the worker checks whether all needed chemical components are available in the required amounts. For some components this check is conducted automatically. In cases components are on hand but not in the correct amounts, CHE tries to vary the

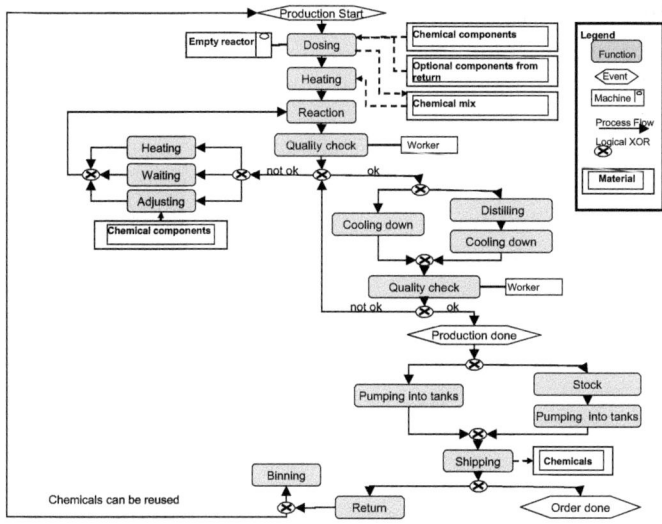

Figure 4.15: Production process for chemicals.

scheduled quantities in the recipe. Each batch contains between 2 and 10 different components. Additionally CHE checks whether all delivered chemical components satisfy the required quality standards. CHE refuses delivered components which do not meet the quality tests. The production gets the needed clearance only when all components are available, their quality checks have been successfully passed, and the specific amounts declared in the recipe can be applied.

After clearance, all components are put into the reactor and heated up to the point of reaction. The chemical mix reacts for a defined amount of time. Then workers take a first sample for the quality check and send it to the laboratory. If the check is passed, the chemical mix may optionally be distilled and then cooled down. If the quality check fails, several steps are possible depending on the specific chemical mix. Either the mixture is left to react for a longer time, or it is heated up to support more reactions or it is adjusted with some more chemical components. The laboratory tells the workers which one of these steps they have to conduct.

For each product the laboratory defines an exact number of samples to be taken during production. They store this information in the recipe. The chemical mix is only allowed to the next production step if the demanded quality checks are satisfactory. The product has to be adjusted as long as the mix does not pass the tests. The exact time when the samples have to be taken is also stored in the recipe. In summary, the workers take at least three samples during production. In the unlikely case that the product needs to undergo several quality tests – and be adjusted with a large amount of more components – the laboratory changes the currently used recipe.

A last quality check is taken after cooling the product down. Then the mix is either directly pumped into tanks for shipment or stays on hold. Generally CHE aims to produce its products as late as possible. By this they try to have resources – tanks and reactors – available as long as possible for other orders.

The shipped products may get returned by the customers if they are not satisfied with the quality. In such cases the returned chemicals may get reused in production. Sometimes they can be further adjusted to meet the customer's requirements or they may get used as components for other products. If none of this is possible, they are binned.

IT Infrastructure

CHE has numerous production plants in several countries. Each plant has its own specific IT processes for production. For instance, several plants use different software solutions for managing and controlling their production. Examples of installed MES solutions are Siemens' Simatic IT, Werum's PAS-X, and Wonderware ArchestrA. Nevertheless, one company-wide service organization manages all these diverse IT processes. On top of these systems, CHE uses one ERP system (SAP) for the company-wide management of its operations.

We now describe one specific production plant. Figure 4.16 shows the deployment diagram with the components of the plant's IT system. In total

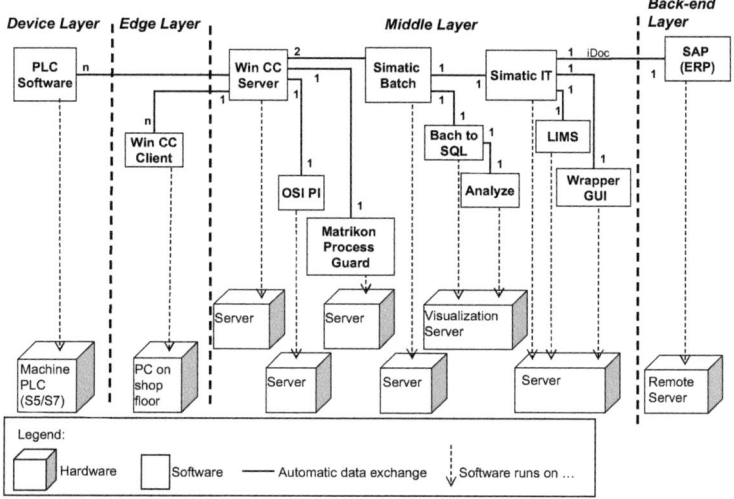

Figure 4.16: Deployment diagram of the software and hardware at CHE.

we identify twelve major software components. These are the SAP ERP, Simatic IT, Simatic Batch, a LIMS, a Wrapper GUI, Batch to SQL, Analyze, OSI PI, Matrikon Process Guard, WinCC Server, WinCC Client, and PLC Software. Table 4.3 gives an overview of these components with a brief description. We drill now down to each system layer.

The device layer at CHE controls hardware such as boilers, tanks, and pipes that are used in the production. The PLCs steer actuators like agitators or valves and capture sensor data like temperature or pressure values from the machines. The PLCs receive control information from the edge layer and pass back event data about sensor measures. Overall, the shop floor of the sample plant has about 2500 actuators and 2500 measuring points. The PLCs are also responsible for running control logic, particularly for safety-relevant checks. (Implementing safety-relevant logic is required by law). About 80% of the used PLCs are either S5 or S7. For communication with higher system layers they mainly use OPC via Microsoft's Component Object Model

Table 4.3: Attributes for quality checks

System Component	Description
SAP ERP	The ERP system at CHE.
Simatic IT	Siemens system for production management.
Simatic Batch	Siemens system for automating and controlling batch processes.
LIMS	Laboratory information management system.
Wrapper GUI	Self-implemented solution for integrating several functionalities of Simatic IT in one user interface.
Batch to SQL	Self-implemented solution for transferring data from Simatic Batch into a relational database.
Analyze	Self-implemented tool for OSIsoft solution for analyzing measured values from machine sensors.
Matrikon Process Guard	Matrikon solution for managing alarms and event messages.
WinCC Server (belongs to PCS7)	Server component of a Siemens solution for process visualization and control.
WinCC Client (belongs to PCS7)	Client component of a Siemens solution for process visualization and control.
PLC Software (belongs to PCS7)	Software for PLCs on machines.

(COM). Specifically OPC Command and OPC A/E are in use. OPC UA is not applied. For time-critical operations CHE uses OPC with UDP and not TCP.

The edge layer at CHE comprises only WinCC clients. A number of WinCC clients is connected to one WinCC server. Workers use these clients for starting/stopping production tasks and for monitoring operations. The clients also integrate interfaces of the Simatic Batch system in the middle layer. The WinCC clients provide user interfaces for monitoring and controlling operations on the plant floor. They receive event data and sensor measurements from the WinCC servers. With this information the clients generate a real-time visualization of the current operations in the plant. Therefore, CHE uses a self-designed interface that graphically represents the plant.

Besides observing production processes, workers use WinCC clients for controlling plant-floor operations. Thus, the clients also embed functionalities from the Simatic Batch in the middle layer.

The middle layer at the investigated plant includes the most system components. Core components are the WinCC server, installations of Simatic IT, and Simatic Batch. Several additional components exist for accessing data in these systems. These are OSI PI, Matrikon Process Guard, a LIMS, and self-implemented components which we refer to as *Batch to SQL*, *Analyze*, and *Wrapper GUI*. From these systems Simatic Batch, OSI PI, and the Matrikon Process Guard directly interact with the WinCC servers.

Two separate WinCC servers run independently in the investigated plant. This is to keep the workload for each server at a moderate level. Due to the central role of the WinCC servers their availability is crucial for the operations at CHE. To ensure reliability, both WinCC servers run redundantly on two separate machines. That is, one machine acts as a master and the other as a slave. The master conducts the actual operations while the slave is only internally replaying the operations. This way both systems keep the same state and the slave can seamlessly take over if the master fails.

The WinCC servers act as hubs for the communication with devices on the device layer, the WinCC clients, and other system components. They receive commands from the Simatic Batch system as well as from the WinCC clients and dispatch them to the respective PLCs. From the PLCs they capture event messages and sensor data. These data are stored in a ring buffer for two weeks and passed on to WinCC clients, OSI PI, the Matrikon Process Guard and Simatic Batch.

OSI PI is used for long-term storage and analysis of measurement data from machine sensors. The WinCC servers in the edge layer store the complete sensor data. Yet, they only keep this data for two weeks. OSI PI retrieves an extract of this data and keeps it permanently. It also provides an interface to Microsoft Excel that is used for data analysis. The system directly communicates with the WinCC servers.

Matrikon Process Guard is used for storing and managing alarms and event messages from the shop floor. It persistently keeps an extract of the event data coming from the plant floor. Furthermore, the Matrikon Process Guard is used for monitoring and controlling error messages. Here, workers can view, edit, and discard error messages before they are passed on to other systems. The system directly communicates with the WinCC servers.

The Simatic Batch system is the central component for controlling the production. That is, it receives the recipes for scheduled production processes from the ERP and controls the execution of the production steps accordingly. From the Simatic Batch system the production steps are scheduled and executed. This system exchanges data with the two WinCC servers. Its interface is also integrated in WinCC and can be controlled via WinCC clients from the edge layer.

The Simatic Batch system interacts with machines on the plant floor via WinCC servers. It passes down commands for executing production steps and receives status reports. Via the WinCC servers it is also integrated in the interface of the WinCC clients. Users of WinCC clients can thereby directly use the functionalities of Simatic Batch.

High reliability of the Simatic Batch system is crucial due to its central role in controlling the shop-floor operations. Consequently it runs redundantly on two independent servers. Similar to the solution for the WinCC servers, Simatic batch servers run in a master and a slave mode. The slave replays the actions of the master and can seamlessly replace the master in the case of a system failure. Systems which interact with Simatic Batch are the self-implemented Analyze tool, and Simatic IT.

The Analyze tool was implemented to graphically evaluate data from Simatic Batch. For this evaluation, data on production tasks (*e.g.*, product-specific production times) are transferred to a relational database. The self-implemented analysis tool provides workers with reports and statistics about the production. Therefore, data from Simatic Batch are extracted to a database via the self-implemented conversion component Batch to SQL.

Communication with further system components is realized via Simatic IT. Simatic IT is used to configure production tasks and recipes. It also facilitates data exchange with the LIMS and ERP system (via iDoc). Simatic IT also provides a user interface for its configuration. However, the actual access is done via the self-implemented Wrapper GUI that provides several functionalities of Simatic IT via a single interface. CHE uses the self-implemented tool Batch to SQL for realizing this transfer. The Analyze tool creates reports on the information in the database, which help workers to evaluate conducted production tasks.

Simatic IT is a system for integrating different software solutions in a manufacturing environment. That is, it enables the description of manufacturing processes and coordinates the functions of involved system components. It serves as the central hub between the Simatic Batch, the LIMS and the ERP system. The system provides graphical interfaces for configuration. However, the IT staff implemented a Wrapper GUI to combine a set of Simatic IT functionalities. Simatic IT, the LIMS and the Wrapper GUI all run on the same server.

The back-end layer only includes the ERP system SAP. The communication with the ERP system varies among different MES. Integration with SAP can be done via BAPI calls, IDoc, or via xMII. Hence, the exchange format and the exchanged data can vary between the MES installations. This is because CHE has no abstraction layer or unified intermediate component for data conversion in place.

The IT processes in the ERP and in the MESs are very loosely coupled. By this the production plants can operate independently from the ERP system. The diverse MESs buffer all messages for the ERP and verify the successful transmission. This is required since availability of the ERP system cannot be guaranteed: the SAP system is regularly shut down for maintenance every week. Thus, the MES must run autonomously to a large extent. Consequently all production-relevant operations run locally in the MES and physically at the plants. The maintenance of each MES is also commonly done locally at the plants. In some cases, VPN connections enable remote access for administrators. Yet, this is not realized for every system. This is because some plants have security concerns to connect their MES via VPN to the internet.

Furthermore, we interviewed the IT staff regarding requirements for the IT infrastructure. The identified requirements are reliability, performance, autarky, open interfaces, and security.

Reliability is crucial for the systems involved in data capturing and production control. The high degree of automation renders this requirement particularly relevant. CHE ensures reliability by running key components redundantly on different servers. That is, identical components run on two different servers.

High system performance is especially relevant for components that are directly involved in the control of production tasks. Steering machines in the plants includes time-critical tasks. CHE implements three main measures to ensure fast response times and scalability of the system. The first measure is to run a great proportion of processing tasks on PLCs. This is even pursued by law, because PLCs are considered as reliable system components. The second measure is to decentralize processing by using multiple servers for certain operations. As the third measure, CHE uses connectionless communication via UDP instead of connection-oriented communication via TCP for time-critical tasks.

Autarky of the systems for production control is required in terms of independence from the ERP back-end. The SAP system has an availability of no more than 99.5 %. The 0.5% downtime is mainly due to maintenance tasks. To ensure seamless operations, CHE only loosely couples the IT processes of the plant floor with the ERP system. That is, the IT systems in the plants store production tasks in advance, run them independent from the ERP, and buffer reporting messages to the ERP until delivery is verified.

Open interfaces are seen as important by the IT staff. This is because they tailor the system to the needs of each production. For instance, they integrate different system components into one graphical user interface or program reporting tools for production data analysis. It is therefore important that proprietary system components are accessible for self-implemented extensions. Consequently, it is perceived as an important advantage if a software solution provides open APIs.

Security of operational systems is important. However, the probability of attacks on the IT system of production plants is perceived as low. This is because the system is operated as a closed system. External connections

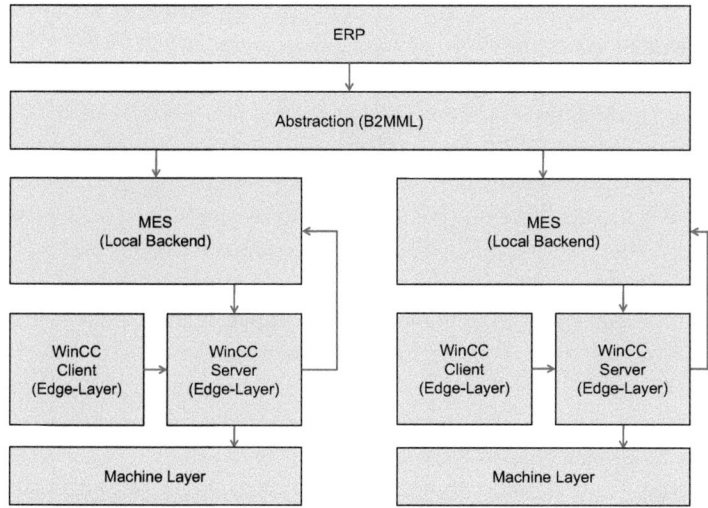

Figure 4.17: The layers pattern at CHE.

are very limited and secured via VPN. Security is therefore not perceived as a primary concern of systems for production data acquisition.

Regarding the interaction of software components, we have identified one predominant architectural pattern: The layers pattern (including indirection layers) is prevalent in the IT Infrastructure of CHE, see Figure 4.17. Yet, the pattern is not strictly applied throughout the whole system. The layers pattern is useful in systems where high-level components depend on low-level components for performing a task. Vertical decoupling in functionalities in layers helps to ensure reusability, modifiability, and portability. To achieve this, each layer provides a set of functionalities via a clear interface to the next upper layer.

Lower-level functionality is only accessed via the interfaces of the adjacent higher layer. Top-down the access hierarchy reads: ERP, Simatic IT, Simatic Batch, WinCC Server, and finally PLCs. This clean-layered structure makes high-level system components independent from lower levels and eases the exchange of system parts. However, the pattern is not strictly applied throughout the whole infrastructure.

The first exception from the strict application of layers is the integration of functionalities from the Simatic Batch System into WinCC clients. That means that higher-level functionality is accessed from a lower layer. At this point, the layers become tightly coupled which reduces reusability, modifiability and portability of the solution. For instance, replacing the lower-level system (WinCC) with an alternative solution impacts how the higher-level system (Simatic Batch) is accessed.

The second exception from the strict application of layers is the coupling of the various MESs with the ERP. At this point, we see a clear logical separation of the layers but no clear interface between them. Here, an indirection layer or intermediate representation would improve the independence of the layers and support reusability, modifiability, as well as portability. The XML-based Business To Manufacturing Markup Language (B2MML) is a good candidate for a common intermediate data representation. The language is part of the ISA-S95 standards and is designed for the data exchange between ERP systems and MES. CHE is currently evaluating the use of B2MML to achieve the abstraction properties of the layers pattern.

Summarizing Case CHE

The IT infrastructure is very well tailored to CHE's needs, both in terms of functionality and architecture. The infrastructure of CHE is an example of architectures with centralized control. That is, a small number of powerful computers are used for production data management. This is in contrast to architectures with distributed control systems on the plant floor.

Centralized control fits well to the high degree of automation and complex interdependent processes at CHE. Process control at CHE requires an integrated view over large parts of the plant within one system. Such architectures can pose challenges for reliability and performance. CHE solves the issue of reliability by running critical system components redundantly. However, performance bottlenecks are avoided, because here CHE does not strictly stick to the centralized approach. That is, communication with the device layer is realized via parallel servers.

4.2.6 Production of Power Plants

POW produces power plants that include numerous pipelines in diverse sizes and dimensions. The production starts after the design of the plant in CAD systems. When the plant design is ready, the company sends the engineering drawings to the state's certification bureau. After receiving a certificate the production can begin. In this study we focus on the processes along the manufacturing of pipes for power plants. This production process comprises seven compulsory steps. The production begins with the material intake and a subsequent check that verifies the correct delivery. This is followed by various repetitions of welding or bending. Subsequent production steps are a mandatory quality check, glowing, a second quality check, and the final assembly of the whole power plant on site, see Figure 4.18. If the check after the bending and welding step is not ok, the product may undergo several adjustments until all certifications have been met.

At the material intake POW receives steel pipelines. When the pipelines arrive POW needs to conduct several verifications before the assembly of the power plant can begin. In the case of maintaining or building a new power plant, the verifications allow POW to start the construction. When an existing plant has to be maintained then POW can start to replace pipelines that are worn out. After the verification arrives, the assembly can begin.

The assembly comprises steps for welding and bending of the pipelines. This is done manually or via machines, depending on whether or not MoPP has a machine that can weld or bend the pipeline into the desired shape. After the pipes have all been bent into the right form and then welded, MoPP conducts quality checks. The pipes are glowed when the quality checks are passed. This step is followed by another quality check. When all quality checks have been passed successfully, the final assembly at the plant can be completed.

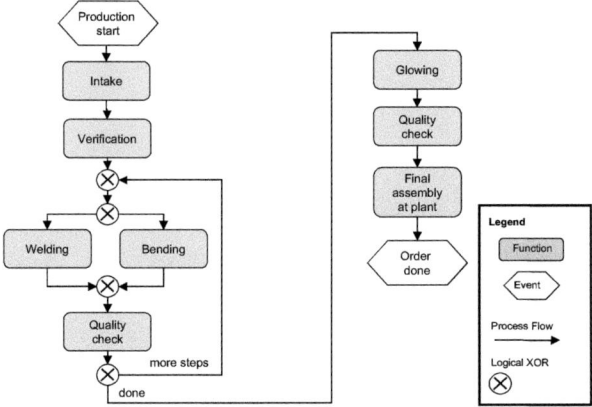

Figure 4.18: Production process at POW.

IT Infrastructure

Figure 4.19 shows the physical deployment of involved software systems along with logical communication links.

The device layer comprises machines and their PLC devices. The only software that runs in the device layer is the PLC software. The company uses no terminals for machine control. That is, workers configure the machines directly. The reason for this thin device layer lies in the nature of the produced products. The company does not use many machines during the welding and bending process. Most work needs to be done manually.

The edge layer includes logging programs that log data from the PLCs. Some customers desire reports about the production process. In such a case POW extracts the desired data from the logging program and feeds them into reports. The data extraction is done on a case-to-case basis with manual queries. Besides the logging program and the reports, the edge layer also comprises ERP clients and BHR clients.

The middle layer comprises the CAD system. The CAD system is, for example, used for design and construction of new power plants. Furthermore, we find the BHR system in this layer. BHR is their self-programmed MES solution. The BHR provides only simple user interfaces on UNIX shelves and become increasingly hard to maintain and to update. Thus, for modernization POW considers the introduction of new solutions in the future.

The back-end layer includes the ERP system, a business intelligence system, and a fileserver. The fileserver is used for all backups of all logged data worldwide.

Two aspects are remarkable about the IT infrastructure at POW: One is the thin edge layer with little IT support on the plant floor. POW has such a thin IT solution because they only produce unique products. For instance, POW only has manual communication between the shop floor and the ERP/MES. There is also no IT support in the coordination of the production. Workers get all the production plans (what they have to weld and bend) on paper documents.

The other aspect is that the IT infrastructure at POW falls into two independent parts. That is, the data flows of the log data and general feedbacks from the workers are completely separated. There is also no connection between the log data and reports in the MES/ERP clients see Figure 4.20. This figure also reveals that the IT infrastructure has a clear dominance of the client-server patterns; there are no layers or tiers in the classical sense.

Conclusion

POW combines several IT systems to manage the production processes. The current solution works well to support the essential data exchange. However, several legacy systems play a central role in the IT solution and the data flows are not fully integrated. For the mid-term IT strategy POW should consider moving toward a standardized system design that integrates the data flows for production data. Consolidation of data flow into one system can ease integration tasks in future IT projects and increase the visibility of shop-floor operations.

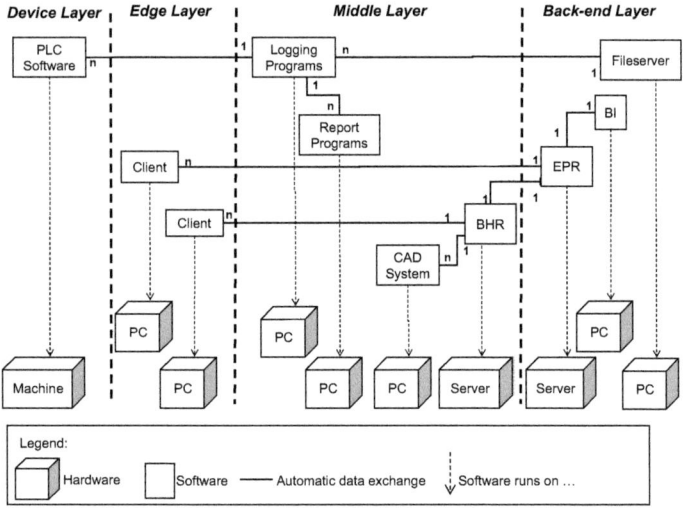

Figure 4.19: Deployment diagram of the software and hardware at POW.

4.2.7 Production of Tires

A tire consists of 15 to 20 different materials. Generally the production of tires comprises the following five steps: assembling carcass, assembling belt, assembling carcass and belt to one unit, vulcanization and finally a quality check. A simplified model of the production process is depicted Figure 4.21.

The carcass assembly itself consists of five production steps. It starts with mixing diverse compounds like different types of rubber together. From this mix, TIR constructs the inner liner in the next production step. The inner liner covers the inside of the future tire. It has to prevent the air from escaping through the tire.

The subsequent step to building the inner liner is the construction of the body ply. The body ply is made out of a single layer of steel cord wire. It is responsible for the solidity of the tire. The steel belts are made in the next step. They also consist of diverse layers of steel cord wires. Depending on the type of tire, one or up to five such belts need to be constructed on top of

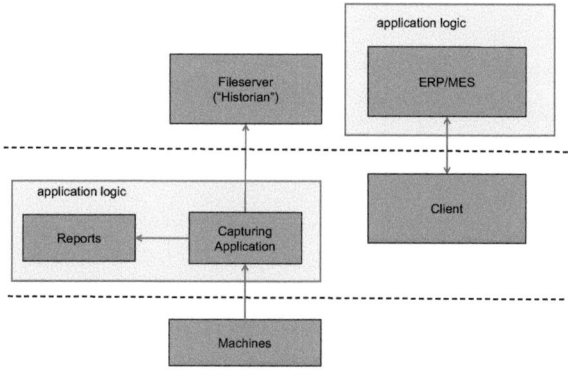

Figure 4.20: Separated dataflows at POW.

each other (off-road tires have more steel belts than city tires). The last step of the carcass assembly is the construction of the side wall. The side wall is a rubber coating on the outer side of the tire.

Parallel to the carcass assembly TIR assembles the tire's belt. The belt consists of the tread and breakers. The tread is – like the inner liner – a specially compounded rubber mix. The breakers are made of nylon or steel wire. They have to provide a protection for the steel belts and body ply.

After the assembly of the carcass and the belt, both components are combined into one piece. This is done via air pressure. Subsequently, TIR vulcanizes the raw tire. During this step the tire is backed for ca. 10 min up to 60 min under a pressure of 22 Bar. The last step is the quality check. This check is party automatic by measuring diverse characteristics via sensors, as well as manually by visual observation.

IT Infrastructure

For analyzing the IT infrastructure we interviewed IT staff regarding the requirements for IT. Relevant requirements are reliability, performance, autarky, open interfaces, and security. TIR implemented its IT infrastructure

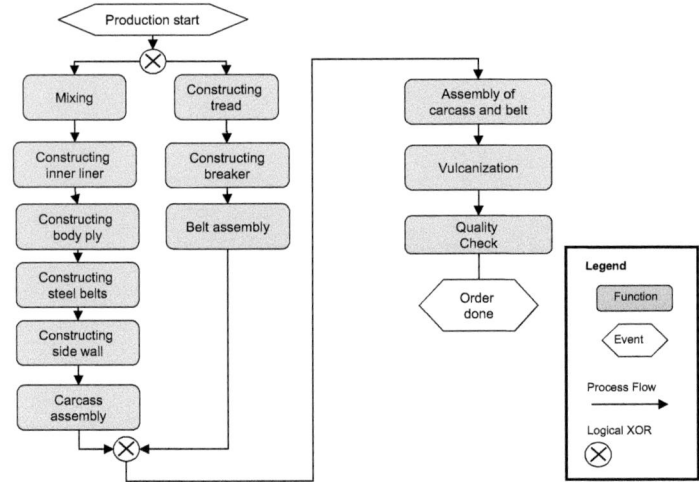

Figure 4.21: Production process at TIR.

based on these requirements. The IT infrastructure and their components can be categorized into four system layers, see Figure 4.22.

The device layer includes all machines and their corresponding PLC devices on the shop floor. Software in the device layer includes the PLC software and the user interfaces of the machine terminals. *The edge layer* at TIR comprises only MES clients. Via these clients plant-floor workers receive descriptions for the production tasks. They also use these MES clients for manual data entry to report about the production.

The middle layer comprises the MES, detailed planning software, and a time-recording application. The MES, time-recording, and detailed planning software are plant specific. *The back-end layer* comprises the MES, ERP, a separate data warehouse, detailed planning software, time-recording application, and a separate specification database. The specification database and the data warehouse each lie on a central server hosting the data of all plants worldwide. The ERP is plant specific.

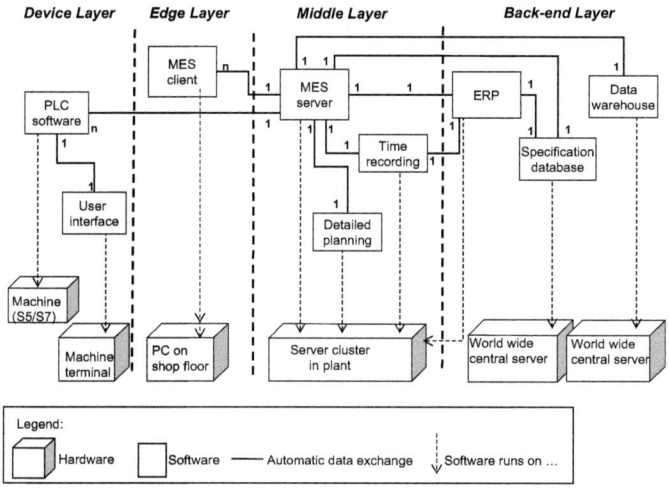

Figure 4.22: Deployment diagram of the software and hardware at TIR.

The infrastructure of TIR is an example of architectures with centralized control. The majority of the systems lie in the middle and back-end layer. This also means that only a small number of powerful computers are used for production data management. This is in contrast to architectures with distributed control systems on the plant floor. Centralized control fits well to the high degree of automation and complex interdependent processes at TIR. However, this design can pose potential challenges to scalability. TIR addresses this issue using buffers on the lower system layers. These buffers prevent data loss in cases of temporary high workload in the back-end database.

Conclusion

TIR combines several systems to realize MES functionality. The current solution works well to support and monitor operational processes on the plant floor. However, several legacy systems play a central role in the IT solution. For the mid-term IT strategy TIR should consider moving toward a standardized system design based on ISA-S95. This can help to increase the flexibility of the IT solution and ease integration tasks in future IT projects.

4.3 Lessons Learned

This section discusses how data acquisition and data flow is accomplished in the case studies. The discussion also includes how activities of production planning are distributed across the different IT systems in common IT infrastructures. In the following, I map the analyzed IT infrastructures and IT requirements to the plant-to-business integrations standard ISA-S95. This enables us to later describe common functionalities which have to be fulfilled when manufacturers aim to embed RFID.

Moreover, the case studies reveal that companies use central or local production control depending on their specific requirements; we discuss this in detail. Then we evaluate which activities can be supported by RFID. Most of them lie in level 3 of the ISA-S95 standard. Therefore, this section concludes with an evaluation of which requirements this level has to fulfill. These requirements are according to the case studies.

4.3.1 Data Acquisition and Dataflow in IT Infrastructures

Activities of production planning are commonly distributed across different IT systems. The ERP system generates the raw production plan, see Figure 4.23. This plan is then finalized in the MES and mapped to concrete machines on the shop floor. During the production, various systems in the device layer collect production data. The sources can be any type of senors, RFID readers, bar-code readers, HMIs or PLCs. Collection of source data from the shop floor provides information about the current state of the processes. In general, it is possible to divide the acquisition of data into the following four groups:

1. short time collection without storing (*e.g.*, current worker, paper that is thrown away)

2. collection on a medium from that the data cannot automatically be written to a back-end system (*e.g.*, paper)

3. collection on a medium that can be read automatically and its data easily linked to the back-end storage (*e.g.*, mobile PDA, RFID chips)

4. direct collection in back-end systems without using a secondary storage (*e.g.*, MES)

After the data is acquired it needs to be fed into the IT systems. This is then followed by various stages of processing, storage and use of the data. Devices on the plant floor communicate the collected production data to the edge layer – into the PDC system or an MES. The PDC systems generally comprise I/O slots for the data collection systems. In summary the PDC system gathers, stores and processes data in order to control or monitor production processes. The PDC system can aggregate the data and forward it to the MES or ERP for production controlling and short-term production planning. Later on, the data is stored, analyzed and further processed in the back-end layer. Particularly, business intelligence tools can evaluate the data for supporting managerial decisions. Figure 4.23 visualizes the described flow of production data.

4.3.2 Mapping Analyzed IT Infrastructures to ISA-S95

Only one manufacturer explicitly applies the ISA-S95 standard for its IT deployment. Most of them have not even heard about this standard. Nevertheless, all infrastructures share common functionalities and software components. Thus I try to match their IT infrastructures as close as possible to this standard. This enables us to later describe – along a well-defined standard – common functionalities which have to be fulfilled when manufacturers aim to embed RFID.

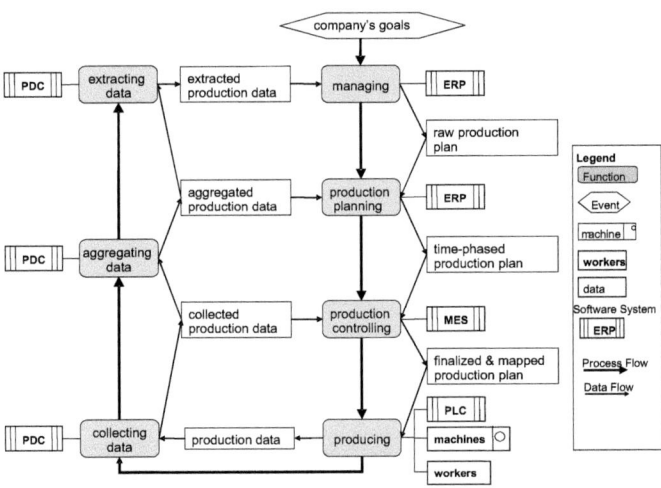

Figure 4.23: Flow of production data between the different IT systems in manufacturing.

In the case studies we use device, edge, middle, and back-end layer for the deployment of IT infrastructures. In this section I map these four layers to the ISA-S95 standard. The device layer comprises user interfaces on the machines, PLC software, and distributed control systems. This layer can be matched to ISA-S95 level 1 and 2.

In the edge layer we put OPC servers and diverse clients like MES or PDC client. This layer is not explicitly elaborated in the standard; it is rather included in level 3. Following the standard level 3 includes the clients and their associated servers. In our case studies the servers are positioned in the middle layer. This includes MES or PDC systems and related software components. The software components can be programs responsible for visualization of the shop floor, logging programs – also referred to as historians, or utility maintenance software. In the back-end layer we position the ERP system, data warehouse, and business intelligence systems. This layer matches to level 4 of the ISA-S95 standard.

When integrating RFID, we would position it into the device layer. According to ISA-S95 RFID readers belong to level 1. Only when a distributed control system is in place would the RFID data then have to be processed already in the device layer, or level 2, respectively. Otherwise the data goes directly to MES systems in the middle layer, or level 3, respectively.

4.3.3 Central Versus Local Production Control

We observed two approaches to production control: production control with a central component, and decentralized production control. It depends on the production environment as to which option is favorable. Production control with a central component is depicted in Figure 4.24. Here the production control is accomplished in three steps. The first step is the generation of a production plan in the ERP system. This can be mapped to ISA-S95 level 4 activities. The production plan is then coordinated in the second step. This includes sending control commands and job instructions to the hardware on the shop floor. These activities fit to ISA-S95 level 3. The instructions are performed on the shop floor and events reported back to level 3.

This approach has little functionality on level 3. It is suitable if a detailed view of all actuators is required. Examples for such IT infrastructures are the case studies 4.2.1 and 4.2.5. It is also suitable for lightweight infrastructures like 4.2.3.

The advantages of this central approach are a straightforward realization of a central view about the whole shop floor or a specific facility. This is because the whole infrastructure is kept simple. However, the drawbacks are poor reliability and scalability. It is possible to increase reliability by embedding redundancies, which in return make the whole infrastructure more complex. Scalability is increased by integrating filters. The fever data are pushed from level 2 to level 4 and instead processed in the lower levels the more scalable the respective infrastructure is.

The second approach is decentralized production control in a hierarchy, see Figure 4.25. Production control is conducted in four steps. The first step is also generation of a production plan in the ERP system. We can also map

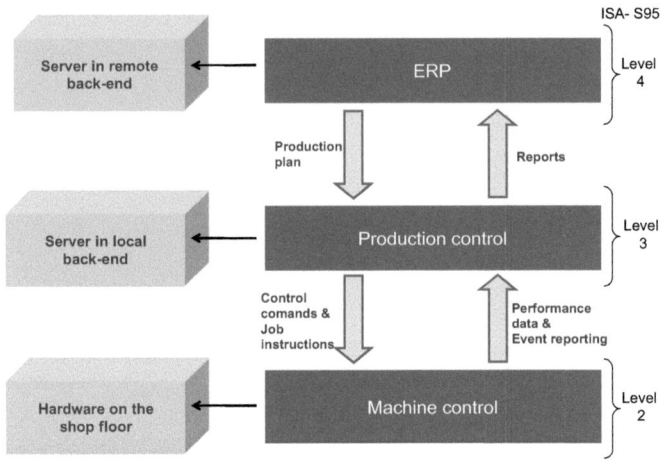

Figure 4.24: Central production control.

this to the ISA-S95 level 4. In the second step a detailed production plan is generated from the production plan. This is then split up and sent to the appropriate PCs on the shop floor. They are responsible for the production control of specific processes and the corresponding machines.

This approach has substantial functionalities in level 3. Information is kept redundant in the system. This enables a high level of scalability. It also supports productions with well-encapsulated tasks. An example is the case 4.2.4. The advantages are higher autarky of all system components, which reduces the problem of bottlenecks. Through this decentralization the IT systems can react faster to changes on the shop floor. Nevertheless, one has to keep the disadvantage in mind that maintenance is more complex. This is also due to the problem of redundant data storage.

For both approaches RFID data processing would have to be embedded into those modules that are responsible for retrieving events and performance data. In the first case the modules would lie on the server in the local back end. In the second case the location would be on the PCs on the shop floor.

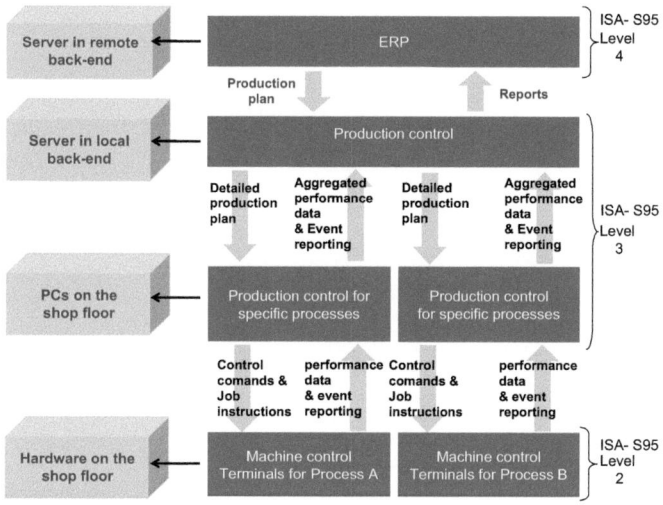

Figure 4.25: Local production control.

4.3.4 Activities Supported by RFID

RFID technology may support most MES functionalities. The typical functionalities of an MES are described by MESA (Manufacturing Enterprise Solutions Association). These include:

- Operations scheduling and production control
- Labor management
- Maintenance management
- Document control
- Data collection
- Quality management
- Performance analysis

161

In operations scheduling and production control, RFID can be used for guaranteeing process safety and interlocking. If a material or material container is equipped with a unique ID (provided via bar code or RFID), the MES can ensure that all proceeding process steps have been conducted successfully before starting the next manufacturing step. Furthermore, production order data and manufacturing parameters may be written to the RFID tag at the first manufacturing step and then read and updated locally, providing fast local data maintenance and redundancy for the MES.

Concerning labor management, plant personnel could automatically be registered via appropriate sensor technologies. Also, it could potentially enable the location tracking of the plant personnel. However, privacy concerns need to be taken into account when considering such measures. In maintenance management, data may be stored locally at the resource in an RFID tag. This may reduce the required paperwork for performing maintenance and updating associated records. Regarding data collection, RFID can help to automate the tracking and tracing of materials, Work In Process (WIP), location of mobile resources, *etc.* In quality management, data about the quality targets may be stored locally at the material within an RFID tag.

Moreover, there are enterprises that prefer not to use an MES and connect the hardware controllers directly to the ERP. This is only possible if the ERP is equipped to do this, *i.e.*, if it contains modules that accept the controller output as input and that perform the necessary modeling and filtering. SAP's Auto-ID Infrastructure Bornhövd et al. (2004) provides such functionalities. Moreover, vendors such as Infosys Dubey (2006) or PEAK Schultz (2007) offer middleware components that serve as interface between the hardware on the shop floor and the ERP. Often, however, this includes only a technical interface without any application and process support as provided, for example, by an MES.

4.3.5 Requirements for the ISA-S95 Level 3

Following the ISA-S95 standard, RFID data are generated on level 1 and collected on level 2. The data must then be integrated into level 3 for processing.

But before one can integrate the data we need to know which requirements level 3 has to meet. Only then is it possible to fully integrate RFID data in a way that manufacturers gain full advantage out of them. As described above, level 3 includes MES or PDC systems and RFID may support most of their functionalities.

In Table 4.4 we summarize which requirements companies have on MES or PDC systems. ++ stands for very important; + for nice to have. We evaluate all requirements from our case studies.

The table shows diverse requirements surveyed companies have on their level 3 activities. For the analyzed companies adaptability of the used PDC or MES system is very important. Four out of seven put a tick here. This is the case in four out of six case studies. The requirement of a lightweight solution is not seen as relevant. We found this requirement explicitly in those cases where a PDC system is not seen as important for maintaining the production processes. The case studies further show that reliability, scalability, and quick response times of the system are often important. Generally security is not considered as important. In two cases we also see that the companies use an event-driven system for communicating data up stream.

In summary all companies have very heterogeneous requirements. Therefore, there is no "one fits all" architecture for level 3. All PDCs are tightly customized to the specific needs of the company if they have not been uniquely built for the specific company. Furthermore, we see that if the analyzed companies have high requirements on reliability, response times and scalability, then the companies push a lot of processing logic down to level 3. In the cases this is realized by pushing substantial activities to the middle layer. However, if a functioning IT is not as relevant for keeping up a running production then the companies use simple solutions keeping most of the production control on level 4 (in the ERP system) and having very few until there are no functionalities in level 3. We can describe such architectures also as client-server solutions, where the ERP system represents the server and hardware on the shop floor of the clients.

Table 4.4: Attributes for quality checks

	Adapt. Open	Light Weight	Relia ble	Fast	Secure	Event Driven	Scal able
MIL	+		++	++			++
ENG	++		++	++		++	++
CHE	++		++	++			++
TIR	++		++	++		++	++
COO	+					++	
REF		+					
POW	++	++					

4.4 Conclusion

In summary, all companies have very heterogeneous requirements. There is no "one fits all" IT deployment. All infrastructures are tightly customized to the specific needs of the company. Also, software components in use are adjusted if not uniquely built for the specific company. Furthermore, we see that if the analyzed companies have high requirements on reliability, response times and scalability, then they push processing logic from the edge to the middle layer, level 3 according to ISA-S95. However, if a functioning IT is not the bottleneck for keeping up the production then the companies have little functionality in layer 3 and rather use simple client-server solutions.

Furthermore, we reveal in this chapter that IT implementations following the ISA-S95 standard and most IT infrastructures in practice differ. Six of the seven analyzed companies do not apply the ISA-S95 standard. Only one manufacturer explicitly applies this standard for its IT deployment. Nevertheless, all infrastructures share common functionalities and software components. Thus it is possible to match their IT infrastructures to this standard. This enables us to describe – along this well-defined standard – common functionalities which have to be fulfilled when manufacturers aim to embed RFID. We identify such commonalities and use them to derive general design guidelines in the next chapter.

Chapter 5

Design Guidelines for Embedding RFID into IT Infrastructures

As Chapter 2 shows RFID technology opens new opportunities to monitor and control manufacturing processes. However, Chapter 3 reveals that IT staff faces various challenges when adapting software infrastructures for RFID. Also Strüker et al. (2008) detected recently by a survey among 102 manufacturers that IT integration is a barrier. Manufacturers attach to the barrier "complex integration into existing IT infrastructures" an importance of 55%. It is seen as the second most important barrier after "complex inntegartion into cross-company business processes. Therefore in this chapter I present design principles which guide application designers in developing and adapting RFID solutions for manufacturing environments. This work was conducted with Holger Ziekow. We published the results in Ivantysynova and Ziekow (2008).

We derive the design guidelines from a Product Line Analysis (PLA). Based on the PLA we present a toolset of standard components and their variations along with guidelines for the application design. These guidelines cover processing paradigms for RFID data and heuristics for distributing data and logic in the IT system. In particular we derive commonalities and variations for IT systems that support RFID applications in manufacturing. This covers reusable assets including requirements and functional components. Beyond this, we provide guidance for implementing the required functionality and heuristics for mapping the software components to the hardware infrastructures.

The next section reviews related work. Section 5.2 presents results of the completed product line analysis of the manufacturing domain. Here we derive common activities and required data when using RFID. Section 5.3 discusses implementation issues. Section 5.4 concludes this chapter.

5.1 Related Work

We categorize existing work on RFID application design into work for horizontal and work for vertical integration of RFID data. The research community has put a lot of effort into defining services for horizontally exchanging RFID data. The most prominent set of standards and propositions for enabling services for horizontal integration is the EPCglobal network. Currently specified services in this network comprise interfaces for inter-organizational data exchange (EPCglobal, 2007) and a lookup service for object-related data (EPCglobal, 2005). However, applications and design guidelines on top of these services target mainly scenarios outside the shop floors of manufacturers (*e.g.*, Angeles, 2005; Främling et al., 2006).

Work on vertical integration of RFID is embedded into the context of RFID middleware (*e.g.*, Bornhövd et al., 2004; Floerkemeier and Lampe, 2005). These approaches focus on functionalities and requirements for reader management and data filtering. Here Moon and Yeom (2007) identified abstract functional components that are common for general RFID applications. They identify general interfaces and functionalities.

In contrast to all these works we explicitly focus on shop-floor applications in manufacturing. For the components that we derive in the domain-specific requirement analysis we provide concrete implementation approaches. Unlike existing work our design guidelines also provide heuristics for physically distributing processing logic and required data within the IT infrastructure of manufacturers. These guidelines will ease the integration of RFID systems and middleware components in manufacturing environments.

5.2 RFID in Manufacturing: Common Functionalities

In this section we present our key findings of the domain analysis. We conduct the analysis based on the method of Moon et al. (2005). Using this method we identify common activities and variations in IT applications supporting RFID in manufacturing. Our results focus on common activities which a software solution for RFID in manufacturing should generally support. We relate these common activities to the required input data from different software systems. Thereby, we provide cornerstones for the architectural design of RFID applications in manufacturing and their integration into existing IT landscapes.

Our domain analysis comprises four steps: (i) identifying requirements in the targeted domain, (ii) analyzing similarities and variations among the identified requirements, (iii) estimating commonalities of the requirements and (iv) modeling the flow of common activities. Subsequently we discuss each step in detail.

5.2.1 Identifying Requirements

In the first step we identify primitive requirements (PRs). Moon et al. (2005) define a PR as "a transaction that has an effect on an external actor". For the domain of RFID applications we define an external actor as any person or IT system that directly or indirectly uses RFID data. For identifying RPs we drew on existing work about RFID in supply chain management (Bornhövd et al., 2004; Moon and Yeom, 2007).

We then evaluate and extend this initial list of requirements with regards to their applicability to the manufacturing domain. Here we use our case studies from Chapter 2 for identifying the PRs: We identify the PRs following the flow of RFID data trough the IT system. We list and describe our derived PRs in Table 5.1; we set them in italics.

As depicted in this table we identify three variations for read activities: manual triggering by plant-floor workers (*e.g.*, with mobile readers), regularly scheduled automatic requests, or requests that are triggered by an event (*e.g.*, reads after a light barrier is triggered). This activity may require a reader schedule or a trigger event as input.

The next PR is *writing data to tag*. This requirement refers to data to the memory of RFID tags. For enriching RFID data we identify three variations. One is semantic enrichment by associating the reads with certain process steps for example. Another requirement is adding reference data such as resolving IDs to corresponding object data. Furthermore, streams of dynamic context information can be correlated with RFID read events (*e.g.*, machine sensor data or current machine settings).

Data filtering refers to removing error from the raw input stream for RFID data. Variations are removal of flickering by low-pass filters or complex inference based on statistical filers. Similar to data filtering, data cleaning removes errors from input data. The difference is that data cleaning is performed on a higher semantic level and with enriched RFID data. Data cleaning exploits process knowledge to infer on the plausibility of RFID-based inputs.

Inference on RFID-based events is either done for process control or monitoring purposes. For process control the inference determines a reaction to the RFID input. Monitoring the inferences filters out certain events of interest.

Activities of notification generation collect and assemble information which must be communicated along with detected events. That is, an event of interest may require additional information for creating meaningful messages.

Notification delivery refers to transmitting captured RFID-based events to the desired destinations. This can involve various systems inside or even outside the manufacturing plant. Examples range from triggering processes on the plant floor over providing workers with RFID-based information to status updates in the ERP systems.

Table 5.1: Description of all derived PRs

Requirements	CV Prop. %
RFID reading activity	C / 100%
manually issuing reads	P / 33%
scheduled reads	C / 100%
triggering reads by events	C / 100%
writing data to tag	P / 67%
data enrichment	C / 100%
semantic enrichment	C / 100%
stream correlation	C / 100%
adding reference data	C / 100%
data filtering	C / 100%
low-pass filtering	C / 100%
statistic filtering	P / 50%
data cleaning	P / 50%
inference	C / 100%
process control	C / 83%
process monitoring	C / 83%
notification generation	C / 100%
aggregation	C / 100%
adding context information	C / 83%
notification delivery	C / 100%
triggering process step	P / 50%
reporting asset position	P / 67%
submitting notifications	P / 50%
reporting history/status information	C / 100%

5.2.2 Analyzing Similarities and Variations

In the second step we group PRs and if possible generalize them to one common PR with variations (in Table 5.1 non-italic requirements). We do this by analyzing the similarity between the PRs. We generalize all identified PRs based on the semantic similarity of their functionalities. For example, *low-pass filtering* and *statistic filtering* are required activities that can be subsumed into the common requirement: *data filtering* (see Table 5.2).

However, for generalizing PRs it is important to consider the level of abstraction on which the respective functionality is applied. Generally, in RFID applications the subsequent processing steps transform the input data to more and more abstract and semantically rich information; having only raw RF data at the beginning and with semantically enriched production information at the end.

Therefore, despite semantic similarity of the respective operations, one cannot generalize PRs for different levels of abstraction. For instance, data cleaning on raw data from an RFID reader is very different from data cleaning of semantically enriched RFID data in a database. Low-pass filtering for omitting false positives and negatives is prevalent in the first case. In the second case, one may check the data against logical constraints on attributes. To account for such differences we do not generalize PRs for data on different semantic levels.

Table 5.2: Example of a Generalized PR derived from other PRs

REQUIREMENTS	CV P. %	AIR	CLU	COO	CAS	CON	PAC
data filtering	C / 100%	√	√	√	√	√	√
low-pass filtering	C / 100%	√	√	√	√	√	√
statistic filtering	P / 50%	√	X	X	√	√	X

5.2.3 Estimating Commonalities of Requirements

In the third step we identify commonalities of the PRs based on the frequency of occurrence in the case studies. Table 5.2 presents how we derive the commonality of the two PRs *low-pass filtering* and *statistic filtering* for some exemplary PRs. The full Table is in appendix 8. The commonality is denoted by the CV property ratio (CV Prob. %). This is the ratio of cases where the requirement exists to the total number of cases. For determining the CV Prop. % we check for each PR in how many case studies it occurs. We consider a requirement as common if it occurs in over 80% of the cases (denoted by C in the Table). If it occurs less than 80%, we denote it as an optional property (denoted by P).

In Table 5.2 we portray CV properties for all PRs. The significant overlap that we have found in the investigated cases gives confidence that reasonable generalizations can be made based on our sample. Table 5.2 includes the CV properties that we found for the identified requirements. This provides an indication about the commonality of RFID requirements in the manufacturing domain. As the table shows, almost all generalized requirements occur in every investigated application scenario. Thus, it is likely that each RFID-based solution in manufacturing will implement at least one variation of functionalities corresponding to these requirements.

However, on the level of PRs we found variations in the commonality. This means that certain functionalities are not mandatory in the manufacturing domain. The least frequent PR that we found (manually reading RFID) occurred in only two of the investigated cases. Though most applications do not require manual reading, it is likely that this requirement will occur repetitively in manufacturing applications. Thus, we render this requirement as optional for the manufacturing domain. 11 out of 17 primitive requirements occur in at least 5 of the 6 investigated cases. Given the high frequency of occurrence, we consider these requirements as common for the manufacturing domain.

5.2.4 Modeling the Flow of Common Activities

In the fourth step we model the common flow of activities and data. Each generalized requirement is denoted as an activity. For each activity we identify the data that is required for performing it. That includes required configuration information and data which is needed in addition to the captured RFID data. By identifying these data items we provide a basis to specify interfaces for integrating RFID applications in existing system landscapes. In Figure 5.1 we present the model of the common flow of activities and data. We also denote required additional input data and the place of its origin (denoted in brackets). Here we point out data sources that can be found in common software systems of manufacturers. This enables situating the common activities in the existing IT landscape.

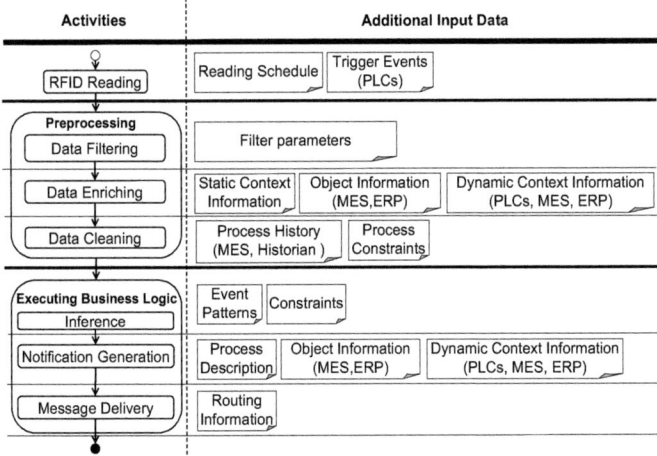

Figure 5.1: Activities and required data in the capturing process.

Throughout the above-presented analysis we have identified commonalities among different RFID applications in manufacturing. We analyzed the commonalities (PRs) by applying the PLA. Within the manufacturing domain the described PRs can be used for deriving IT architectures for each specific RFID application.

5.3 Implementation Issues

In this section we present guidelines for developing RFID software in manufacturing. That is, we provide guidelines for implementing the common activities which we identified above. This includes a discussion about processing paradigms for each of the common activities in and a presentation of heuristics for deciding on the distribution of data and logic within the IT infrastructure.

5.3.1 Technologies for Implementing the Common Activities

For processing RFID data we have found three classes of common activities. These classes are Reading Activities, Pre-processing, and Executing Business Logic. Note that manufacturers which do not apply RFID also perform activities in class three: Executing Business Logic (*e.g.*, using manually recorded data). Thus, synergies with existing software solutions (*e.g.*, an MES) may exist. Therefore, these existing systems are candidates for performing the RFID-specific class-three activities as well. Reading and Pre-processing activities are to a large extent RFID specific. These activities require dedicated or specially adapted solutions. Subsequently we discuss technologies for implementing each activity in all three classes in detail.

Reading Activities

The first activity is capturing raw read events, see Figure 5.1. This activity occurs in the device layer. In general there are three options for capturing read events. These are regularly polling read requests, event-triggered reads, and manual reads. For regular polling one must create schedules that avoid collisions between readers with overlapping signal fields. For example, a central control system can avoid signal collisions (Goyal, 2003). Alternatively, it is possible to use a decentralized solution where agents on the readers negotiate a schedule (Spiess, 2005).

For event-triggered reads it is necessary to couple readers with an external actuator. Especially in the production environment, activities in the production process can trigger reads: a tag on a material carrier is read out when a machine loads the carrier. However, this requires coupling the machine sensors to the controller of the RFID reader. For manual reads, workers need an interface to readers. This is commonly the case for mobile readers which typically come to be used in scenarios with manually issued RFID reads.

Data Filtering Activities

After capturing the raw read events, the data must be filtered. Existing solutions in the device layer use low-pass filters to avoid flickering and cancel out double reads (Bornhövd et al., 2004). However, simple low-pass filtering with fixed filter windows is not suitable in every application.

In our case studies we frequently found conditions on the plant floor that are challenging for RFID installations. This includes presence of metal and spatial proximity of different reading points. This causes the need for more advanced filters that can be configured to account for particularities of shop-floor conditions. Such filters must be implemented in the software positioned in the edge layer.

Jeffery et al. (2006) have proposed an adaptive filtering solution based on characteristics of the underlying data stream. Brusey et al. (2003) use statistical filters that weight read events to account for particular physical conditions in a specific application scenario. The applied RFID system should therefore provide the option of embedding a range of highly configurable filtering solutions.

Data Enriching Activities

A simple solution for enriching filtered RFID events with additional data is using a relational database. Here one could dump the incoming data in a table and run batch processes for creating the correlations. This is mainly conducted in the middle layer. However, this approach does not account for the streaming nature of RFID events. One disadvantage of the batch-driven paradigm is that it decouples execution time from the arrival time of events. Batch processing is therefore contrary to real-time requirements.

Furthermore, query languages for databases have poor support for operations on data streams (Babu and Widom, 2001). Dedicated stream engines exist that are designed for real-time correlation of data streams with additional data (Abadi et al., 2003). These approaches match the requirements for the data-enriching activity. Stream operators can correlate RFID read events with static information about their sources and dynamic information from machine sensors. Expressive high-level languages for defining such stream operations are available, *e.g.*, Arasu et al. (2006). Thus, the stream-oriented processing paradigm is suitable for realizing the activity of data enrichment; especially for applications with real-time requirements.

Data-Cleaning Activities

The data-cleaning activity is for checking the plausibility of detected events and making corrections where possible. For instance, previous scans of the pallet can allow completing missing reads in pallet scans. Also, duplicate reads from different sensors may be dropped. Jeffery et al. (2006) present a framework for such cleaning based on stream-processing operations and predicate checks. Here, the predicates implicitly encode process knowledge. The peculiar conditions on many plant floors make cleaning steps on this level necessary. Software systems for RFID applications in this domain should therefore support the definition on semantic-rich rules for constraint-based data cleaning. This software would normally lie in the edge layer.

Pattern Matching and Notification Generation Activities

The fifth activity in the flow of common activities is inference on input data for detecting events of interest. The sixth is for generating corresponding notifications. From the computational point of view these are different processing tasks that are conducted in the middle layer. Yet, techniques of CEP (Luckham, 2001) cover both tasks.

CEP is of relevance whenever the events of interest result from a set of input events rather than from single events. The semantic aggregation of CEP is necessary to avoid information overload. This applies specifically to notifications to the back-end layer, *e.g.*, notifications from the MES to the ERP. Thus, direct support for defining and running CEP rules within the RFID solution is beneficial in many manufacturing applications.

CEP evaluates rules which define an event pattern, constraints on the pattern, and an action. In that sense CEP is similar to ECA rules in active databases. However, CEP rules can be triggered by arbitrary event messages and are not limited to database-specific events (such as insert or update). This supports formulation event patterns on RFID events captured in a production process and fits to the event-driven nature of RFID data. Using state machines for complex event processing (Gehani et al., 1992) or adapted Petri nets (Gatziu and Dirtrich, 1993) are options for implementing this kind of pattern evaluation.

Notification Delivery Activities

The last activity for RFID data capturing is delivering notification messages to the respective addressees in all three layers. Here we distinguish four different communication styles. The dimensions for the distinction are push- vs. pull-based communication and direct vs. indirect addressing schemes. Periodic pull-based loading of data chunks in the manner of an ETL process is appropriate for analytic applications. Though, push-based communication is a better fit to the event-driven generation of notification messages.

Furthermore, monitoring and control applications need more timely updates. This applies in particular if control applications directly steer operations on the plant floor. These are arguments for applying the push-based communication scheme for RFID data acquisition at manufacturers. Both, push-based and pull-based communication can be combined with direct or indirect addressing.

Direct addressing requires to explicitly denote the destinations of each notification type. Indirect addressing via an intermediate service decouples data provision from data consumption. This decoupling enables flexible adaptation of notification delivery because data sources and recipients can be managed separately. Event-based systems use a notification service and publish/subscribe mechanisms combine the push-based communication scheme with indirect addressing (Mühl et al., 2006). Using such a notification service matches to the requirements of many of the investigated application scenarios and should therefore be available in RFID-enabled IT infrastructures for manufacturing.

5.3.2 Distributing Data and Logic

I now provide heuristics for decisions on the distribution of the functional components. This goes in hand with the distribution of corresponding input and output information. Writable memory of RFID tags enables pushing data management down to lower system layers.

RFID memory can store production data – such as recipes or production records – right at the object (*e.g.*, the product). This allows running several operations solely in the device or edge layer, *i.e.*, consistency checks can run locally on station control servers or on PCs on the shop floor without back-end interactions.

However, throughout the case studies we found reoccurring arguments for, as well as against decentralization. The benefits are better scalability, performance, reliability, and an eased data association with objects. The drawbacks of decentralization are worse redundancy, maintainability and inconsistency. We now describe each of the identified key benefits of decentralization and the drawbacks.

Scalability

Decentralized systems distribute the total workload on several devices is the system. As the system grows, the number of devices that share a task grows as well. Furthermore, pushing aggregation and filter functions down the hierarchy to the information sources reduces network traffic and avoids overloading higher system layers.

Performance

Performance bottlenecks in the IT can impact the productivity on the plant floor. We found that the tolerable delay is typically about 0.5 sec for a manually issued request and in the order of milliseconds for machines. The cause for longer delays can be delays for accessing remote systems or peaks in the workload. Placing the logic and required data close to the point of operation avoids the problem of network delay. Furthermore, decentralization of processing tasks mitigates peaks in the workload.

Reliability

system failures that cause a breakdown of the production can account for major expenses. Decentralization can help to avoid single points of failure and limit the number of affected production tasks.

Eased Data Association With Objects

Through the RFID-enabled decentralized information storage it is ensured that the information is available at the point of operation. This helps to avoid that the wrong information is associated with an object.

Redundancy

A lot of data that is collected on shop floors is not only used for steering the production but also to document the conducted steps. That is, a certain percentage of the data must be available in the back-end layer. Distributing this data to lower system layers consequently results in a certain degree of redundancy.

Maintainability

Distributing logic across system layers adds complexity to the management of the IT systems. This is because maintenance tasks cover systems that run at several locations and possibly different platforms. If most functionality resides on a central system, the majority of maintenance tasks are done on the same platform.

Inconsistency

Information on tags can only be read if the item is in the proximity of a reader. Thus, for applications that require data access independently from the corresponding object, it is necessary to have the information available in the network as well. Keeping data redundantly on the tags and in the network bears the risk of inconsistency.

Application designers can decide on the distribution of data and logic within the system along these listed arguments. It depends on the particular application how much these arguments weigh. In our case studies we found that RFID applications fall into two major categories regarding the trade-off between centralization and decentralization. These categories are applications for *monitoring/analyzing* and *controlling/steering* processes. For each application category we derive guidelines for distributing processing functionally. We base our analysis on the three previously identified main activities: RFID Reading, Pre-processing and Executing Business Logic, see Figure 5.1.

Applications for *controlling/steering* processes perform checks in the running processes and steer the operations on the shop floor. These applications commonly have strong real-time constraints. That is, the production processes slow down if machines or workers have to wait for responses from the IT system, *e.g.*, case study 2.3.1. Thus, performance is typically the main concern. Consequently, it is often desirable to run the three activities RFID Reading, Pre-processing and Executing Business Logic in the edge and middle layer and without back-end interaction. The guideline is to push the operations as close to the physical processes as possible.

Applications for *monitoring/analyzing* processes support management decisions and help spot potentials for improvements in the production processes. Here, no real-time requirements apply. Typically, solutions like data warehouses or reporting tools extract, process, and visualize data from several sources on the plant floor. Such applications are often integrated in MES or ERP systems. Consequently, the activities of Executing Business Logic for monitoring/analyzing processes with RFID should run in the back-end.

However, in order to ensure scalability it is desirable to reduce the input data on lower system layers; *i.e.*, the edge layer. Particularly data cleaning and data filtering (part of the activity Pre-processing) reduce the amount of transmitted RFID data. Filtering raw read events can take place within device controllers (Bornhövd et al., 2004). These may run on terminal PCs in the edge layer.

Data enriching and data cleaning (part of the activity Pre-processing) can require information from the back-end and other sensors on the plant floor, see Figure 5.1. Such context information is particularly relevant for monitoring and analyzing production processes.

A suitable placement of enriching and cleaning operations is therefore where RFID data and required context information join. This point depends on the targeted system environment. Yet, we found that station control servers in the middle layer are suitable for enriching and cleaning operations in many cases. Therefore, the guideline is to join information as close to their sources as possible and run operators of data enriching and data cleaning at this point.

Note that design decisions on the distribution of data and logic are heavily dependent on the targeted manufacturing environment. In our case studies we found that hardware infrastructures at manufacturers are very heterogeneous. That is, not every device type depicted in Figure 1.1 is always in place; *e.g.*, not every manufacturer has PCs on the shop floor or station control servers for controlling several machines. Yet, most IT systems at manufacturers have some sort of a hierarchically structured hardware landscape. Our guidelines help the placing of operations for RFID data processing into this hierarchy.

5.4 Conclusion

The design guidelines for embedding RFID into IT infrastructures developed in this chapter take the particularities of manufacturing into account. This includes typical applications as well as typical IT systems in this domain.

Focusing on production-specific issues, we identify core components and technology paradigms. Following a product line engineering approach we derive common activities and variation points for respective RFID infrastructures. The guidelines comply with IT environments as they are typically found in manufacturing plants and as they are characterized in Chapter 4. That is, components relate to components of existing software systems; the guidelines indicate where RFID data processing can be integrated into software systems.

Beyond defining functional components, we investigate which processing paradigms and technologies are most suitable for challenges in manufacturing environments. Furthermore, we discuss the mapping of software components to hardware in the infrastructure. This is because RFID allows to store data and execute computations on the chips, which is a driving factor for using RFID in several cases. Overall the design guidelines presented comprise aspects of (i) functional components, (ii) interfaces and interaction with external components, (iii) processing paradigms, and (iv) distribution of data and logic.

Chapter 6

Costs and Benefits of RFID Investments

The previous chapters show that RFID promises to improve a broad range of processes in manufacturing. However, market acceptance of RFID is developing slower than anticipated. One likely reason is the difficulty to evaluate the resulting effects beforehand (see Strüker et al., 2008). Strüker et al. (2008)'s survey reveals that manufacturers see "lacking possibilities for forecasting and measuring the benefits" as one of the three main barriers regarding RFID deployments in their enterprise.

Substantial research has already been conducted on assessing costs and benefits of RFID investments. But until now the focus has mainly been on logistic applications. The manufacturing domain still lacks dedicated models for evaluating costs and benefits of an RFID rollout especially concerning the intangible, non-quantifiable aspects of such an investment. Therefore, this chapter provides guidance for assessing both the quantifiable and the non-quantifiable aspects of RFID in manufacturing. I conducted this work with Oliver Günther, Seckin Kara, Michael Klafft, and Holger Ziekow. I published parts of the results in Ivantysynova et al. (2007). The complete results are currently under review.

The next section reviews related work. In Section 6.2 we discuss quantifiable costs and benefits resulting from the seven typical RFID advancements

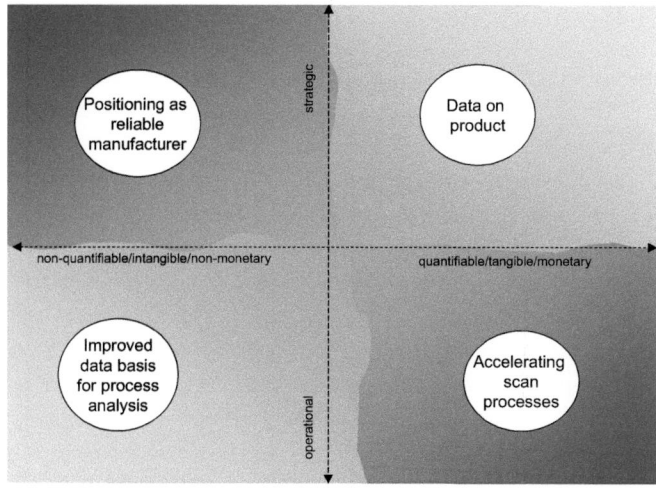

Figure 6.1: Aspects of an RFID rollout in manufacturing.

evaluated in Chapter 2. Section 6.3 describes non-quantifiable aspects of an RFID investment. Section 6.4 deals with the question of how to combine tangible and intangible costs and benefits. Section 6.5 concludes this chapter.

Note that we use the terms quantifiable, tangible, and monetary interchangeably as opposed to the terms non-quantifiable, intangible, or non-monetary. As we will discuss later, this taxonomy is independent of the taxonomy classifying certain measures into being operational vs. strategic. Figure 6.1 gives examples for all four possible cases. The boundaries between operational and strategic are somewhat fuzzy, as are the boundaries between quantifiable and non-quantifiable. Especially the latter classification should not be seen as a dichotomy, but as a spectrum.

6.1 Related Work

For decades, researchers have been working on the challenge to assess investments in IT. As a result, a large number of models and frameworks have been developed (*e.g.*,see Pietsch, 1999; Costello et al., 2007). As RFID is an information technology, these general IT investment models are of interest for the assessment of RFID investments, even though they are often quite conceptional, arguing mostly on a meta level. Thus, they are not directly applicable to concrete investment decisions on the introduction of RFID in the manufacturing domain.

One of the earliest models was Rockart (1982) critical success factor approach. According to Rockart (1982), there are four key factors determining the success of IT investments: quality of the system's service, communication between management and users, human resources in the company, and the new system's ability to reposition the information system's function from an "automated back office to a [...] ubiquitous function involved in all aspects of the business".

Although published almost 30 years ago, Rockart (1982) already identified the ubiquity of information systems as a key factor for IT investment success – a strong argument for the introduction of RFID throughout the company, including manufacturing processes. However, Rockart's set of factors also indicates that *ubiquity* alone is not sufficient and needs to be accompanied by other components, such as technology acceptance, intense communication, and management skills.

A more recent model along these lines is the balanced scorecard approach developed by Kaplan and Norton (1992, 1993, 1996). The balanced scorecard was initially conceived as a general management tool, but was soon adapted to the specific needs of IT investments, where it comprises the following four evaluation dimensions: user orientation, corporate contribution, operational excellence, and future orientation van Grembergen and van Bruggen (2000).

Other popular IT investment evaluation approaches are the information systems effectiveness matrix from Seddon et al. (1999), DeLone and McLean (2003)'s model of information systems success, or Farbey et al. (1995)'s information system benefits evaluation ladder. However, all these approaches do not take into consideration the very specific challenges of RFID-related IT investments.

During the last few years, more RFID-specific evaluation methods have been developed. One recent stream of research addresses the issues of imprecise and uncertain information by applying fuzzy logic to solve the underlying investment decision problems. Bozdag et al. (2007), for example, propose a fuzzy analytic hierarchy process with a hierarchy of four main criteria (scientific and technological merit, potential benefits, project execution and project risk) and 11 sub-criteria. However, AHP-based approaches are impractical if a large number of decision criteria needs to be covered, as usually is the case in the manufacturing domain. A second approach by Üstündag and Tanyas (2005) focuses on fuzzy cognitive maps to "model causal relations in a non-hierarchical manner for an RFID investment evaluation".

However, in order to apply Üstündag and Tanyas (2005)'s method, relationships between causes and effects as well as their impact on costs and benefits have to be clearly known, which is not always the case beforehand. Furthermore, Üstündag and Tanyas (2005) focus on applications in distribution logistics rather than manufacturing. Additionally, fuzzy-logic approaches like the ones discussed here include complex mathematical computations and therefore do not meet the simplicity and clarity criteria which we focus on. Although being very valuable for specialists, they are not ideally suited for applications in small and medium-sized enterprises where the management often has little decision-modeling experience.

The same needs to be said about proposals to apply option models from financial theory (Cox et al., 9791) to IT and RFID investment decisions (Lucas, 1999; Curtin et al., 2007). In order to be applicable to a wide range of companies, less sophisticated approaches are needed, such as value benefit analyses, as discussed by Tellkamp (2003).

Other methods take a more fine-granular approach and focus on the effect that RFID has on atomic activities. Laubacher et al. (2005), for example, conduct an activity-based performance measurement. GS1 (2007) show the impact of RFID on logistic processes with their MS EXCEL®-based calculation tool for cost benefit analysis of RFID rollouts in supply chains. The tool takes various steps in the supply chain into account and calculates the payback period of the investment. The steps considered range from the packaging supplier to the point of sale.

The Auto-ID Center developed a web-based tool for estimating the impact of RFID (Tellkamp, 2003). However, only the EPC Value Model (Lee et al., 2004) focused more on the role of manufacturers. The tool uses a cause-and-effect analysis to assess the impact of RFID on various business goals. Unlike our work this MS EXCEL®-based tool targets mainly benefits in the manufacturers supply chain rather than on the shop floor. In several survey sheets it captures basic business information about the company, information on the implementation cost, and information about the impact of RFID on expected improvements. A summary sheet presents the overall results of the cost and benefit calculations.

Still, all these methods are not tailored for RFID rollouts in the manufacturing domain, and they strongly focus on financial issues, omitting to a large extent the unquantifiable benefits and risks that RFID may have. Specialized models for RFID rollouts in the manufacturing domain have rarely been discussed so far. Automation (2004) and Chappell et al. (2003) discuss potentials of RFID on the plant floor. However, they provide no concrete equations for calculating monetary effects, do not address strategic potentials of RFID and nor do they propose a corresponding evaluation model.

In summary, existing RFID assessment approaches still do not provide a concrete method to assess the tangible and the intangible aspects of an RFID rollout in manufacturing. We address this problem by presenting a detailed guide for assessing monetary and non-monetary costs and benefits of RFID applications on the plant floor. We provide guidance to assess RFID potentials that go beyond purely operational improvements. Our method is suitable for applications in most manufacturing enterprises.

6.2 Quantifiable Costs and Benefits

In this section we first discuss quantifiable costs and benefits of RFID investments along the identified RFID use cases from Section 2.4. We structure this discussion along three parts: fixed costs, variable costs, and benefits.

One part of the fixed costs arise only in the first period T_0. These are, for instance, costs of an RFID reader R or costs for additionally needed software S. However, another part of the fixed costs are uniformly distributed between T_1 and T_n. This are in particular maintenance costs M.

Also, variable costs and benefits are basically uniformly distributed between T_1 and T_n. If the proportion of the fixed costs in comparison to the total costs in T_0 is low then a calculation of one period is sufficient, otherwise not. When conducting the calculation for more than one period the amount for each T_i with $T_0 < T_i < T_n$ must be discounted. When discounting, the correct discount rate has to be chosen. This can be done with the capital asset pricing model.

Note that the implementation of RFID has a lot in common with any generic IT project: the IT project's costs for integration, support, training, and maintenance are much higher than the actual purchase price of the required hardware and software. Therefore, the costs should be calculated with the Total Cost of Ownership (TCO) analysis (Wolf and Holm, 1998).

A complete TCO analysis spans over a specific period of time (such as 5 years) and includes expectation values for all costs to be encountered by the specific company in question. Therefore, a TCO analysis cannot be done at a general level; it has to be case specific. In this section we restrict the discussions to aspects that apply to any manufacturer.

6.2.1 Fixed Costs

Some fixed costs are common to practically all RFID applications in manufacturing. Equation 6.1 captures these costs by summing up the cost for software, hardware, training, maintenance, and system integration:

$$C_{Fixed} = S + R + N + A + O + F + M + I \tag{6.1}$$

with

A	Cost per reusable RFID tag
$C...$	Cost per reusable RFID tag
F	Cost for training staff
I	Integration cost in the introduction phase of RFID
M	Average cost per hour of maintenance
N	Cost for network technology
O	Cost per PC on the shop floor
R	Cost of an RFID reader
S	Cost for additionally needed software

Of course these fixed costs must be compared to the fixed costs of (existing or potential) alternative solutions.

If RFID is used as a replacement for an existing bar-code solution, for example, Cfixed needs to be offset by the fixed cost of the existing infrastructure.

6.2.2 Variable Cost

When considering variable costs of an RFID application, one needs to distinguish closed-loop and open-loop scenarios. In closed-loop applications, RFID tags do not remain on the product post-sale. They are recycled, typically at the point of sale, and reused in future production cycles. It is possible to compute the variable costs as the product of the expected lifetime of the application, the number of items labeled per time unit, and the cost of applying and later recycling an RFID tag:

$$C_{VarClosed} = T \times L \times (E + D + G) \qquad (6.2)$$

with

$C...$ Cost per reusable RFID tag
D Cost of removing an RFID tag from an object
E Cost of applying an RFID tag to an object
G Cost for transporting tags
L Number of items per hour labeled with RFID tags
T Expected service life of the application in hours

Note that if RFID tags are applied directly to a specific part of the product, the number of tags (L) equals the number of manufactured products per hour. However, one may also apply RFID tags to several parts of the product or to material carriers which hold more than one object. In many use cases, RFID tags could be applied to transportation units which cycle on the plant floor (*e.g.,* material carriers). In such cases, tags are applied only once.

However, the data written on the tag (or associated with the tag) must be changed in each cycle. Depending on the particular setup, this task may require manual intervention which results in variable labor costs. D refers to costs per tagged item which occur if RFID tags are removed at the end of the production process. Removing tags accounts for additional labor costs. However, no removal is necessary if tags cycle on transportation units on the plant floor.

G refers to the cost per object for transporting reusable RFID tags between the points of application and removal. Tags may just be transported within the plant floor in applications that are restricted to one plant. Yet, advanced RFID applications may span several production steps in the supply chain and tags may need to be transported between different plants.

In open-loop applications, the RFID tags are only used once and subsequently discarded (or left with the customer). In this case we adapt the calculation of variable costs as follows:

$$C_{VarOpen} = T \times L \times (E + J - K) \qquad (6.3)$$

with

$C...$	Cost per reusable RFID tag
E	Cost of applying an RFID tag to an object
J	Cost per non-reusable RFID tag
K	Cost savings per tag due to cost-sharing models or discounts
L	Number of items per hour labeled with RFID tags
T	Expected service life of the application in hours

Note that K represents cost discounts per tag due to cost sharing models or discounts. Cost-sharing models are typical of complex supply chains where RFID tags are used by several supply chain partners at once, which then share the related expenses.

6.2.3 Benefits

In the following we discuss and provide equations for all use cases for RFID listed in Table 2.2 except no. 2 (extending scan processes for quality and efficiency), because here the monetary effects cannot be quantified in a general manner.

Accelerating Scan Processes

One reason for applying RFID is to accelerate or to completely automate the scanning of identifiers. This allows reducing labor costs. Resulting total benefits can be quantified as the product of the expected application lifetime T, the number of identifiers scanned per hour Q, the time saved by RFID $(U - W)$, and the relevant labor costs P:

$$B_{AcceleratingScanProcesses} = T \times Q \times (U - W) \times P \qquad (6.4)$$

with

$B...$	Used to denote various types of benefits
P	Labor cost per hour for scanning labels
Q	Number of identifiers scanned per hour
U	Time which is needed for scanning identifiers with RFID alternatives
W	Time for scanning an RFID tag
T	Expected service life of the application in hours

Extending Scan Processes for Narrowing Recalls

Equation 6.5 estimates the monetary benefits of reducing the batch size for tracking. In the considered case, errors occur at a known single point in time and only affect a single item. Total benefits are the product of the expected application lifetime T, the error frequency X, the improvement in batch sizes $(Y - Z)$, and the cost for recalling an item n:

$$B_{NarrowingRecalls} = T \times X \times (Y - Z) \times n \qquad (6.5)$$

with

$B...$	Used to denote various types of benefits
T	Expected service life of the application in hours
X	Frequency of errors which result in a product recall
Y	Tracked batch sizes without RFID
Z	Tracked batch sizes with RFID
n	Cost for recalling an item

Reducing Paper-Based Data Management

As described above, improving data maintenance by RFID may reduce costs which result from errors in collected production data. This is because RFID can help to automate data maintenance in some applications and thereby reduce the impact of human mistakes.

Equation 6.6 captures the potential savings due to improved data maintenance, taking into account various types of data maintenance errors and related costs. For instance, wrongly configured machines may produce waste

($m \times c_m$), or forgotten bookings of finished steps may delay the production ($f \times c_f$). Furthermore, RFID may accelerate or automate data maintenance tasks, thus saving labor costs ($e \times (a - r) \times P$).

$$B_{ReducingPaperBasedDataManagement} = T \times (m \times c_m + f \times c_f + w \times c_w + e \times (b-r) \times P) \tag{6.6}$$

with

	$B...$	Used to denote various types of benefits
	P	Labor cost per hour for scanning labels
	T	Expected service life of the application in hours
	b	Time for making a data entry without RFID support
	$c...$	Used to denote various costs resulting from false or missing data entries
	e	Frequency of manual label scans
	f	Frequency of forgotten data entries
	m	Frequencies of data mix-ups
	r	Time for making a data entry with RFID support
	w	Frequency of wrong data entries

Automating Asset Tracking

Having the right assets available at the right time is crucial for seamless operation of a production plant. The expected monetary benefits can be computed as the product of the expected application lifetime T, the improvement regarding missing assets ($b - d$), and the related costs ($o + p$):

$$B_{AutomatingAssetTracking} = T \times (a - d) \times (o + p) \tag{6.7}$$

with

$B...$	Used to denote various types of benefits
T	Expected service life of the application in hours
a	Frequency that assets are missing without RFID-based tracking
d	Frequency that assets are missing with RFID-based tracking
o	Opportunity cost resulting from production downtimes
p	Penalties for delays resulting from production downtimes

Reducing Back-End Interactions

RFID allows storing data with the corresponding object rather than in back-end databases. Applications that work on data from RFID tags are less vulnerable to system failures than centralized solutions (no single point of failure). We estimate the monetary value of this effect as the product of the expected application lifetime T, the improvement regarding back-end system failures ($k \times g \times t - s \times u \times v$), and the related costs ($o + p$):

$$B_{ReducingBack-EndInteractions} = T \times (k \times g \times t - s \times u \times v) \times (o + p) \quad (6.8)$$

with

$B...$	Used to denote various types of benefits
T	Expected service life of the application in hours
g	Number of production tasks affected by a back-end system failure
k	Frequency in which back-end systems fails
o	Opportunity cost resulting from production downtimes
p	Penalties for delays resulting from production downtimes
s	Frequency of failures in an RFID-based system
t	Time back-end system failures lasts
u	Number of products affected by a failing RFID tag
v	Time until a broken RFID tag is replaced

Unifying Labels

One cost driver for printing labels are specialized multi-format printers. Another cost factor that is related to label handling, concerns the penalties for labels which cannot be read by the customers. We estimate the monetary effect as the product of the expected application lifetime T and the improvement regarding unreadable labels $((i-j) \times x)$, plus some label transportation costs $(y \times z)$:

$$B_{UnifyingLabels} = T \times ((i - j) \times x + y \times z) \qquad (6.9)$$

with

	$B...$	Used to denote various types of benefits
	T	Expected service life of the application in hours
	i	Frequency that bar-code labels are unreadable
	j	Frequency that RFID tags are unreadable
	x	Penalty per unreadable label
	y	Cost for transporting a bar-code label from the printer to a packing station
	z	Number of labels applied per hour

6.3 Non-Quantifiable Costs and Benefits

Despite the advantages of RFID, adoption by the marketplace proceeds slower than expected. Among the main reasons for not implementing RFID are the high implementation costs, *e.g.*, Ivantysynova and Ziekow (2007), and the lack of foreseeable benefits (Schmitt and Michahelles, 2008). Taken together, this often leads to a negative expected return on investment in the short and medium term. It is, however, necessary to consider not only quantifiable (tangible, monetary) aspects but also non-quantifiable, intangible benefits and costs.

Yet, another challenge in making investment decisions is to assess incorporate factors that are hard to quantify or not quantifiable at all. As we observed in the case studies this results in companies' tendency to adopt

RFID for operational improvements first. For such applications it is possible to determine the breakeven point based on the equations presented in Section 6.2. However, the potential of RFID in manufacturing goes beyond operational benefits and can be a means to achieve strategic goals (Knebel et al., 2007). In particular with increasingly tighter supply chain integration RFID may become a distinguishing factor in collaboration.

In this section, we first analyze potential operational benefits, then strategic benefits, and intangible risks and costs manufacturers have to take into account before adopting RFID. We also present a method for how to assess such intangible aspects.

6.3.1 Operational Benefits

The case studies show that operational benefits are the main driver in most RFID projects. They provide short-term positive returns on investment, which should convince every controller. However, some RFID applications can leverage additional intangible benefits on top, which may tip the scale in favor of adoption, even though the short-term ROI may be negative. We have observed the potential for such effects regarding improved *production planning (PP)*, *process optimization (PO)*, and *IT management (IT)*. Table 6.1 shows in which case studies we observed these three potentials.

Table 6.1: Intangible objectives for RFID in manufacturing.

Case Study	Operational			Strategic		
	1.PP	2.PO	3.IT	4.IQ	5.IR	6.II
AIR			√	√	√	√
CLU		√		√		√
COO			√	√	√	√
CAS	√					
CON		√				
PAC	√	√	√	√	√	

Production Planning

Production planning requires accurate information on the availability of resources. RFID enables better control of assets and materials through its tracking functionality, thus reducing loss and search times. The direct effect of this is easy to quantify. However, these applications open up new opportunities by enabling the introduction of more flexible planning methods, such as switching to shorter planning periods (case 2.3.4). The same applies to RFID-enhanced methods for material tracking and inventory management. In combination with these methods, RFID can reduce uncertainty in planning (case 2.3.6). However, the resulting benefits are rarely quantifiable beforehand.

Process Optimization

Process optimization is often a driver for RFID introduction; *e.g.*, manufacturers exploit properties of RFID (like reads without line of sight) to increase process automation and speed up manual scanning tasks (case 2.3.1, 2.3.2, 2.3.5). This kind of process optimization does not necessarily lead to intangible benefits. However, RFID can also facilitate more detailed data capturing (cases 2.3.2, 2.3.5, 2.3.6). This enhanced business intelligence might enable data analysts to get more insight into the processes and potentially reveal unexpected potentials for improvements.

IT Management

IT management in a plant is certainly affected by RFID introduction. Introducing RFID components into an existing IT landscape allows for a novel distribution of data and logic as well as for new means of data exchange. RFID-based architectures also improve the autonomy of system components (case 2.3.6), encapsulate data management tasks (case 2.3.3), and support a system's scalability (case 2.3.1). As a result, RFID may improve the robustness and availability of the production system. However, the degree of improvement is often unknown before an actual implementation takes place, thus making this benefit very hard to quantify ex-ante.

6.3.2 Strategic Benefits

The decision as to whether or not a manufacturer should adopt an RFID has impacts beyond the operations on the plant floor. Depending on the specific industry, RFID may be a distinctive factor in a company's strategy. Strategic potentials of RFID may concern *improving quality and customers' service (IQ)*, *increasing reputation (IR)*, and *improving inter-organizational collaboration (II)*. Table 6.1 shows in which case studies we observed these three strategic potentials.

Improving Quality and Customer Service

Improving quality and customer service are both important strategic means to gain an advantage over one's competitors. The introduction of RFID possibly affects the quality and the range of customer services that a manufacturer can provide to its clients. As a side effect of operational improvements, better control of shop-floor processes can improve the quality of a manufactures output. For instance, RFID-based process monitoring could enhance the detection and correction of production errors before products are shipped (case 2.3.2).

Moreover, RFID can improve production quality by helping to ensure that shipments are complete, consistently documented, and that all products passed through the production process correctly. As an additional service, the manufacturer may share the captured RFID data with its clients (case 2.3.3). This could streamline operations and leverage benefits at the client side (*e.g.*, better planning due to updates on the production status).

Another potential for additional services is to leave RFID tags on the shipped products (case 2.3.1). This leverages RFID applications at the client side. For instance, clients could benefit from RFID at their material intake. Manufacturers may also store production data on the RFID tags. This service could help clients to route products through their production and facilitate consistency checks on the plant floor (case 2.3.2, 2.3.6).

Increasing Reputation

Reputation is another strategic benefit that RFID can contribute to. A company's reputation can profit from new technology advancements – such as RFID – because the company is perceived as innovative by its business partners (case 2.3.1, 2.3.3). Additionally, RFID enables narrowing and avoiding recalls for some products (case 2.3.2), thus limiting adverse reputation effects associated with production problems.

Improving Inter-Organizational Collaboration

Inter-organizational collaboration can leverage optimization across value chains and strengthen the position of partner networks. Depending on the market structure, good positioning in such a partner network is a crucial strategic issue. RFID is developing more and more into a technology for inter-organizational collaboration. Collaboration infrastructures – such as the EPCglobal network (EPCglobal, 2007) – are increasingly based on RFID technology. Early adopters may have the opportunity to improve their strategic position in the market.

A manufacturer may strengthen its market position by offering new services that are enabled by the RFID technology. Possible options include providing detailed tracking information to clients or storing production data right at the products. In one of the case studies we already observed such a client request. Prominent examples where RFID was demanded are the supply chains of Wal-Mart and Metro. Moving towards RFID today can make a manufacturer ready to participate in RFID-driven value chains. This may become a distinguishing factor or even a requirement for getting new contracts if value chains move towards more RFID-based collaboration (Günther et al., 2006).

An RFID rollout provides the strategic option to opt into RFID-based collaboration networks and become part of RFID-enabled value chains. Dominant players in a value chain may even force their suppliers into RFID adoption (see Chapter 7). These market forces influence manufacturers as well. Thus, getting ready for RFID is of strategic importance for many manufacturers, see 2.3.1, 2.3.2, 2.3.3.

6.3.3 Risks and Costs

Any IT project bears intangible risks with associated costs that decision makers must weigh against expected benefits. In the following, we discuss specific intangible risks that are related to RFID technology. We identified three major risk categories concerning *technology integration*, *privacy and security*, and *standardization*. While these general risk categories also exist in supply chain processes, manufacturing shows different particularities within these categories. Specifically the importance of concrete risks differs from supply chain applications.

Technology Integration

Technology integration for RFID systems comprises two levels: the software level for back-end integration, and the hardware level for physical integration in the process. At the software level it is necessary to connect RFID middleware with two systems (*e.g.*, an ERP or MES, see Chapter 5). Like in any IT integration project this poses challenges: *e.g.*, in finding suitable interfaces and organizing the migration to new solutions. A special challenge of RFID data integration is data quality. Compared to identification technologies such as bar codes, RFID reads require more advanced pre-processing and filtering of the input. It is important to understand that raw RFID data can include false-positive and false-negative reads (Derakhshan et al., 2007). It is therefore crucial to define the required data quality and to implement appropriate cleaning mechanisms. This causes the demand for advanced middleware (Bornhövd et al., 2004).

Achieving the required data quality can be a serious obstacle in some projects and may pose the risk of failure. We found such challenging conditions in several of our case studies (case 2.3.1, 2.3.2, 2.3.3, 2.3.6). In many cases the products and production environments contained a lot of metal which can distort the RFID signals. Particularly in cases 2.3.2 we found different process steps in very close spatial proximity. This makes it difficult to associate the RFID reads with the correct process step.

RFID is affected by the environment, especially if metal or liquids are present. Solid objects (especially metal) can absorb and reflect RFID signals. Thus, tags may be missed or captured at positions outside the intended reader scope (*e.g.*, at a different process step). Possible effects include shielding of signals or detuning of the communication frequency. Furthermore, RFID signals may travel unexpected ways due to reflection causing readers to capture tags outside their intended scope. These properties of RFID make it necessary to test the physical integration of RFID into the production processes carefully. The same may apply if production processes are changed or physically rearranged.

Privacy and Security

Privacy and security continues to be a controversial aspect of RFID applications. Privacy concerns mainly arise in B2C markets and after-sale applications (Spiekermann and Ziekow, 2005). Depending on the application context, this has to be taken into account when implementing RFID. It may be advisable, for example, to remove or even destroy the tags at the end of the production line.

Additionally, the (in-)security of RFID data potentially jeopardize the confidentiality of business operations. Most RFID solutions are vulnerable to unauthorized reads or to eavesdropping tag-reader communication (Hancke, 2006). The possibility to read out tags without line of sight exposes RFID data to anyone who can come close to the tag (*e.g.*, staff of logistic service providers). It is therefore important to assess the confidentiality of data on RFID tags, to weigh the risks, and to possibly implement counter measures.

Beyond protecting information on RFID tags, security analysts must carefully evaluate network-based exchange of RFID data. The standards that are currently under discussion for querying RFID information sources can leak information (Fabian and Günther, 2007). Again, one must trade the confidentiality of RFID data against the security risks of the technology used. However, compared to risks regarding technology integration and technology development the risks for privacy and security are less important in the manufacturing domain.

Even though RFID-related privacy concerns mainly occur in the B2C market (Günther and Spiekermann, 2005), RFID can affect the privacy of plant-floor workers as well. Thus, workers may perceive the technology in a negative way.

Technology Development

Standardization is essential for the sustainability of an application and for leveraging network effects. The global standardization consortium GS1 plays a major role in developing standards for the RFID technology. With Gen2 GS1 has released a well-known standard for UHF tags that is already applied by major retailers. Yet, unsolved standardization questions exist until today. The authorized frequency spectra for RFID must still be harmonized and dominating standards for HF technology are still missing. Even though the standardization situation is improving, there remains a degree of uncertainty for some solutions. These aspects specifically play a role when the production process requires RFID-based information from suppliers.

Another threat of early adoption is that having RFID in place may lead to an unfavorable negotiating position for cost-sharing models. This is a threat many companies mentioned during the case studies. In such models partners in the value chain share costs of applying RFID tags if the benefits occur in several steps of the value chain. However, the manufacturer bears the risk of taking most of the cost for RFID while most of the benefits are obtained in subsequent steps of the value chain.

6.3.4 Assessment

In previous sections we have evaluated non-quantifiable, intangible aspects of RFID in manufacturing. As the reader could see, not all aspects occur in each RFID rollout. Moreover, if they occur, their importance may differ substantially. In order to assess non-quantifiable costs and benefits, we suggest a lightweight multidimensional decision model where one assigns weights to the different aspects, specific to each case. Aspects and weights are represented by a tree whose root represents the specific RFID rollout (Figure 6.2).

The nodes and leaves of the tree correspond to the non-quantifiable factors discussed above Note, that on a coarse-grained level some – yet not all – factors are also known from RFID applications in supply chain management. Furthermore, some effects in supply chain management (like improved demand forecast) cannot be achieved by using RFID on the shop floor. Therefore, the relative importance of the various aspects is domain specific. Even though in manufacturing each aspect weighs differently depending on the case, we found some general trends in the case studies. In Figure 6.2, these tendencies are denoted as ++ (for very important) + (for important), and − (for less important).

The tree should be traversed first top-down, then bottom-up. While traversing the tree, each node should be assigned with a relative importance and a score, respectively. The relative importance will typically be assigned by management, while the improvement will be evaluated by domain experts. We assign positive scores for benefits and negative scores for risks and their associated expected cost.

Traversing Top-Down

Managers proceed top-down using their corporate knowledge when assigning weights for the relative importance of each node. For example, production planning may be considered more important than IT management or process optimization. During the top-down traversal, managers assign weights to all descendant nodes in relative importance to each other by using Value Benefit Analysis (VBA), which is a common scoring model (Bernroider and Koch, 1999). The goal of the pairwise comparison method is to create a rank table among the children for each node.

Traversing Bottom-up

Subsequently, domain experts traverse the tree bottom-up and give each node a score for an expected improvement or occurring risk. They start by analyzing all leaves of the tree and assigning each leaf a score. The score denotes the impact of RFID on this particular aspect. We use a standard equidistant scale for the scores. After completing all scores for the leaves, we use the ranking data (the relative importance) created by the management. We calculate a weighted average score for each leaf. Then we assess the final score of the analyzed investment by recursively calculating the scores bottom-up; *i.e.*, for all interior nodes we multiply each child node's score with its relative importance, add the scores of all children, and pass the total score to the parent.

I calculate the overall score for the planed RFID rollout by traversing the tree both ways. An analogous approach can be used to evaluate possible alternatives, such as bar-code-based solutions. Hereby it is irrelevant whether the competing technology is already in use. If the competing technology is bar code, then the tree can be used as it is. If the RFID rollout should be compared with some other technology, like OCR, the tree would need to be adjusted accordingly.

After having evaluated competing alternatives from the perspective of non-quantifiable costs and benefits, evaluation results need to be integrated with the results from the monetary evaluation. This combined assessment then serves as the basis for the final investment decision.

6.4 How to Combine Tangible and Intangible Costs and Benefits

Integrating monetary and non-monetary assessments has always been a challenging task, due to the heterogeneity of decision-relevant factors, as well as the diversity of possible investment scenarios. In general, it is hardly possible to use one type of approach for all types of investment (Andresen, 2001). Therefore, we propose to apply different decision techniques, depending on the investment's main focus and motivation. The following investment types – adapted from Lucas (1999) – can be distinguished in the manufacturing domain:

1. Direct returns as the main investment focus: In the manufacturing domain, this is, for example, the case if RFID is implemented to accelerate scan processes. In such a case, the financial assessment is the key to the management's investment decision. Out of several proposed solutions, the one with the highest calculated return is selected. The intangible assessment is secondary and mainly focuses on the assessment of risks, which must not exceed risk limits predefined in the company's policy.

2. Indirect returns as the main investment focus: Here, the ROI is not quantifiable reliably beforehand. Examples include the implementation of RFID in manufacturing to improve the data accuracy due to more scanning points. This may help to analyze and streamline processes more effectively, which could improve a company's reputation and trust versus its suppliers and customers. In this type of investment, the management should allocate a budget for the envisaged implementation, look for implementations meeting these budget constraints, and then select the implementation with the maximum non-quantifiable evaluation score.

3. Strategic investments that open up new opportunities: As strategic aspects are of utmost relevance, the key factor for the investment decision is the strategy score determined in the non-monetary assessment (see Figure 6.2). Preferably, the alternative with the best score is selected, as long as the investment meets budgetary constraints and the risks identified are deemed as manageable. If alternative solutions have significantly different risk scores, the management is advised to do a trade-off analysis between strategic impact and risk.

4. Transformational RFID investments: These are RFID investments that facilitate a complete reorganization of manufacturing processes. In such investments, all tangible and intangible parameters may be relevant. As a result, the management needs to define minimum thresholds for all criteria. In the first step, all investment alternatives not meeting the thresholds are discarded from further evaluation. For the assessment of

the remaining solutions, decision makers may use a modified balanced scorecard approach combining the financial perspective, the operational perspective, the strategic perspective and the risks perspective.

5. RFID as unique solution to implement a functionality: In manufacturing, RFID is often the only possible solution to achieve a certain functionality (*e.g.*, to identify products reliably in dirty environments, or in environments where a line of sight cannot be achieved). Here, the key issue is how much the management is willing to pay for the RFID-enabled functionality. Therefore, in the first step, the management defines target costs not to be exceeded. In the second step, all RFID implementations meeting the defined thresholds are assessed from a non-monetary perspective. Finally, the management performs a trade-off analysis between the remaining solutions' intangible scores and their calculated financial returns.

6. Mandatory RFID investments: required by law or contracts, *e.g.*, if suppliers have to meet contractual requirements of the OEM. If the investment is mandatory, non-quantifiable aspects play a secondary role (as the investment is required anyway) and the focus of managers will be on cost reduction. In terms of the non-monetary aspects, managers will primarily look at the risks of the proposed solution and make sure that these do not exceed predefined, critical values. Out of the solutions that meet non-quantifiable risk requirements, the cheapest one is selected, unless very large differences in the non-monetary score have been determined.

In combination with the evaluation methods presented before, these guidelines offer decision makers a basis for a comprehensive RFID investment analysis in the manufacturing domain.

6.5 Conclusion

Building upon experiences from the case studies in Chapter 2, we outline the most crucial tangible and intangible risks and benefits for RFID in manufacturing. Moreover, we present an assessment scheme for tangible and intangible aspects, using value benefit analysis. The goal of our work was to develop a guideline for RFID assessments that can be applied by managers and experts in the field without lengthy training and within a reasonable time frame.

Note, however, that it is "not possible to cost the total impact of an IT project" (Costello et al., 2007). This means that investment appraisal techniques alone are unsuitable for assessing IT investments reliably (see criticism by Millis and Mercken, 2004). Nevertheless, these methods are frequently used by managers, as a survey by Bernroider and Koch (1999) revealed.

In their survey 70.6% of all decision makers used static investment appraisal techniques which do not even take into consideration the time value of money. More suitable multidimensional evaluation approaches, however, were only used in 28.5% of all cases. These figures indicate that managers are reluctant to use complex decision models and prefer simple assessment methods. Managers want models that are clear, efficient, and simple – and they strive for security, avoiding risky investments with insecure returns. Unfortunately, however, some investment decisions cannot be performed rationally using just simple models.

With our decision model for RFID rollouts in manufacturing we address these four desires – clarity, efficiency, simplicity, and security. We do so by presenting a holistic evaluation approach that takes into account both quantifiable (tangible, monetary) and non-quantifiable aspects of the investment. Our aim is to provide managers with means to estimate the benefits of RFID when making rollout decisions. We thus address the main obstacle that leads to decisions against RFID, viz., the inability to foresee concrete benefits (Schmitt and Michahelles, 2008).

The guidelines that we have developed meet clarity, efficiency and simplicity criteria. However, it is not possible to meet the reliability criterion as of now. This is not a drawback of our guidelines but inherent in the underlying investment decision problem. Little available experience with the technologies and related organizational solutions, as well as the heterogeneity of application scenarios, make a reliable assessment of tangible and intangible risks and benefits impossible.

However, by guiding managers and experts through the decision process, our approach assures that most important aspects will be reflected in the decision taken, thus reducing the remaining degree of uncertainty. In the future, when more experience with RFID applications in manufacturing becomes available, the remaining uncertainties may be reduced further, thus making RFID investments a less risky venture.

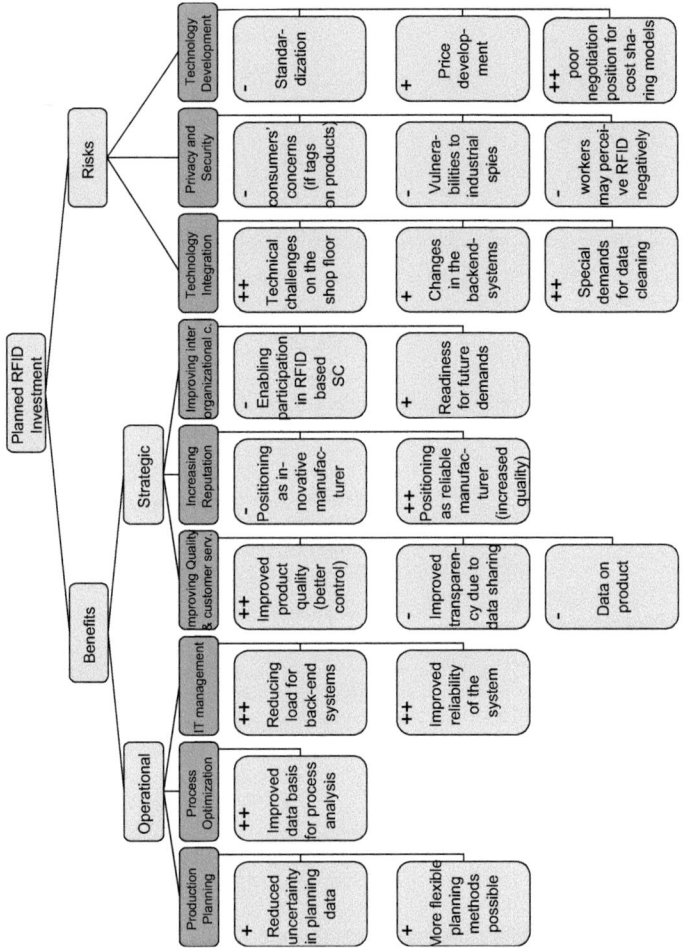

Figure 6.2: Tree classifying the non-quantifiable, intangible aspects of RFID in manufacturing.

Chapter 7

Beyond Manufacturing: RFID in the Automotive Supply Chain

In addition to closed-loop applications, RFID technology can also be implemented as an inter-organizational system (IOS) along the supply chain to ensure real-time information sharing (Sharma et al., 2007). However, besides the intra-organizational challenges of applying RFID in production processes – as described in the previous chapters – one can also observe an inter-organizational reservation of embedding RFID in supply chains. For instance, even though most OEMs and their suppliers are currently engaged in RFID-related pilot projects, which involve both internal and IOS scenarios, the technology has not yet made the decisive step from the meeting room to real-life implementations. It is therefore valuable to understand which factors influence RFID adoption in the automotive industry.

I conducted this work together with Hanna Krasnova and Lorenz Weser. Lorenz Weser has conducted the ten interviews during his master thesis in 2007. The results of this chapter have been published in Krasnova et al. (2008).

Building on existing inter-organizational system adoption models (*e.g.*, Chwelos et al., 2001; Sharma et al., 2007) tailored to RFID specifics we identify important determinants of an RFID adoption decision. Our investigation has an explorative nature and is based on ten interviews conducted with executives from the automotive industry (3 OEMs and 7 suppliers).

The next section provides an overview of existing research on the adoption and diffusion of inter-organizational systems. Section 7.2 describes factors which potentially play a role in RFID adoption decisions in the automotive industry. In Section 7.3 we present our research method and the results of the conducted interviews. Section 7.4 concludes this chapter.

7.1 Related Work

Strassner and Fleisch (2003) consider the value of RFID applications to be even higher if the technology is introduced in a collaborative manner. Similar to Sharma et al. (2007), we view driving forces for adoption of RFID for internal use to be a sub-group of factors relevant for RFID introduction in an inter-organizational context.

In the past few decades, a large number of researchers have attempted to identify the factors influencing IOS adoption. For instance, Iacovou et al. (1995) have studied the impact of perceived benefits, organizational readiness and external pressure on the electronic data interchange (EDI) adoption among small firms.

Based on the work from Iacovou et al. (1995), Chwelos et al. (2001) have empirically studied the impact of various factors on EDI adoption decisions. They have shown that perceived benefits of the EDI, organizational readiness factors (such as financial resources), IT sophistication and trading partner readiness as well as the two external pressure factors competitive pressure and enacted trading partner power, are significant determinants of EDI adoption.

Sharma et al. (2007) have applied the model from Chwelos et al. (2001) to the RFID context and qualitatively assessed it. The study shows that technology-related factors such as perceived benefits and costs as well as the dominant partner pressure are the main determinants behind RFID adoption. Additionally, Whitaker et al. (2007) provide empirical evidence that IT integration and firm size are significant determinants of RFID adoption.

There also exist studies which specifically explore RFID adoption decisions in the automotive industry (*e.g.*, Schmitt et al., 2007; Fleisch et al., 2004; Strassner, 2005). For example, Schmitt et al. (2007) have singled out technological factors, such as compatibility, costs, complexity of the technology and its implementation as well as top-management (TM) support, as relevant RFID adoption drivers for the automotive industry.

Most of these studies are either technology-centric or mainly concentrate on internal RFID application scenarios. However, Strassner (2005) provides a comprehensive analysis of RFID potentials in the automotive industry in the collaborative context. We build on his study and explore RFID adoption dynamics in the supply chain of the automotive industry through the lens of a technology adoption model in the B2B context. Thereby we take a broader view of supply chain relations and their dependencies.

7.2 Toward an RFID Adoption Model in the Automotive Industry

In order to structure and subsequently analyze the conducted interviews, we take the model of Sharma et al. (2007) and adjust it for the automotive industry. Sharma et al. (2007) have classified the potential adoption drivers along four dimensions: technology-related, organizational readiness, external environment, and inter-organizational pressure factors.

I adjust potentially relevant factors for each dimension, as shown in Figure 7.1 and describe each factor in the following.

7.2.1 Technology-Related Factors

I see perceived benefits and technology uncertainty as important technology-related determinants of RFID adoption. Therefore, we now discuss both in detail.

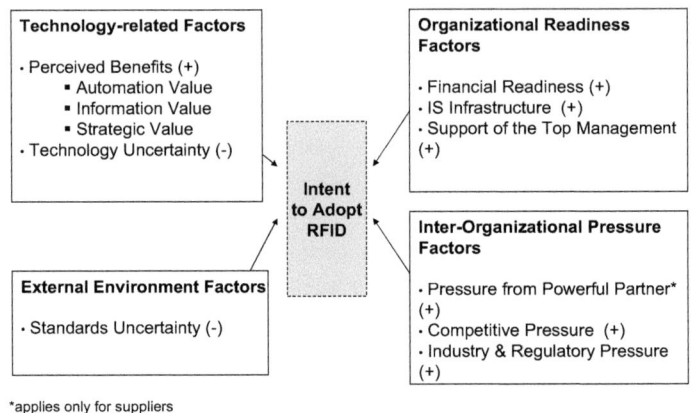

Figure 7.1: Exploratory RFID adoption model based on Sharma et al. (2007).

Perceived Benefits

Perceived benefits were consistently found to have a significant positive effect on the intention to adopt IOS technology (*e.g.*, Chwelos et al., 2001; Iacovou et al., 1995; Premkumar and Ramamurthy, 1995). For the purposes of our study we differentiate between automation, information and strategic benefits of RFID. Automation benefits arise when efficiency gains or cost savings (*i.e.*, labor costs) are achieved resulting from automation of previously non-automated processes.

Information value can be created through improved transparency of processes in the enterprise and along the supply chain, *e.g.*, improved inventory visibility. Strategic benefits result from a potential first-mover advantage as well as innovation-leader acknowledgment. For example, an original equipment manufacturer (OEM) might aspire to the innovator image, similar to METRO AG in the retailing industry.

Technology Uncertainty

Schmitt et al. (2007) single out technology uncertainty factors, such as compatibility and complexity as relevant impediments of RFID adoption in the automotive industry. Due to the characteristics of RF signals the readability of RFID tags depends on the environment (Finkenzeller, 2003). Consequently, all RFID applications need to be sorely tested and the downstream software system – capturing the data – may need to be adjusted to deal with incomplete or false data.

7.2.2 Organizational Readiness Factors

Organizational readiness factors encompass, but are not limited to, financial readiness, information systems (IS) infrastructure as well as the support of the top management. We discuss all three factors in the following.

Financial Readiness

Financial readiness has consistently been found to be positively linked to the intent to adopt IOS (*e.g.*, Chwelos et al., 2001) and implies having enough resources to pay for the technology. Financial readiness is especially crucial for suppliers, because they have to bear the costs of necessary changes in the infrastructure, the production process, and the RFID hardware costs, see Chapter 6. The suppliers' financial readiness can be supported through appropriate cost-benefit-sharing schemes with OEMs (Strassner and Fleisch, 2003; Iacovou et al., 1995). OEM's investment is limited to installing a reader infrastructure and having RFID integration costs (Strassner and Fleisch, 2003).

Information Systems Infrastructure

(Sharma et al., 2007, p.7) define information systems infrastructure readiness as "firm possessing appropriate technology infrastructure, people and expertise to support easy adoption". An advanced IT infrastructure has been consistently found to be a significant positive determinant of IOS adoption (*e.g.*, Chwelos et al., 2001; Premkumar and Ramamurthy, 1995).

Top-Management Support

Introduction of RFID is associated with significant financial investments and costly process changes and therefore can be a strategic decision requiring top-management support. We consistently found top-management support to be a significant positive determinant of IOS adoption (*e.g.*, Premkumar and Ramamurthy, 1995).

7.2.3 External Environment Factors

Sharma et al. (2007) have additionally pointed out RFID-specific external environment factors such as standards convergence and privacy concerns. Whereas privacy discussion mainly concerns daily consumer goods (*e.g.*, Rothensee. and Spiekermann, 2008), RFID standards convergence is an intensively debated issue in the automotive industry. Standards uncertainty (data on tag vs. data on network) can be an impediment of RFID adoption.

7.2.4 Inter-Organizational Pressure Factors

According to Sharma et al. (2007), RFID-related external pressure can take the following forms: competitive pressure, pressure from powerful partners or industry organizations. All three pressure factors are discussed in the following.

Competitive Pressure

Competitive pressure in the automotive industry can take two appearances. On the one hand, sheer competition intensity at both OEM and suppliers' levels can induce organizations to adopt RFID to gain competitive edge. On the other hand, competitive pressure can manifest itself in the organizational desire not to be left behind if the rest of the industry adopts the technology (*e.g.*, Premkumar and Ramamurthy, 1995; Chwelos et al., 2001) have shown that competitive pressure is a relevant factor of EDI adoption. On the contrary, Sharma et al. (2007) have not found any evidence that RFID adoption is driven by the competitive pressure.

Pressure from Powerful Partners

Pressure from powerful partners can be an important determinant of RFID adoption for the suppliers, who often perceive net benefits of the technology as negative. Hart and Saunders (1997) differentiate between persuasive and coercive approaches to power *exercise*. A persuasive approach can, for example, take the form of information exchange and recommendations with the aim to change the perception of the supplier towards RFID (Frazier and Summers, 1984). Furthermore, *coercive* approaches focus on punishment and threats. Whether and which type of influence strategy is exercised depends on the type of relationship between partners.

Hart and Saunders (1997) state that coercive power is often applied in situations when suppliers can be exchanged easily. For example, upstream the automotive supply chain, producers of low-cost spare parts can be exchanged without difficulty due to low sophistication of their products. However, not all suppliers can be replaced in such an easy manner.

Due to increasing outsourcing trends and therefore growing reliance of OEMs on supplier's expertise, successful collaboration and coordination becomes the key to market success (Kalmbach and Kleinhans, 2004). Supplier's expertise (*expert power*) is becoming the most important determinant of their bargaining position against OEMs. (Crook and Combs, 2006, p. 547) even suggest "that stronger firms forbear [from the] use of bargaining power when exercising it [...] would threaten the chain's ability to coordinate". Thus, when a relationship with a particular supplier is important for the OEM, persuasive sources of power will be preferred (Frazier and Summers, 1984).

Industry and Regulatory Pressure

This type of pressure manifests itself in certain regulations which promote technology use. For example, the US TREAD Act obligates OEMs to assure transparency of the production processes. Such regulations can facilitate RFID adoption along automotive supply chains.

7.3 Method and Results

Taking into account the early stage of RFID adoption, we choose an explorative approach to fulfill the aim of our study. We conduct ten interviews: three with OEMs and seven with suppliers at different tiers. We interview high-level executives with relevant RFID and supply chain management expertise. All interviews were conducted in Germany between September and November 2007, either personally or by telephone. Each interview took between 18 and 93 minutes.

Despite a commonly low sample size and resulting lack of generalizability, research interviews are a widespread instrument of qualitative research. We adopt this method because of the explorative nature of the subject. Moreover, due to the personal nature of interviews as opposed to surveys, we are able to collect opinions and impressions rather than just clear facts.

We structure the interviews along the lines of the model described above. We ask the participants about their current RFID experiences, RFID benefits in internal and IOS applications, as well as the main factors of their RFID adoption decision. The analysis of the interviews allows the above-suggested RFID adoption model to be modified, as shown in Figure 7.2.

All excerpts from the interviews are translated from German into English. In the following we first describe each participant and then discuss each factor from OEMs' and suppliers' viewpoints. Tables 7.1 and 7.2 provide an extracted summary of the interviews. In Table 7.1 we depict the RFID standing of the company: whether they have RFID pilots or also real-life implementations. Moreover, one can see on what their adoption decision mainly and secondarily depends on, and why they intended to adopt RFID.

OEM 1's position to the suppliers is that they first want to the suppliers to voluntarily participate in pilots; using their persuasive power. Later coercion may also be possible. OEM 1 thinks that RFID is beneficial for both sides; seeing cost-benefit sharing as a possible opportunity. Here the competitive

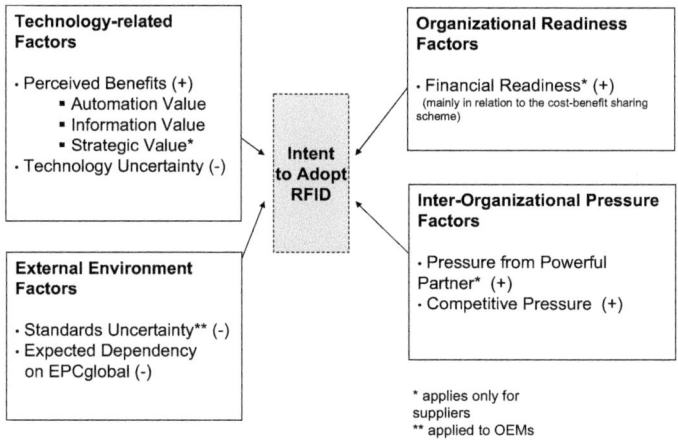

Figure 7.2: Exploratory RFID adoption model based on interview results.

pressure on suppliers supersedes OEM's coercive power. Additionally, this OEM sees that the supplier might be negatively impacted if EPC becomes a standard.

OEM 2 thinks that RFID is beneficial for both sides. He does not intend to apply cost-benefit-sharing models for the long-term. OEM 3 also shares the opinion that RFID is beneficial for both sides. Furthermore, he thinks that the main driver for the suppliers is competitive pressure.

Supplier 1 belongs to the first tier: systems integration. He develops electronics and entertainment systems. Supplier 2 is a first- as well as second-tier supplier: systems integration and developer. They produce car bodies and chassis frames. Supplier 3 manufactures brakes, steering, suspensions, and safety systems. Therefore they belong to the developers in the second tier. Supplier 4 is also a second-tier supplier, developing interior air-conditioning systems. Supplier 5 and 6 are both in the first tier: 5 produces tires, and 6 car bodies and chassis frames. Supplier 6 does not belong to the second tier;

his customers are only OEMs. Supplier 7 is a first- and third-tier supplier, having as customers both the OEMs and second-tier suppliers. He produces components for engines, transmissions, and power trains.

7.3.1 Technology-related Factors

The interviews show that both previously discussed technology-related factors – technology uncertainty and perceived benefits – are relevant. Nevertheless, the strategic value from the perceived benefits only applies to suppliers. We discuss perceived benefits for OEMs and suppliers separately.

Perceived Benefits for Original Equipment Manufacturers

All OEMs in the sample pointed out benefits of RFID as the most important adoption driver. All respondents were asked to rank automation (A), information (I) and strategic (S) benefits of RFID. All OEMs ranked automation benefits higher than information benefits. OEMs see most automation benefits in the process optimization through time and labor cost reductions: *"Bar codes had to be placed under a bar code scanner, and there were workers who managed the check-out gate [...]. We reduced costs by cutting down almost ten workers [through RFID]"*.

Nevertheless, information benefits which RFID can provide along the supply chain are also in the focus of the OEMs. Information value was stressed in the context of traceability and process documentation: *"Again and again it happens that suppliers say they don't have our containers any more. But according to our calculations, there should be enough(...)"* or: *"Our vision is: when the car is completely assembled, to see at an electronic glance that all parts in the car are appropriate"*.

Being an "innovation leader" was not the main motivation for the OEMs: *"RFID has never been an end in itself"*. This is despite the fact that OEMs recognize that RFID can potentially cut costs and improve their competitive position.

Perceived Benefits for Suppliers

All OEMs implied that RFID can bring mutual benefits to them as well as their suppliers: *"Normally, the reasons for "lost" containers can be found at both sides; looking for them costs time, resources, and a lot of money"*. However, most of the suppliers in our interviews evaluated RFID benefits to be too low or absent, especially compared to the costs: *"We don't see any radical advantages, so that the investments into hardware and software implementation are worth it"*.

Despite their importance for the financial plausibility of the investment, only suppliers 3, 5 and 6, who had a relatively strong market position, recognized that perceived benefits would be the most important criteria in their adoption decision. Interestingly, when asked to rank specific RFID benefits, three out of five suppliers placed automation before information benefits. This result is unexpected, because automation benefits are usually derived in internal applications. Conversely they all reported having a low internal value from RFID. Informational benefits of RFID were seen in the area of process documentation and traceability: *"Our customer demands that we are able to relate which component is placed into which module"*.

Some suppliers saw RFID introduction as a strategic investment into their relationship with the OEM. Suppliers who adopt RFID can potentially be evaluated as more trustworthy by the OEM and therefore can hope for more cooperation: *"There is more trust in collaboration with those suppliers who already use RFID. Others have to prove that they are able to fulfill our [the OEM's] requirements"*. Similarly, mutual investment into RFID infrastructure might create higher switching costs for the OEM and therefore bind it: *"RFID represents strategic value when one cooperates better with the OEM, for example when both invest into hardware, which can be seen as a specific investment."*

Technology Uncertainty

RFID adoption is still hindered by physical problems in some areas: *"The question is how exact the tag stability and readability is. If we cannot assure it, we won't do it"*. Similarly, one OEM recognized: *"At the moment, we are in a learning phase. We are running the first RFID projects to see if it makes sense to continue with this technology. Actually we want to know if the technology is even mature"*. Two suppliers could also predict possible readability issues.

7.3.2 Organizational Readiness Factors

We have evaluated that for OEMs organizational readiness factors do not play an important role. However, suppliers mentioned financial readiness as an important factor for RFID adoption. Many of them see no benefits in RFID but have to finance it. Interestingly only some low- and moderately dependent suppliers (3, 5 and 6) explicitly mentioned high costs of RFID introduction. To alleviate the problem of high investments, many suppliers expect the OEM to partly share the costs of RFID introduction. This is independent of their OEM's dependency: *"If OEM says, we want you to introduce RFID, we will do so. But we will then negotiate price with them. At the end it is their requirement"*.

Although OEMs generally agree to support their suppliers during pilots, their support will diminish or stop after the pilot phase ends: *"If we want to use RFID permanently after the pilot phase and we would have to provide all suppliers with the hardware [...] then all cost savings will be gone"*.

7.3.3 External Environment Factors

Based on the literature review we have identified uncertainty about standards as an external environment factor. The interviews have shown that OEMs are indeed negatively influenced by standards uncertainty. Their absence is an obvious impediment of RFID introduction: *"When we later adopt the new standards [...], we would be confronted with huge IT problems [in our company]"*.

Additionally, expected dependency on EPCglobal emerged as an impediment of RFID adoption. EPC dependency risks represent a two-sided problem. Some OEMs do not want to depend on EPC: *"I want cryptography on the tag that allows me to identify if the parts inside the car are original. I don't want to use any IT infrastructure [...]"*.

Furthermore, adoption of EPC standard might result in extra costs for suppliers who have to buy identification number area from EPCglobal. This can become a significant financial burden for small suppliers: *"The identification number area will impact suppliers considerably"*.

7.3.4 Inter-Organizational Pressure Factors

The interviews show that industry and regulatory pressure factors have no significant relevance. However, pressure from powerful partners and competitive pressure do play a role.

Pressure from Powerful Partner

This is a decisive factor of RFID introduction for OEM-dependent suppliers (1, 2). They feel that they have no choice but to adopt RFID, if the OEM demands it: *"If OEM demands RFID introduction, we will for sure do so"*.

Suppliers (3, 4, 5) with a better bargaining position saw estimated benefits of RFID as an important factor in their decision to adopt. Even so, these suppliers acknowledged that their OEMs still remain their customer. Thus, his wishes are to be respected: *"If for example an OEM sends a request regarding RFID, then we have a different situation"*. Suppliers in this category expected the OEM to share upcoming RFID-related costs with them: *"If OEMs say: we would like you to introduce RFID – no bar code any more – then it will be done. [...] but we can conduct price negotiations. At the end of the day it is their requirement and it has its costs"*.

Suppliers in the third category (6, 7) viewed themselves as an equal partner with their OEM either due to their size or unique expert power. These suppliers were mainly guided by estimated benefits and competitive pressure in their decision to introduce RFID. For example, supplier 6 mentioned that they *"would invest into RFID introduction and process re-engineering once OEMs show RFID benefits to them"*.

Despite differences in the dependency structure between interviewed suppliers, most of them expected the OEM to adopt a persuasive approach first: *"Such things are medium-term and long-term strategies. As a rule they are clearly communicated, so that one can prepare oneself for the new business model"*. Only supplier 1 did not have illusions regarding its role in the RFID adoption process. Answering the question of whether an *"OEM is likely to recommend RFID adoption kindly!"*, he answered: *"I have never experienced it in this form. There are clear requirements, which state that this and that information should be placed at the deliverables. And we simply have to fulfill it. There is no other alternative"*.

The OEMs were also asked how they plan to enforce RFID adoption at their suppliers. Being in the pilot phase now OEMs are trying to win the suppliers on their side by using persuasive influences: *"We have to persuade our colleagues in the motor-producing factories that they will also have value added [from RFID]. [...] Gradually we can win more suppliers by showing the savings that can be achieved along the supply chain"*.

Coercive power is not applied at the moment: *"We try to win the suppliers [...]. At the moment we don't coerce them to adopt RFID"*. Once the value of RFID has been proved in the pilot projects, OEMs are likely to request RFID for the next contract: *"Once we persuade ourselves that RFID makes sense and offers a lot of benefits for all, but we have partners who are not on the same line, then we will say: we demand this"*. Most OEMs confirmed that if, in this case, their demands are not met, they are likely to change the supplier for the next contract.

Competitive Pressure

Competitive pressure was an important factor for OEMs and as well as suppliers. Throughout the interviews OEMs recognized high cost pressure indicating intensive competition. One OEM stated that competitive pressure will be the main factor for suppliers to adopt RFID so that no coercive influence is necessary: *"the pressure is already so high that people start to go in this direction by themselves [...] without the need to use the "brutal brute force" [coercive power]"*. This potential rotation threat also translates into competitive pressure for the suppliers: *"Since most suppliers know quite well that RFID will come sooner or later, they are currently preparing themselves, so that they do not fall behind the competition"*.

Supplier 7 saw no internal benefits of RFID. Nevertheless, he will be ready to introduce it due to competitive pressure: *"When one of our customers asks for RFID, it is a signal for us that the trend is going in this direction. As [...] at some point another customer will come, and then the third and the fourth"*.

7.4 Conclusion

In this chapter we analyzed RFID adoption dynamics in the automotive industry. We show that perceived benefits, technology uncertainty, pressure from a powerful partner as well as competitive pressure play an important role in RFID diffusion in the automotive industry. Moreover, dependency on the organization for defining RFID standards – EPCglobal – emerged as an additional determinant of RFID adoption decision. For OEMs standards uncertainty is an industry-wide impediment. Financial readiness of the suppliers was mentioned mainly in relation to cost-benefit-sharing schemes. Other determinants, such as top-management support, were mentioned only sporadically.

In our interviews we found that OEMs consider competitive pressure as a self-enforcing mechanism for RFID diffusion at suppliers. This will make the exercise of coercive power by OEMs redundant. Being primarily motivated by perceived benefits OEMs persuade suppliers to find meaningful RFID applications at their site.

However, only two suppliers with a relatively strong market position recognized that perceived benefits would be a key determinant in their decision to adopt RFID. Some suppliers consider pressure from the OEM as the key adoption determinant, independent of their RFID benefits. Moreover, once OEMs fully recognize the usefulness of RFID in collaborative scenarios, they will demand it coercively. But until now they prefer to use persuasive power.

Finally, cooperation in common RFID projects creates more trust between partners and increases the supplier's chances of gaining future contracts.

From our study we see the following implications for an RFID adoption in the automotive industry. The use of a coercive approach could be redundant because of the market-driven RFID adoption among many suppliers. This is also the reason why OEMs could promote their RFID activities more openly and already integrate suppliers at early stages. Furthermore, suppliers should adopt a more global view when considering RFID adoption. Suppliers implementing RFID now can gain an early-mover competitive advantage by developing higher trust in their relationship with the OEM as well as accumulating unique expertise in this area.

Our study furthermore shows that RFID adoption can be accelerated and further enhanced by cost-benefit-sharing arrangements, such as, for example, cross payments or non-monetary compensation. This is not contingent upon the level of supplier dependency. However, the forms which these arrangements should take is subject to further research.

Summing up, our key findings are that the use of a coercive approach by the OEM could be redundant because of the market-driven RFID adoption among many suppliers. Furthermore, suppliers implementing RFID can now gain an early-mover competitive advantage by developing higher trust in their relationship with the OEM as well as accumulating unique expertise in this area.

Table 7.1: Summary of Interview Results with OEMs

OEM	RFID: PILOT	RFID: REAL-LIFE	1. ADOPTION DECISION DEPENDS ON	2. ADOPTION DECISION DEPENDS ON	INTEND TO ADOPT RFID
1	✓ intra and IOS	✓ intra and IOS	Perceived benefits: A<I<S	Industry and regulatory pressure (Traceability) Top-management support Technology uncertainty	Evaluating Preparing Integrating diverse suppliers
2	✓ intra and IOS	✓ intra and IOS	Perceived benefits: S<A<I Strategic competitive advantage with increased visibility	Technology uncertainty	Evaluating Preparing Integrating few suppliers
3	✓ intra	✓ intra	Perceived benefits: A=I>S Standards		Evaluating Preparing Waiting

Table 7.2: Summary of interview results with the automotive suppliers.

Sup.	Dependency on OEM	Estimated RFID Benefits	Adoption Decision Depends on	Expectation Towards OEM
1	High	Low I>A>S	Pressure from OEM	OEM will use coercive and persuasive power. Cost-benefit sharing is expected
2	High	Low	Pressure from OEM Industry pressure Technology readiness (incompatibility)	Technology uncertainty
3	Moderate	Medium A>S>I	Perceived benefits Pressure from OEM	Cost-benefit sharing is expected.
4	Moderate	Low A>I>S	Perceived benefits Pressure from OEM	
5	Moderate	Low A>I>S	Perceived benefits Pressure from key customers Competitive pressure Technology readiness (incompatibility)	
6	Low	Potentially high I>S>A	Perceived benefits	OEM will initiate RFID introduction using persuasive power.
7	Low	Low	Competitive pressure	Expects persuasive power (information sharing) from OEMs.

Chapter 8
Conclusion

This thesis evaluates the use of RFID in the manufacturing industry. Based on case studies we analyze seven use cases for RFID. They occurred frequently during our evaluation and are typically either a replacement of bar-code technology or an application that can only be realized using RFID. These RFID use cases are: accelerating scan processes, extending scan processes for quality and efficiency, extending scan processes for narrowing recalls, reducing paper-based data management, automating asset tracking, reducing back-end interactions, and unifying labels.

However, despite all the potential benefits these use cases promise, RFID technology is not yet widely adopted in intra-enterprise applications. This is because manufacturers face various challenges when embedding RFID into shop-floor processes. This includes physical hindrances on the shop floor as well as software issues, and the difficulty to evaluate quantifiable and non-quantifiable costs and benefits of RFID investments beforehand.

Hostile physical conditions on the shop floor or the presence of metal can be solved using appropriate hardware. Concerning software issues, companies need to integrate RFID into their existing IT infrastructures. Only a tight integration with existing ERP and MES facilitates that RFID leads to concrete and local productivity improvements. Integrating RFID data into IT-enabled business processes results in a more precise match of the shop floor with the companies' IT processes. This leads to more visibility about production processes; permitting faster adaptations to production variations. Additionally, the software has to be robust and scalable for handling the processing of RFID data streams. Thus, besides the evaluation of RFID use cases, another contribution of this thesis is the identification of RFID-specific constraints that IT infrastructures in manufacturing have to provide. An additional contribution is to give guidelines for the construction of IT infrastructures that satisfy these constraints.

By conducting seven more case studies we evaluated that IT implementations following the ISA-S95 standard and most IT infrastructures in practice differ. Most of the analyzed companies do not follow the ISA-S95 standard. Nevertheless, the seven case studies show that all infrastructures still share common functionalities and software components. It was even possible to at least partially match their IT infrastructures to this standard. This means that manufacturers share common parts in their IT infrastructure even though their productions differ in diverse ways. This enabled us to generally describe – along the well-defined ISA-S95 standard – common functionalities which have to be implemented for an integration of RFID technology.

We evaluated how and where RFID-specific requirements should be deployed in IT infrastructures specific to the manufacturing sector. Overall, the design guidelines comprise which functional components the IT has to provide for RFID, which interfaces and interactions with external components are needed, and which RFID-specific technologies have to be implemented. Moreover, we developed guidance on how to decide where RFID data should be integrated in the four layers of IT infrastructures.

Another impediment of RFID adoption is the lack of dedicated models for evaluating costs and benefits of an RFID rollout. This concerns especially the intangible, non-quantifiable aspects of such an investment. Therefore, this thesis provides guidance for assessing both the quantifiable and the non-quantifiable aspects of RFID in manufacturing.

The analysis is based upon experiences from the RFID case studies. The thesis outlines the most crucial tangible and intangible risks and benefits. We also present an assessment scheme to assess tangible and intangible aspects, using value-benefit analysis. The approach assures that the most important aspects will be reflected in the decision taken, thus reducing the remaining degree of uncertainty.

Furthermore, the RFID use cases also reveal that manufactures' motives for an RFID adoption are operational uses within manufacturers' enterprises. Five out of the six evaluated companies would like to use this technology mainly to improve processes and productivity on the shop floor. Motivations to use RFID as a strategic enabler of data exchange between enterprises along the supply chain were found much less frequently. However, this focus on operational, intra-enterprise applications fails to exploit the full potential of RFID technology.

A hindrance when considering RFID introduction in a supply chain is that costs and benefits are not always correlated. Some participating companies may incur considerable costs that outweigh the local benefits, and vice versa. This can lead to a classical prisoner's dilemma: It could well be possible that an existing supply chain could benefit from introducing RFID technology. These gains, however, are never realized because some participants would need to incur costs that are not justifiable in comparison to their local benefits. As a result, they decide – for completely rational reasons – not to adopt the new technology.

Therefore, we also conducted ten semi-structured interviews with OEMs and suppliers analyzing if and how this deadlock not to adopt RFID in supply chains could be resolved.

We show that RFID adoption can be accelerated and further enhanced by cost-benefit sharing arrangements, such as, for example, cross payments or non-monetary compensation. This is not contingent upon the level of supplier dependency. However, the forms these arrangements should take are subject to further research.

Perceived benefits, technology uncertainty, pressure from a powerful partner as well as competitive pressure play an important role in RFID diffusion in the automotive industry. Moreover, dependency on the non-profit standardization EPCglobal emerged as an additional determinant of the RFID adoption decision. For OEMs standards uncertainty is an industry-wide impediment.

We could also observe that cooperation in common RFID projects creates more trust between partners and increases suppliers' chances of gaining future contracts from their OEMs. If OEMs more openly promoted their RFID activities and communicated that they give RFID-interested suppliers privilege treatment, suppliers would be more encouraged to talk about their RFID motivations. OEMs and suppliers could then solve upcoming hindrances collectively.

If manufacturers implement RFID now, they can gain an early-mover competitive advantage by developing higher trust in their relationship with the OEM as well as accumulating unique expertise in this area.

Bibliography

Abadi, D., D. Carney, U. Çetintemel, M. Cherniack, C. Convey, C. Erwin, E. Galvez, M. Hatoun, A. Maskey, A. Rasin, A. Singer, M. Stonebraker, N. Tatbul, Y. Xing, R. Yan, and S. Zdonik (2003). Aurora: A data stream management system. In *Proceedings of the ACM SIGMOD International Conference on Management of Data*, pp. 666.

Andresen, J. (2001). *A Framework for Selecting an IT Evaluation Method – in the Context of Construction*. Ph. D. thesis, Danmarks Tekniske Universitet, Lyngby, Denmark.

Angeles, R. (2005). RFID technologies: Supply-chain applications and implementation issues. *Information Systems Management 22*(1), 51–65.

Arasu, A., S. Babu, and J. Widom (2006). The CQL continuous query language: semantic foundations and query execution. *The VLDB Journal 15*(2), 121–142.

Arasu, A., B.Babcock, S. Babu, M. Datar, K. Ito, R. Motwani, I. Nishizawa, U. Srivastava, D. Thomas, R. Varma, and J. Widom (2003). STREAM: The stanford stream data manager. *IEEE Data Eng. Bull. 26*(1), 19–26.

Auto-ID-Center (2002). Technology guide. Technical report, Auto-ID Center.

Automation, R. (2004). RFID in manufacturing. Technical report, Rockwell Automation.

Babu, S. and J. Widom (2001). Continuous queries over data streams. *SIGMOD Record 30*(3), 109–120.

Bernroider, E. and S. Koch (1999). Empirische Untersuchung der Entscheidungsfindung bei der Auswahl betriebswirtschaftlicher Standardsoftware in österreichischen Unternehmen. In H. Hansen and W. Janko (Eds.), *Diskussionspapiere zum Tätigkeitsfeld Informationsverarbeitung und Informationswirtschaft*, Volume 20, Wien, Austria.

Bornhövd, C., T. Lin, S. Haller, and J. Schaper (2004). Integrating automatic data acquisition with business processes – experiences with SAP's Auto-ID infrastructure. In *Proceedings of the VLDB – Very Large Data Bases*, pp. 1182–1188.

Bozdag, E., R. Ak, and T. Koç (2007). Development of a justification tool for advanced technologies: An example for RFID. In *Proceedings of RFID Eurasia*, pp. 1–4.

Brandl, D. (2000). ANSI/ISA-95.00.01 enterprise-control system integration part 1: Models and terminology. Technical report, ISA Research Triangle Park, North Carolina, USA.

Brandl, D. (2001). ANSI/ISA-95.00.02 enterprise-control system integration part 2: Object model attributes. Technical report, ISA Research Triangle Park, North Carolina, USA.

Brandl, D. (2005). ANSI/ISA-95.00.03 enterprise control system integration part 3: Activity models of manufacturing operations management. Technical report, ISA Research Triangle Park, North Carolina, USA.

Brusey, J., C. Floekermeier, M. Harrison, and M. Fletcher (2003). Reasoning about uncertainty in location identification with RFID. In *Proceedings of the Workshop on Reasoning with Uncertainty in Robotics at IJCAI*.

Chang, Y., D. McFarlane, R. Koh, C. Floerkmeier, and L. Putta (2002). Methodologies for integrating Auto-ID data with existing manufacturing business information systems. Technical report, Auto-ID Labs.

Chappell, G., L. Ginsburg, P. Schmidt, J. Smith, and J. Tobolski (2003). Auto-ID on the line: The value of Auto-ID technology in manufacturing. Technical report, Auto-ID Center.

Chwelos, P., I. Benbasat, and A. Dexter (2001). Research report: Empirical test of an EDI adoption model. *Information Systems Research 12*, 304–321.

Coral8 (2006). Complex event processing: Ten design patterns. Technical report, Coral8 Inc.

Costello, P., A. Sloane, and R. Moreton (2007). IT evaluation frameworks – do they make a valuable contribution? A critique of some of the classic models for use by SMEs. *The Electronic Journal Information Systems Evaluation 10*(1), 57–64.

Cox, J. C., S. Ross, and M. Rubinstein (19791). Option pricing: a simplified approach. *Journal of Financial Economics 7*(3), 229–263.

Cox, P. and J. Camps (2002). Regulation (ec) no 178/2002 of the european parliament and of the council of january 2002 – laying down the general principles and requirements of food law, establishing the european food safety authority and laying down procedures in matters of food safety. *Official Journal of the European Communities 31*, 1–24.

Crook, T. and J. Combs (2006). Sources and consequences of bargaining power in supply chains. *Journal of Operations Management 25*(2), 546–555.

Curtin, J., R. Kauffman, and F. Riggins (2007). Making the most out of RFID technology: a research agenda for the study of adoption, usage and impact of RFID. *Information Technology and Management 8*(2), 87–110.

DeJong, C. (1998). Material handling tunes in. *Automotive Manufacturing and Production 110(7)*, 66–69.

DeLone, W. H. and E. McLean (2003). The DeLone and McLean model of information systems success: A ten-year update. *Journal of Management Information Systems 19*(4), 9–30.

Derakhshan, R., M. Orlowska, and X. Li (2007). RFID data management: Challenges and opportunities. In *Proceedings of the IEEE International Conference on RFID*.

Dubey, P. (2006). Tagging the supply chain. *SAP INFO 141*.

EPCglobal (2005). EPC generation 1 tag data standards version 10 1.1 rev.1.27, standard specification. Technical report, EPCglobal powered by GS1.

EPCglobal (2006). EPCglobal tag data standards version 1.3. Technical report, EPCglobal powered by GS1.

EPCglobal (2007). EPCIS standard version 1.0. Technical report, EPCglobal powered by GS1.

Fabian, B. and O. Günther (2007). Distributed ONS and its impact on privacy. In *Proceedings of the IEEE International Conference on Communications*.

Farbey, B., F. Land, and D. Targett (1995). A taxonomy of information systems applications: the benefits' evaluation ladder. *European Journal of Information Systems 4*(1), 41–50.

Finkenzeller, K. (2003). *RFID Handbook: Fundamentals and Applications in Contactless Smart Cards and Identification* (2nd ed.). New York, NY, USA: John Wiley and Sons, Inc.

Fleisch, E., J. Ringbeck, S. Stroh, C. Plenge, and M. Strassner (2004). From operations to strategy: The potential of RFID for the automotive industry. Technical report, M-Lab, St. Gallen, Switzerland.

Floekermeier, C. (2006). *Infrastructure Support for RFID Systems*. Ph. D. thesis, ETH, Zurich, Switzerland.

Floerkemeier, C., D. Anarkat, T. Osinski, and M. Harrison (2003). PML core specification 1.0. Technical report, Auto-ID Center Massachusetts Institute of Technology, Cambridge.

Floerkemeier, C. and M. Lampe (2005, October). RFID middleware design: addressing application requirements and RFID constraints. In *Proceedings of the sOc-EUSAI – Smart Objects Conference*, Grenoble, France, pp. 219–224.

Flyvbjerg, B. (2006). Five misunderstandings about case study research. *Qualitative Inquiry 2*, 219–245.

Frazier, G. and J. Summers (1984). Interfirm influence strategies and their application within distribution channels. *Journal of Marketing 48*, 43–55.

Främling, K., M. Harrison, and J. Brusey (2006). Globally unique product identifiers – requirements and solutions to product lifecycle management. In *Proceedings of the 12th IFAC Symposium on Information Control Problems in Manufacturing*, pp. 855–860.

Fruness, A. (2006). Data carriers for traceability. In A. Fruness and I. Smith (Eds.), *Improving Traceability in Food Processing and Distribution*, Cambridge, England: Woodhead Publishing, pp. 199–237.

García, A., D. McFarlane, M. Fletcher, and A. Thorne (2003). Auto-ID in materials handling. Technical report, Auto-ID Center.

Gatziu, S. and K. Dirtrich (1993). Events in an active object-oriented database system. In *Proceedings of the International Conference on Rules in Database Systems*, pp. 23–39.

Gatziu, S. and K. Dirtrich (1994). Detecting composite events in active database systems using petri nets. In *Proceedings of the Workshop on Research Issues in Data Engineering: Active Database Systems*.

Gehani, N., H. Jagadish, and O. Shmueli (1992). Event specification in an active objectoriented database. In *Proceedings of the ACM SIGMOD International Conference on Management of Data*.

Günther, O., L. Ivantysynova, M. Teltzrow, and H. Ziekow (2006). Kooperation in RFID-gestützten Wertschöpfungsnetzen. *Industrie Management*.

Günther, O., W. Kletti, and U. Kubach (2008). *RFID in Manufacturing* (1st ed.). Berlin, Heidelberg, Germany: Springer.

Günther, O., W. Kletti, U. Kubach, L. Ivantysynova, and H. Ziekow (2008). RFID in manufacturing: From shop floor to top floor. In O. Günther, W. Kletti, and U. Kubach (Eds.), *RFID in Manufacturing* (1st ed.)., Berlin, Heidelberg, Germany, pp. 1–23. Springer.

Günther, O. and S. Spiekermann (2005). RFID and the perception of control: The consumer's view. *Communications of the ACM (CACM) 48*(9).

Goyal, A. (2003). Savant guide. Technical report, Auto-ID Center Massachusetts Institute of Technology, Cambridge.

GS1 (2007). Der RFID Kalkulator im Überblick. Technical report, GS1 Germany.

Gyllstrom, D., E. Wu, H. Chae, Y. Diao, P. Strahlberg, and G. Anderson (2007, Jan). SASE: complex event processing over streams. In *Proceedings of the 3rd Biennial Conference on Innovative Data Systems Research*, Asimolar, CA, USA.

Hancke, G. (2006). Practical attacks on proximity identification systems. In *Proceedings of the IEEE Symposium on Security and Privacy*, pp. 328–333.

Hart, P. and C. Saunders (1997). Power and trust: Critical factors in the adoption and use of electronic data interchange. *Organization Science 8*(1), 23–42.

Iacovou, C., I. Benbasat, and A. Dexter (1995). Electronic data interchange and small organizations: Adoption and impact of technology. *MIS Quarterly 19*(4), 465–485.

IDTechEx, 2007 (2007). IDTechEx RFID forecasts, players and opportunities 2007-2017. Technical report, IDTechEx, Cambridge.

ISO/IEC-15438 (2001). Information technology – automatic identification and data capture techniques – bar code symbology specifications –

PDF417. Technical report, ISO – International Organization for Standardization.

ISO/IEC-16022 (2006). Information technology – automatic identification and data capture techniques – data matrix bar code symbology specification. Technical report, ISO – International Organization for Standardization.

ISO/IEC-18000 (2004a). Information technology – radio frequency identification for item management – part 1: Reference architecture and definition of parameters to be standardized. Technical report, ISO – International Organization for Standardization.

ISO/IEC-18000 (2004b). Information technology – radio frequency identification for item management – part 6: Parameters for air interface communications at 860 mhz to 960 mhz. Technical report, ISO – International Organization for Standardization.

ISO/IEC-4909 (2000). Bank cards – magnetic stripe data content for track 3. Technical report, ISO – International Organization for Standardization.

ISO/IEC-7813 (2006). Information technology – identification cards – financial transaction cards. Technical report, ISO – International Organization for Standardization.

Ivantysynova, L. and H. Ziekow (2007, September). RFID in der Produktion: eine Fallstudie aus der Airbagindustrie. In *Proceedings of the GI Workshop RFID-Einsatz in kleinen und mittelständischen Unternehmen*.

Ivantysynova, L. and H. Ziekow (2008). Design guidelines for RFID-based applications in manufacturing. In *Proceedings of the ECIS – European conference on informations systems*, Irland.

Ivantysynova, L., H. Ziekow, and O. Günther (2007, December). A guide to assess costs and benefits for RFID investments in manufacturing. In *Proceedings of ICIS 2007 Workshop on E-Business*, Montreal, Canada, pp. 420–432.

Ivantysynova, L., H. Ziekow, O. Günther, W. Kletti, and U. Kubach (2008a). Case studies. In O. Günther, W. Kletti, and U. Kubach (Eds.), *RFID in Manufacturing* (1st ed.)., Berlin, Heidelberg, Germany, pp. 61–111. Springer.

Ivantysynova, L., H. Ziekow, O. Günther, W. Kletti, and U. Kubach (2008b). Lessons learned. In O. Günther, W. Kletti, and U. Kubach (Eds.), *RFID in Manufacturing* (1st ed.)., Berlin, Heidelberg, Germany, pp. 113–151. Springer.

Jaroszewicz, S., L. Ivantysynova, and T. Scheffer (2007). Schema matching on streams with accuracy guarantees. *Intelligent Data Analysis special issue on Knowledge Discovery from Data Streams 12*(3), 253–270.

Jeffery, S., G. Alonso, M. Franklin, W. Hong, and J. Widom (2006). Declarative support for sensor data cleaning. In *Proceedings of the Pervasive Conference*, pp. 83–100.

Kalmbach, R. and C. Kleinhans (2004, April). FAST 2015: Zulieferer auf der Gewinnerseite. *Automobil-Produktion 48*, 4–8.

Kaplan, R. and D. Norton (1992). The balanced scorecard measures that drive performance. *Harvard Business Review 70*(1), 71–79.

Kaplan, R. and D. Norton (1993). Putting the balanced scorecard to work. *Harvard Business Review 71*(5), 134–142.

Kaplan, R. and D. Norton (1996). The balanced scorecard as a strategic management system. *Harvard Business Review 74*(1), 75–85.

Knebel, U., M. Leimeister, and H. Krcmar (2007). Wahrgenommene strategische Bedeutung von RFID aus Sicht von IT-Entscheidern in Deutschland. In *Proceedings of the 8. Internationale Tagung Wirtschaftsinformatik*.

Krasnova, H., L. Weser, and L. Ivantysynova (2008). Drivers of RFID adoption in the automotive industry. In *Proceedings of the AMCIS – American Conference on Information Systems*.

Kärkkäinen, M. (2003). Increasing efficiency in the supply chain for short shelf life goods using RFID tagging. *International Journal of Retail & Distribution Management 31*(10), 529–536.

Lampe, M. and M. Strassner (2003). The potential of RFID for moveable asset management. In *Proceedings of the Workshop on Ubiquitous Commerce in conjunction with the UbiCom Conference.*

Laubacher, R., S. Kothari, T. Malone, and B. Subirana (2005). What is RFID worth to your company? Measuring performance at the activity level. *MIT Center for eBusiness Research Brief 7*(2), 1–6.

Lee, H., B. Peleg, J. Paresh, S. Sarma, M. Schoonmaker, and B. Subirana (2004). EPC value model. Technical report, Board of Trustees of Leland Stanford Junior University.

Lucas, H. C. (1999). *Information Technology and the Productivity Paradox - Assessing the Value of Investing in IT* (2nd ed.). Oxford et al.: OUP.

Luckham, D. (2001). *The Power of Events: an Introduction to Complex Event Processing in Distributed Enterprise Systems* (1st ed.). Addison-Wesley Longman Publishing Co., Inc.

Malakooty, N. (2005, october). Rosettanet:the organization and the system. Technical report, Personal Computing Industry Center University of California, Irvine, http://www.rosettanet.org/cms/sites/RosettaNet/.

MCBeath, B. (2006). RFID for manufacturers: How manufacturers are improving processes by using RFID. Technical report, ChainLink Research.

Mühl, G., L. Fiege, and P. Pietzuch (2006). *Distributed Event-Based Systems* (1st ed.). Springer-Verlag, Inc.

Millis, K. and R. Mercken (2004). The use of the balanced scorecard for the evaluation of information and communication technology projects. *International Journal on Project Management 22*, 87–97.

Moon, M. and K. Yeom (2007). Product line architecture for RFID-enabled applications. In *Proceedings of the BIS Conference*, pp. 638–651.

Moon, M., K. Yeom, and H. Chae (2005). An approach to developing domain requirements as a core asset based on commonality and variability analysis in a product line. *IEEE Transactions on Software Engineering 31*(7), 551–569.

OAGIS (2007). Open applications group integration specification (OAGIS). Technical report, OAGIS, http://www.openapplications.org.

OICA (2007, December). Organisation internationale des constructeurs d'automobiles. http://oica.net/.

Paton, N., F. Schneider, and D. Gries (Eds.) (1998). *Active Rules in Database Systems* (1st ed.). New York: Springer-Verlag, Inc.

Pietsch, T. (1999). *Bewertung von Informations- und Kommunikationssystemen: ein Vergleich betriebswirtschaftlicher Verfahren*. Berlin: Erich Schmidt Verlag.

Premkumar, G. and K. Ramamurthy (1995). The role of interorganizational and organizational factors on the decision mode for adoption of interorganizational systems. *Decision Sciences 26*(3), 303–336.

Rankl, W. and W. Effing (2008). *Handbuch der Chipkarten. Aufbau – Funktionsweise – Einsatz von Smart Cards* (5th ed.). Germany: Hanser Fachbuchverlag.

Remenyi, D., A. Money, M. Sherwood-Smith, and Z. Irani (2000). *The effective measurement and management of IT costs and benefits* (2nd ed.). Oxford et al.: Butterworth - Heinemann.

Rockart, J. (1982). Sloan working paper 1297-82: The changing role of the information systems executive: A critical success factors perspective. Technical report, MIT, Cambridge, USA.

Rothensee., M. and S. Spiekermann (2008). Between extreme rejection and cautious acceptance – consumers' reactions to RFID-based IS in retail. *Social Science Computer Review 26*, 75–86.

Schmitt, P. and F. Michahelles (2008). Economic impact of RFID report. Technical report, BRIDGE.

Schmitt, P., F. Thiesse, and E. Fleisch (2007). Adoption and diffusion of RFID technology in the automotive industry. In *Proceedings of the ECIS – European Conference on Information Systems*, St. Gallen, Switzerland.

Scholz-Reiter, B., K. Windt, and M. Freitag (2004). Autonomous logistic processes - new demands and first approaches. In L. Monostori (Ed.), *Proceedings of the 37th CIRP International Seminar on Manufacturing Systems*, Budapest, pp. 357–362.

Schultz, C. (2007). A roadmap to rfid integration on an sap-centric platform. *SAP NetWeaver Magazine*.

Seddon, P., S. Staples, R. Patnayakuni, and M. Botwell (1999). Dimensions of information systems success. *Communications of the AIS 2*(20), 1–60.

Sharma, A., A. Citurs, and B. Konsynski (2007). Strategic and institutional perspectives in the adoption and early integration of radio frequency identification (RFID). In *Proceedings of the HICSS – 40th Annual Hawaii International Conference on System Sciences*, Hawaii, USA.

Spiekermann, S. and H. Ziekow (2005). RFID: A 7-point plan to ensure privacy. In *Proceedings of the 13th ECIS – European Conference on Information Systems*.

Spiess, P. (2005). Collaborative business items: Decomposing business process services for execution of business logic on the item. In *Proceedings of the European Workshop on Wireless Sensor Networks*.

Üstündag, A. and M. Tanyas (2005). Evaluating an RFID investment using fuzzy cognitive map. Technical report, Technical University – RFID Research & Test Center, Istanbul.

Stockman, H. (1948, October). Communication by means of reflected power. In *Proceedings of the IRE Conference*, pp. 1196–1204.

Strassner, M. (2005). *RFID im Supply Chain Management: Auswirkungen und Handlungsempfehlungen am Beispiel der Automobilindustrie*. Wiesbaden: DUV.

Strassner, M. and E. Fleisch (2003, February). The promise of Auto-ID in the automotive industry. Technical report, Auto-ID Center Massachusetts Institute of Technology, Cambridge.

Strüker, J., D. Gille, and T. Faupel (2008). RFID report 2008. Technical report, Alber-Ludwig University, Friedrichstr. 50, Freiburg im Breisgau, Germany.

Tellkamp, C. (2003). The Auto-ID calculator: An overview. Technical report, Auto-ID Centre.

van Grembergen, W. and R. van Bruggen (2000). Measuring and improving corporate information technology through the balanced scorecard. *Electronic Journal of Information Systems Evaluation 1*(1).

Walsham, G. (1993). *Interpreting Information Systems in Organizations* (1st ed.). U.K.: Wiley.

Wamba, S. F. and H. Boeck (2008). Enhancing information flow in a retail supply chain using RFID and the EPC network: A proof-of-concept approach. *Journal of Theoretical and Applied Electronic Commerce Research 3*(1), 92–105.

Wang, F., S. Liu, P. L. P, and Y. Bai (2006). Bridging physical and virtual worlds: Complex event processing for RFID data streams. In *Proceedings of the EDBT*.

Whitaker, J., S. Mithas, and M. Krishnan (2007). A field study of RFID deployment and return expectations. *Production and Operations Management 16*(5), 599–612.

Wilde, T. and T. Hess (2007). Forschungsmethoden der Wirtschaftsinformatik – eine empirische Untersuchung. *Wirtschaftsinformatik 4*, 280–287.

Williams, T. (1992). The purdue enterprise reference architecture – a technical guide for CIM planning and implementation. Technical report, ISA Research Triangle Park, North Carolina, USA.

Wiltschi, K., A. Pinz, and T. Lindeberg (2000). An automatic assessment scheme for steel quality inspection. *Machine Vision and Applications 12*, 113–128.

Wolf, K. and C. Holm (1998). Total cost of ownership: Kennzahl oder Konzept? *Information Management 13*(2), 19–23.

Wu, E., Y. Diao, and S. Rizvi (2006). High-performance complex event processing over streams. In *Proceedings of the ACM SIGMOD International Conference on Management of Data*.

Ziekow, H. and L. Ivantysynova (2006, June). Stream processing in networks of smart devices. In *Proceedings of ACS/IEEE International Conference on Pervasive Services, ICPS*, Lyon, France, pp. 269 – 272.

Appendix – PLA: Table of Primitive Requirements

Table 1: Generalized PR derived from other PRs

REQUIREMENTS	CV P.	AIR	CLU	COO	CAS	CON	PAC
RFID reading act.	C/100%	√	√	√	√	√	√
manual reads	P/ 33%	X	X	X	X	√	√
scheduled reads	C/100%	√	√	√	√	√	√
triggered reads	C/100%	√	√	√	√	√	√
writing data to tag	C/ 67%	√	X	√	X	√	√
data enrichment	C/100%	√	√	√	√	√	√
semantic enrich.	C/100%	√	√	√	√	√	√
stream corr.	C/100%	√	√	√	√	√	√
adding data	C/100%	√	√	√	√	√	√
data filtering	C/100%	√	√	√	√	√	√
low pass	C/100%	√	√	√	√	√	√
statistic	P/ 50%	√	X	X	√	√	X
data cleaning	C/ 50%	√	X	X	X	√	√
inference	C/100%	√	√	√	√	√	√
process control	C/ 83%	√	√	√	√	√	X
process monit.	C/ 83%	√	√	√	X	√	√
notif. generation	C/100%	√	√	√	√	√	√
aggregation	C/100%	√	√	√	√	√	√
ad context inf.	C/100%	√	√	X	√	√	√
notif. delivery	C/100%	√	√	√	√	√	√
triggering p. step	C/ 50%	√	X	X	X	√	√
reporting asset pos.	C/ 67%	X	√	X	√	√	√
submitting notif.	C/ 50%	√	√	X	X	√	X
reporting	C/100%	√	√	√	√	√	√

List of Abbreviations

AIR	manufacturer of airbags
ALE	application level events
API	application programming interface
ASN	advanced shipping notification
ATP	available-to-promise
ATS	automated transport system at ENG
Auto-ID	automatic identification technology
B2B	business-to-business
B2MML	business-to-manufacturing mark-up language
B2C	business-to-customer
BPP	business process platform
ECA	event condition action
CAS	manufacturer of cast parts
CEP	complex event processing
CHE	manufacturer of chemicals
CIM	computer integrated manufacturing
CLU	manufacturer of sliding clutches
COO	manufacturer of engine cooling modules
COM	component object model
CON	manufacturer of connectors
CNC	computerized numerical control
DAX	deutscher Aktienindex; German stock index
DC	device controllers
DCOM	distributed component object model
DCS	distributed control system

DNS	domain name service
ECA	event condition action rules
EDI	electronic data interchange
ENG	manufacturer of engines
EPC	electronic product code
EPCIS	EPC information services
ERP	enterprise resource planning
ETL	extract transform load
FCS	facility control system at ENG
HF	high frequency
HMI	human machine interface
ID	identification
IOS	inter-organizational system
IT	information technology
JIS	just-in-sequence
LF	low frequency
MDAX	Mid-Cap-DAX; stock index
MES	manufacturing execution system
MESA	manufacturing enterprise solutions association
MIP	manufacturer of milk products
MM	materials management
OCR	optical character recognition
OEM	original equipment manufacturer
OLE	object linking and embedding
ONS	object name service
OPC	OLE for production control
OPC-UA	OLE for production control - unified architecture
P2B	plant-to-business
PAC	manufacturer of packaging
PDC	production data collection
PLA	product line analysis
PLC	programmable logic controller
PML	physical mark-up language

POW	manufactuer of power plants
REF	manufacturer of refractories
RF	radio frequency
RFID	radio frequency identification
ROI	return on investment
SC	supply chain
SCS	station control system at ENG
SCADA	supervisory control and data acquisition
SOA	service-oriented architecture
TCO	total cost of ownership
TIR	manufactuer of tires
TM	top management
UHF	ultra high frequency
VBA	value benefit analysis
VIS	visualization system at ENG
VDI	Verein deutscher Ingenieure
WIP	work in process
XML	extensible mark-up language

Acknowledgment

I wish to thank everyone who helped me with my studies and contributed to my thesis. In particular, I wish to thank and express my deep and sincere gratitude to my supervisor, Professor Oliver Günther, Ph.D., Head of the Institute of Information Systems, Humboldt-Universität zu Berlin, Germany. He has always fully supported and encouraged me during the more than three years of this thesis's work. He has provided an optimum working environment for me at the Institute.

I wish to express sincere thanks to Professor Dr.-Ing. Frank Straube, Head of the Logistics Department at the Institute of Technology and Management, Technical University Berlin, Germany, who has agreed to be my second reviewer.

I warmly thank Dr. Jochen Rode from SAP Research Dresden, for his valuable advice and ideas. His discussions regarding the work of all case studies have always been very helpful for this study.

The conducting of five of the six case studies about RFID in manufacturing has been supported by MPDV Microlab GmbH, Moosbach, Germany. With their support, I was able to approach several of their customers, who are interested in applying RFID. Here I would especially want to thank Jochen Schumacher of MPDV Microlab GmbH. He established many of the corporate contacts and contributed to the case studies about RFID.

I would also like to thank the whole team at the Institute of Information Systems for the great working environment they provided. Here I would like to thank especially my colleague Holger Ziekow. I carried out all of the case studies together with him and also parts of my research. Furthermore, I would also like to thank Hanna Krasnova with whom I conducted my research on RFID in the automotive industry.

I had the pleasure to supervise and work with several students who did their graduation work around the topic of my Ph.D. thesis. Deria Saki, Mert Sengüner and Matthias Schmidt helped with three case studies about RFID applications in manufacturing. Martin Lehman worked on the identification of functional components and technical services for RFID applications. Helio Pereira helped with the analysis and a market survey about production data collection systems. Seckin Kara's master thesis contributed to the analysis of intangible aspects of RFID rollouts in manufacturing. Lorenz Weser conducted the ten interviews on which Chapter 7 is based.

I owe my loving thanks to my partner and lecturer Tobias Scheffer for his constant encouragement, great advice, and loving support. My special gratitude goes to my parents for inspiring and guiding me on my path to my Ph.D. They have always been there for me and supported me whenever possible.

The work reported here has been supported and funded by SAP Research Dresden, Germany.

Die VDM Verlagsservicegesellschaft sucht für wissenschaftliche Verlage abgeschlossene und herausragende

Dissertationen, Habilitationen, Diplomarbeiten, Master Theses, Magisterarbeiten usw.

für die kostenlose Publikation als Fachbuch.

Sie verfügen über eine Arbeit, die hohen inhaltlichen und formalen Ansprüchen genügt, und haben Interesse an einer honorarvergüteten Publikation?

Dann senden Sie bitte erste Informationen über sich und Ihre Arbeit per Email an *info@vdm-vsg.de*.

Sie erhalten kurzfristig unser Feedback!

VDM Verlagsservicegesellschaft mbH
Dudweiler Landstr. 99
D - 66123 Saarbrücken

Telefon +49 681 3720 174
Fax   +49 681 3720 1749

www.vdm-vsg.de

Die VDM Verlagsservicegesellschaft mbH vertritt

Printed by Books on Demand GmbH, Norderstedt / Germany